EDUCATION

IN

CENTRAL

AMERICA

EDUCATION

IN

CENTRAL

AMERICA

by
George R. Waggoner
and
Barbara Ashton Waggoner

The University Press of Kansas/Lawrence/Manhattan/Wichita

The research reported herein was performed pursuant to a contract with the Office of Education, U.S. Department of Health, Education, and Welfare, under Project No. 4141-6708, Contract No. OEC-1-7-071124-5148. Contractors undertaking such projects under Government sponsorship are encouraged to express freely their professional judgment in the conduct of the project. Points of view or opinions stated do not, therefore, necessarily represent official Office of Education position or policy.

PREFACE

Regional cooperation of the kind that exists among the national universities and among the ministries of education of the six Central American countries is unique in the Western Hemisphere. International cooperation in most endeavors is uncommonly difficult to achieve, and voluntary cooperation among educational institutions and systems is uncommon even within national boundaries. This remarkable movement, therefore, should interest both those concerned with education and with international affairs as well.

Because educational systems are what they are by virtue of a variety of geographical, historical, and social factors we have tried to give some description of the physical and cultural environment of Central America, and to offer in this background some analytical comments to show the complexity of the problems which confront the region. These are not offered as judgments but rather reflect the concern of writers who, on the whole, do not urge simple panaceas. The major part of the book is devoted to a description of the educational systems of Guatemala, El Salvador, Honduras, Nicaragua, Costa Rica, and Panama, and the efforts toward regional cooperation. Such evaluations as are included are largely those of Central Americans themselves.

Our effort has been to present a Central American view of its own educational patterns in the belief that an understanding by interested outsiders should comprehend not only the structures and details of these systems but also the Central American evaluation of educational progress and problems. Hence the study includes comparisons among the Central American countries but not comparisons between Central America and other regions.

v

This study has confronted us with problems of various kinds. There is constant change among the public and private universities of the six countries, among the ministries of education, and among the regional organizations. We have not tried to describe the many imaginative and important plans under way in many parts of the Isthmus but have tried to describe the reality as of early 1969.

Affairs in a state of change are hard to describe and, even as the study must arbitrarily end, there are important developing situations whose outcomes are not clearly foreseeable. It is not possible, for example, to predict the future of the University of Panama, closed by the Military Junta in 1968, even after its reopening and reorganization; nor to assess the probable impact of the educational television program for the first three years af secondary education in El Salvador, a program that began in 1969; nor to predict the consequences of abolition of the general studies program in the University of San Carlos of Guatemala or the outcome of proposed secondary school reform in Honduras. Education is subject in an extreme degree to the vagaries of national and international politics. We have tried to present an accurate, still photograph of the systems as we found them.

In many areas there is a lack of statistics or a contradiction among existing statistics. But our study seems feasible, despite this problem, because there has been a great improvement, quantitatively and qualitatively, in available data during the last two or three years.

There have been problems, too, of describing in English a Latin American system where often Spanish terms have no English equivalents or where apparent equivalents are misleading. For example, *educación secundaria* usually means, not the level of education between primary and higher education, but academic as opposed to vocational secondary education. We have not tried to mix the two languages but have translated *educación media* (intermediate education) as *secondary education* and *educación secundaria* as *academic secondary education*.

A major sponsor of this study was the Institute of International Studies of the U.S. Office of Education by means of a contract with the University of Kansas. Because the scope of the project greatly exceeded the support that could be offered by the contract, we want also gratefully to acknowledge invaluable additional support by the University of Kansas and by the Ford Foundation.

Many persons have assisted us in this project: officials in the Central American ministries of education, in the Central American universities both public and private, in U.S. embassies and AID missions, in foundations, and in regional organizations both Central American (such as CSUCA and ODECA) and international (such as UNESCO).

John F. Helwig and Ana Herzfeld of the University of Kansas assisted us in the collection of data and offered useful criticism of portions of the manuscript. We are particularly indebted to Ovidio Soto Blanco of ODECA for both his publications and his comments, and to Dr. William Harrell of the U.S. Office of Education for his cooperation. We are grateful to scores of other persons who supplied us with information, comments, criticism —so many persons that it is not possible to list them here.

For nearly a decade we have enjoyed the stimulus and friendship of a group of Central American educators, their interest in the future of their countries and the region, their realism about and persistence in the face of incredible problems, and their willingness to innovate. They have given us new and useful insights. For us, to be in Central America is to be in the company of friends.

George R. Waggoner
Barbara A. Waggoner

CONTENTS

1

WHAT IS CENTRAL AMERICA?

Central America is a relatively small piece of the earth's surface. It is two words for a group of countries not especially well known to its own neighbors in the hemisphere to the north or south. Central America is also a concept of a set of relationships among peoples once arbitrarily unified by Spanish rule, long divided and frequently quarreling, and in the late twentieth century struggling to achieve a new, voluntary unity.

Bordering Mexico on the north and Columbia on the south, the region, however unified it was in the past or may be in the future, has varieties of landscapes, climates, and cultures which do not make for easy communion. Furthermore, most of the countries have histories which make internal cohesion and national unity difficult as well. There are even discrepant views as to how many countries comprise Central America: some map makers, some historians, and more politicians, for example, call the disputed territory Belize a part of Guatemala, while others give it recognition as British Honduras. Panama has quite a different history from that of the countries to the north, yet increasingly it becomes linked in practical ways to Costa Rica, Nicaragua, Honduras, El Salvador, and Guatemala. There is logic for treating these six countries as comprising contemporary Central America. By the same reasoning, British Honduras (Belize) will be excluded here because not only does it reflect an English colonial heritage of language and social institutions, but it has few significant functional ties with its neighbors.

These six separate nations of Central America occupy a total territory equivalent to a little more than one-fourth of that of modern Mexico. Here, as in Mexico, there have been the problems of reconciling Spanish language and culture with those of the Indians; here, too, are volcanos and jungles with their attendant problems and riches. But Central America is six nations, not one, and Central America's people today still suffer the consequences of political divisions which aggravate the problems of a landscape hostile to easy communication.

Mountains and coastlines dominate the lives of Central Americans. The *cordillera central,* some of whose mountains reach to over 12,000 feet, is forbiddingly rugged, making travel from east to west in any one country difficult enough, and scarcely less easy from north to south and country to country.

Simón Bolívar said of that land from Panama to Guatemala that it could be the Byzantium of the New World, in time the marketplace of the world. "Then why has it not even succeeded in unifying itself, but remains in sorry stagnation while its brother countries of Spanish America are in a period of such obvious improvement?"[1] This was the anguished question put by Alberto Herrarte, Guatemalan intellectual. He blames in part the easy access to the sea, which left each country unneedful of its neighbors. From all its promise in the long ago, Central America slipped into relative obscurity except as what Herrarte calls "a shock point of races, civilizations, interests and ambitions of every kind."[2]

Historian Lewis Hanke wrote, "Central America catches the world's attention only when one of its volcanos erupts, when communism is believed to be about to take over one of its republics, or when an archaeological expedition uncovers another ancient city."[3] A wry jest in part, but also a perceptive summary of three elements ever present in the lives of more than 15,000,000 people who live there.[4] One map shows a chain of 26 volcanos active since 1500, but a new one must be added as of 1968, and these visible signs of crustal instability are reminders of the earthquake potential of the region as well.[5]

Hanke alludes to still another kind of instability, that of the social order, whose inquietudes are nearly constant, and which the world watches if there are real or imaginary threats of change. The United States, of course, has most often intervened in the twentieth century on one pretext or another to guard its interests in the present Panama Canal and to assure access to potential canal sites; and both U.S. government and business interests have had rather fixed ideas of what the social order of Central America ought to be.

Those archaeological treasures of which Hanke speaks, still being discovered and interpreted, are testimony to the high level of artistic achievement of their long-ago creators and eloquent evidence as well of the highly developed social organization which made them possible. Contemporary Central America's institutions, including education, are comprehensible only with some knowledge of the region's past, for certainly the descendants of those who fashioned the old cultures have made and still make their mark on most aspects of the land and the living.

The Indians

The early settlers of Central America made their way southward from the Bering Strait in a journey of unknown beginnings and countless generations. Franklin Parker's summary of what he calls the remains of antiquity puts a date of the second millennium B.C. for the oldest ruins in this region, on sites in Honduras and Guatemala.[6] Various civilizations flourished and fell in different areas, but it was undoubtedly the Maya culture that directly or indirectly left the strongest imprint on the peoples and land of Middle America: "Here, from the fourth to the sixteenth centuries, flourished the most brilliant civilization of the New World in pre-Columbian times."[7] That civilization, of course, was the end product of a long pioneer period. There was a large area and a common language, forms of which are the language today of many of Guatemala's citizens. There was well-established agriculture. "Corn, perhaps first developed and improved by the ancestors of the Maya on the highlands of Guatemala, was the chief food of the people. And corn, because its production was generous and easy, gave man leisure to build pyramids and temples. The surplus of corn flowed over into the cities and financed the priest-scientists who probed the mysteries of earth and stars, and created a cosmology, an astronomy, and a system of writing and of mathematics."[8] Conflict and corn failures perhaps account for the decline of this civilization, which once extended over much of southern Mexico, modern Guatemala, Honduras, and British Honduras.

Numerous less sophisticated cultures were found in other areas to the south, peoples speaking a variety of languages, and with many customs and languages showing influences from South America. If their archaeological remains are fewer, it may have been that their materials were perishable and that their technology and societies were weaker. The golden artifacts of Costa Rica are testimony of a high level of artistic imagination and accomplishment.

The Aztec empire of Mexico had reached a high level of material accomplishment and social organization when the Spaniards came out of the east in 1519 to overwhelm it. The confrontation took place in what is now modern Mexico, and by 1522 Hernan Cortes was the ruler of the "New Spain of the Ocean Sea." By somewhat over a decade later, the

Spaniards were in legal control of what is now Central America. Real control would be another matter.

It is naïve to suggest that the kinds of religious and economic domination which the Spaniards brought were unknown styles of behavior to the Indians themselves, or that the Spaniards interrupted some serene and comfortable body politic which was homogeneous throughout all the Isthmus. Little pockets of people with their separate though related languages and religions were scattered throughout the region, and communication was not fostered by the rugged land.[9]

It is also naïve to praise or vilify the conquerors who came in the name of Cross and King. It is more useful to say that the Conquest had its own logic as part of a history which began in Spain long centuries before. We look now briefly at the land which lay then several weeks of sailing to the east.

The Iberian Heritage

The Iberian Peninsula, separated by mountains from easy communion with its northern neighbors, was a land which challenged its early and late inhabitants to survive.[10] There is evidence of Cro-Magnon culture, perhaps out of Africa, and waves of other peoples: Celts, Phoenicians, Greeks, Carthaginians, Romans. Each came in its time; not without violence was Roman rule overthrown by the Visigoths out of the north in the fifth century.

Spain was long a battleground of contending religious forces, first over Christian doctrine, and then between the forces of Roman Christianity and the conquering Moslems. The Moslems dominated the peninsula from 711 to 1031, bringing with them sophisticated ideas in science, technology, and philosophy, and high art that forever left its mark on Spain and its colonies.

The inevitable divisiveness among rulers which weakened the Moslem rule came at a time when Iberians subdued their own ambitions to achieve the beginnings of national unity. By the thirteenth century Spain had its own language, thriving cities, a high level of social organization, and a powerful and wealthy church. Universities with scholars from all of Europe also welcomed the high intellectual contribution of Jewish and Moslem scholars. There were still dynastic battles between the houses of Aragon and Castile to be resolved. A confluence of events was building up to forthcoming religious and patriotic upswelling that was to complete the Reconquest of Spain and drive out or dominate non-Catholic elements.

The union of Castile and Aragon, with the marriage of Isabel and Ferdinand in 1469, was followed by a consolidation of power, and by the forging of that instrument, the Spanish Inquisition, which completed the purging of alien people from country and from church. The last Moslem stronghold fell in 1492.

Spain's interest in the new worlds her explorers found should be seen against the background of her national development, and her unhappy and costly conflicts in Europe. There was no time or inclination to care if artistic treasures of far-off heathens were melted into ingots to pay the bills for wars with France and England. Spain was in her golden sixteenth century, first under Charles I and then Philip II, and that century was a continuous contest for dominance in Europe.

Her monarchs and her church, threatened by the rise of Protestantism, undertook further purgations of church and society, and the fervent nature of Catholicism grew more so with a new advent of mysticism. The proselytizing Jesuit order came into being as well in the first half of this century.

"The Spain that set its stamp upon America was thus deeply in earnest about religion. Of course the Spaniards were intent upon conquest and empire, upon winning gold and silver and trade, but they had a genuine zeal for carrying the true faith to the ends of the world. The Conquest and colonization of Spanish America cannot be understood except in the light of this compulsion."[11]

It will become evident as we discuss contemporary Central America that many of the values of the period of the conquest remain dominant today. What is important to us is what the Spaniard is and what he has done, for his achievements are indissolubly wedded to his misfortunes and failures. Rebellious to law and to any norm of the state, the Spaniard was docile to the voice of tradition and to the imperative of his absolute person. . . . The Spaniard welded himself to his legendary, religious, and artistic beliefs, as did no other European people. He fortified himself in the castle of his own person, and in his own person he found the impetus and faith to build a strange and immense colonial empire that lasted from 1500 to 1824. . . . The Spaniards did not let themselves be rationally unified by means of reason, knowledge, law, or a net of economic links, but rather by beliefs which enfolded and motivated them.[12]

Spanish historian Américo Castro thus describes some of the unique values and personal qualities the conquerors implanted in their lands and peoples. However different from each other are the countries and institutions of Central America, there are common patterns of behavior so unmistakably different from those of northern Europe or North America that it is useful to describe some of them. Useful not so much as a descriptive exercise but as an explanation for some of the anomalies that sometimes exasperate Latin Americans themselves when they try to change such institutions as their educational systems.

Hard work, good deeds, material rewards, progress, and problem solving were never the roots on which Latin American institutions flourished, and it is an error to condemn them for not achieving what is incompatible with their basic values.

It was almost inevitable that various Spanish conquerors attributed their successes in the Americas not to horses and superior weapons but to the magic intervention of St. James in their battles. (Even St. James' horse helped by biting and kicking. Moreover this intervention demonstrated to the Spaniards the righteousness of their cause.)[13] After centuries of day-to-day living in the belief that superhuman not human effort shaped events, it was unlikely that new lands and peoples would abruptly change the way of seeing the world. The Spaniards who stumbled upon a new world had, after centuries of reliance on divine forces, Jewish financial and technical skills, and Arab science, developed certain characteristics. From both Christian and Moslem sources, there was derived a belief in the absence of free will, the belief in fatalism, and a fusion of things of this world and the other. What was long important was the inner life, what a man felt. (As an example of misunderstanding among educators one may cite the ever-present concern on the part of Latin Americans who often mean, when they speak of *formación básica,* the creation of the integrated and essentially inner-directed person, rather than a plan of study which gives some introductory courses.)

Castro quotes from a number of sixteenth-century Spanish writers who describe the Spanish proclivity for avoiding manual labor. It had nothing to do with laziness but simply with the need to play the role of *hidalgo,* the gentleman. There was in Spain the servant with money to buy a *real*'s worth of fruit who must give half of it to a porter to carry it.[14] Those porters are there today in Latin America, in ministries and university offices, homes and businesses: little men who open and close doors, carry messages, make and serve coffee.

The need for virtual slavery of first Indians and then Negroes accorded with social and psychological values. It was a Franciscan priest who sent a letter to Philip II lamenting the awful state of affairs in Buenos Aires. Argentinians, without gold, silver, or available natives, had found it necessary for ". . . Spanish women, noble and of high quality [to] . . . carry their drinking water on their own shoulders." The men had to care for "their cattle with their own hands, . . . and it is a pitiable state of affairs; the people wait on themselves as if it were the tiniest village in Spain."[15] In many very modest households in Central America today it is not a part of the life style for manual tasks to be performed by anyone but servants.

There is a host of examples to be found of the forces from Spain which shaped family life, education, social organization, and political attitudes in the New World of Latin America. We have already mentioned the importance of the inner life, the concept of the *hidalgo,* a hierarchical society, the importance of religion. The ancient hatreds of Jews and Moslems, coupled with the Spaniard's dependence upon them for everything from banks to boots, carried over to the New World in at least two manifestations: conquest was still a holy and honorable business; and the Spaniards continued to be dependent on someone else, or to do without; when it came to coping with practical affairs ". . . deeds and accomplishments were seen as valuable while those who performed them were held in low esteem. Artisans, businessmen, technologists, scholars, etc., produced all manner of good things, but these products were tainted from birth by the fact that their producers came from castes deemed inferior . . . . Social functions had to be differentiated not according to their objective value but according to the castes that carried them out."[16]

And so it is today in varying degrees in Central America that to be the land*owner* (generally absentee) matters more than to be the one who makes the land produce. (This shows up in taxation policies, for example, and the widespread nonuse of land.) Education to deal with everyday concerns was not an end that fit the traditional values. What has mattered is to be educated, to possess a certain title. Material rewards may be smaller for the man entitled to call himself *ingeniero* or *licenciado* than for the businessman, but money is not the traditional sign of the Lord's blessing as it was in the Protestant tradition.

If there was no need to understand nature or cope with things, there was little incentive to scientific curiosity or methodology in problem solving, and scant interest in innovation. It is no accident that universities in Spanish-speaking lands today have not generally devoted themselves to research in either the natural or social sciences, or even that textbooks in the sciences *translated* into Spanish are hard to find. Likewise, if fear of rather than reward for innovation is a deep-rooted characteristic, it should not be surprising that Latin Americans have little modified their social, educational, or political institutions; nor should it seem curious that they sometimes resent the patterns they must borrow from other traditions. It would be strange, indeed, if such value systems went so far as to produce radically new kinds of institutions.[17]

The Spanish in Central America

The Colonial era in Central America, which in the legal sense lasted until the early nineteenth century, gave way only to new men, not to new institutions. Panama was almost immediately important to the Spanish as a transit zone between Atlantic and Pacific. From here exploration and conquest moved northward into Costa Rica and Nicaragua. (Names, of course, and boundaries were to come later.) Almost at once, Indians were put to work mining gold, cutting timber, raising stock, and cultivating indigo and cacao; land use patterns in Nicaragua's lowlands continued for some 400 years.[18] Racial mixing of Indians and Spaniards began, for the Spaniards did not customarily bring wives to their colonies. Only in parts of the *meseta central* of Costa Rica, where Indians had been mostly overcome by disease, did a primarily white population prevail, and with it, a system of small farms worked by their owners; that pattern of land use flourished and spread to other parts of the highland. "At the end of the colonial period, the density of the population in the *meseta central* exceeded 100 persons per square mile, and the expansion of white settlements into other parts of the forestcovered highlands and adjacent escarpments, which is still going on in Costa Rica, began."[19]

One might well pause here to anticipate what will clearly show up as educational systems are described later. Costa Rica was and is different from the other countries. Essentially Spanish values attached to landowning still prevail—who of the old families in San José or even the newer middle class does not have his *finca* somewhere? But without slaves and in a country without large mineral deposits, the people simply had to make the land produce, and they developed social and political patterns different from other parts of the region.

Mexico was the other center from which exploration and conquest spread; by the number and nature of the Indian population which lay to the south into Honduras, a system of social patterns and land use was developed which has its consequences into the present era. *Encomiendas* —land and the Indian villages on it—were awarded the conquerors. The Indians had known bondage before, and the need for making payments to their overlords in service or goods. Later on, the Indians became technically free of the demand of enforced work, but the system of tribute of goods prevailed longer. What is important for our purposes is that both economic and social patterns were set in a mold which has contemporary consequences.

If Spain's colonies were to serve her, they must of necessity be controlled, and that they were, but with varying degrees of success. Most physically conspicuous, perhaps was the town or city plan dictated from Spain with its characteristic plaza, flanked by church and municipal buildings in the center of a grid pattern of streets. A pattern of administration, likewise imposed from Spain, was put into effect when the Captaincy-General of Guatemala was established in 1543 under rule of the Viceroyalty of New Spain in Mexico.[20]

Cabildos or town councils were responsible for local affairs, while the overall regional agent of the king was the viceroy. The *Audiencia de Guatemala,* a court with administrative and consultative responsibilities, also exercised the royal power over the provinces, except for Panama, which now make up Central America. In theory, at least, policies for the colonies were made in Spain by the Council of the Indies, with the all-important regulation of commerce in the hands of its agent, the *Casa de Contratación.* Historian Herring describes some of the minutiae of daily living the Spaniards sought to control from afar and cites 400,000 edicts in effect in 1635 for the colonies.[21]

But conflicts of interest and countervailing powers early set the stage for loss of control by Spain and the division of the region. There were conflicts between Spanish-born Spaniards and the *criollo* or American-born Spaniards they came to rule. Those who achieved power in the villas or cities guarded it zealously, and so did those who owned the land, the *hacendados.*

> We can see, then, that Spain's control over her subjects in Central America was not so effective as is generally believed. . . . the rough topography and inadequate internal communications as well as the enormous distance from Spain to Central America militated against the establishment of a highly centralized system of government, a feat which would be difficult enough under modern conditions. Moreover, Spanish theory of government broke down in practice because the mother country depended upon her colonials to defend and hold the far-flung empire from the attacks of envious foreign nations . . . . Concessions had to be made to home rule with the result that the decentralization of power became characteristic . . . .[22]

Mario Rodríguez goes on to point out that it was at the local level that the colonists gained experience in self-government as a means of circumventing Spanish control in order to further the interests of their own local aristocracies; that experience of self-government would only add to the centrifugal tendencies of the later era.

Through most of Central America, the *meseta central* and parts of the west coast were the most attractive to the Spaniards for minerals, Indians, and agricultural potential. To the inhospitable climate of the Atlantic coast there was the added problem of continuous depredations by English, French, and Dutch pirates from their footholds in the Antilles.

Lacking any rational plan of colonization, the towns were founded, according to Rodrigo Facio, "only on the will or individual caprice of captains and lieutenants." The more important fact, as he says, is that "they never behaved in an organized way, nor were they united by a sense of collaboration; on the contráry, in a form completely anarchic and many times even opposed to each other by personal or jurisdictional questions, the towns they founded remained scattered . . . the length of the Isthmus, in mesas and valleys independent, isolated and far apart, a tragic condition which has lasted till the present day."[23]

If Facio also, in his own words and those of others, calls "the kingdom . . . a group of entities that didn't add up," and describes the lack of even internal development of these separate entities, he is even more vigorous in ascribing the blame. "Abandonment [and] oppressions" characterized Spanish policy, for Spain imposed "exaggerated taxes ordinary and extraordinary, monopoly decrees, and prohibited all industry and commerce in each of these unhappy provinces."[24] Nor were roads or ports developed. Commerce with foreign nations was prohibited, and Central America lay outside the most important sea lanes to north and south.

Administration from Guatemala and other centers was chaotic, inconsistent, and often in conflict on the civil side; Facio found the ecclesiastical organization equally confused and obstructive. It is not strange that Guatemala was regarded with resentment and jealousy as a by-product of its power and also greater prosperity. To some extent these feelings linger still.

It is outside our scope to detail the events of the colonial era except to mention some which have been of prevailing significance. The establishment of towns and mining camps, and the development of certain kinds of agriculture led to, among other things, the interbreeding of Indians, Caucasians, and African Negroes to produce the *mestizo* people who populate all except predominantly Indian Guatemala and predominantly white Costa Rica.[25] Both land and climate were factors in the use of Negro labor, slave or free, along the Atlantic Coast.

As minerals were depleted, agriculture became dominant. Crops and the tools to produce them were introduced from Europe to add to indigenous agriculture. Dyestuffs, wheat, fibers, cane, tobacco, and cattle were of early commercial importance. One could safely generalize that much land was used and abused, much was underused, and if there could be anything termed an agricultural policy it was simply to get the product and/or their cash yields to local power centers or to Spain. The patterns of land use, of land tenure, and of transportation have been slow to change in Central America even into the present century.

The system of large landholdings, the use of Indians caught up in a never-ending debt peonage, and an economy tied to external markets are heritages that to varying degrees characterize the region still. The introduction of coffee and bananas in the nineteenth century and of cotton in the twentieth century was the basis for commercializing agriculture, now bringing in some 80 percent of the value of Central America's export. Yet, as West and Augelli point out, the region cannot feed itself.[26] What it earns from export goes in part for buying food abroad. The economic dependence on a few crops and the vagaries of foreign market prices, plus the fact that several of the countries produce the same crops, do not conduce to economic stability.

Before turning to events of the nineteenth century in Central America, it is useful to show the nature of a common pattern of economic behavior which appears as a continuous theme. Argentine historian Luis Vitale argues that it was not a set of feudal relationships which Spain imposed on the colonies, but a mercantilist capitalist one: "the exploitation and commercialization of precious metals,"[27] which applied to other raw materials as well, and the development of markets for manufactured goods. The creole bourgeoisie, which was gaining economic and a limited political power in local isolated centers in the region, was soon to seek political freedom from Spain and the control of its own commerce. But the land and the people on it would not be basically changed, for the land would continue to yield wealth for those who owned it and a marginal existence for those who worked it. Landowners would continue their political power, and there would be little incentive either to use land rationally or to reinvest the profits from it for national, much less regional, development.

Vitale points out that the rationalist thought of the eighteenth century, which aided a new industrial class in Europe, "in Latin America was the temporary ideology of the land holders, mine owners, and traders."[28]

All that we have observed thus far about Spanish values, the problems of civil and ecclesiastical organization, the conflicts between crown and *criollo,* are exemplified in the founding and early years of Central America's first university. When, on January 7, 1681, the Universidad de San Carlos de Guatemala formally opened, over a century of struggle lay behind it. Quarrels among religious orders, chaos in communication with Spain, and rivalries with Mexico, were among the delaying factors. Once the university was established, the disorders, if anything, increased. Historian John Tate Lanning describes the cutting of classes by professors and the "disdain" of the students for the university. He also tells some useful things about university governance, which remained a profoundly controversial issue in the nineteenth and twentieth centuries.

"The affairs of Spanish universities were conducted by rigid statutes, which, while reducing administration to a minimum, also reduced change and flexibility to something less than a minimum." The King was the patron of the royal and pontifical universities; the Captain-General was the vice-patron. The academic electorate, called the *claustro,* was "composed of all licentiates, masters of arts, and doctors graduated from it or incorporated in it, and from this fountainhead sprang all academic authority."[29] Meetings were secret, and even the dress was prescribed. The rector was elected, but it was often hard to find a willing candidate. The chancellor, who conferred degrees, was certified by the King. "The chief element of continuity in the colonial university was the secretary . . . ."[30] The bedel was a "combination janitor, mace-bearer, and handyman." To qualify, he had to know how to read and write.[31]

But nothing speaks more eloquently of the social history of the times than certain other of Lanning's descriptions, nor gives more evidence that universities are closely linked with the values of their cultures. For example, he comments on the strict regimen imposed upon the university treasurer:

> This vicious circle of suspicion surrounding University finance, made necessary by centuries of malfeasance and by troublesome litigation in an age when the king was trying to grasp and hold all purse strings, in no way reflected upon San Carlos; it was basic in the Spanish theory and practice of government, whether among the doctors of Salamanca or the collectors of the port of Vera Cruz.[32]

The university was not exempt from the contest between King and Church, for in 1767 there was a quarrel "over the placing of the papal arms alternately with the royal ones along the top of walls of the new university building."[33] But the issue was not even that simple.

> On the surface a conflict between church and state, this whole controversy was in reality something else . . . the state aimed to control, not the church, but the university! In both Spain and America university cloisters held tenaciously to the "prerogatives, exemptions, and franchise" of their guild as crown officials overrode them. At Salamanca freedom from royal dictation in internal matters was the issue with the King in the eighteenth century, not reluctance of the university to accept "modernization," as Anglo-Saxon historians and many others have it. The cloister of San Carlos was not worried about the Pope. It merely did not wish to permit the civil government, particularly the local branch, to dictate to it in an ancient matter of privilege.[34]

It is misleading to emphasize only negative aspects, for between 1625 and 1821 San Carlos and its antecedent institutions had produced these numbers of badly needed graduates: bachelor's degrees in arts, theology, law, common law and medicine, 2006; *licenciados*, 256; master's degrees, 32; and doctor's degrees, 216.[35] For a time the doctorate was a largely ceremonial achievement, featuring costly parades, dress, feasts, and fireworks. Citizens complained of the noise and drunkenness. The length of traces

on horses to draw the coaches for the parades was a matter of correspondence with Spain.[36]   But these are more than amusing anecdotes.

> Beneath the love of pomp . . . lay a factor far more basic. The
> lines of development of state and university, were opposite and
> contradictory. As the modern age dawned, the national govern-
> ment became absolutist and centralist at the expense of corporate
> privilege. Thus, the university, while waging a running fight to
> prevent encroachment upon the privileges it had acquired as a
> medieval guild, indirectly supported the modern principle of
> autonomy in learning and science. Unfortunately, the state with
> its capacity for quick action, was some times so far ahead of the
> university that it could impose progress by fiat. *Even more
> fundamental than this struggle was the economic stringency,
> which cast a lasting pall upon the university, preventing its
> physical growth and retarding its intellectual development.*[37]

The university continued to mirror values and social conflicts of its
society in the years to come. Certainly much of the rationalistic thought
which fueled the independence movement and which had some impact on
emerging constitutions was brought from Europe by the intellectuals of
the university. But it could prove as difficult to change an essentially
elitist institution of higher education as to change the social structure in
which it was embedded.

Independence and its Aftermath; the New Colonialism

A great deal of eighteenth-century rhetoric lives on in the ceremonial
acts and documents of Central America, but the face of the land and the
faces of the people seem to have been only little affected. If we are to
give credence to any of Américo Castro's description of Spanish values
and virtues, we should not be surprised.

The nineteenth century got off to an uneasy start in Central America.
There was a genuine ferment of new, liberal ideas. There was also
restlessness with the secondary roles American-born Spaniards and their
descendants were forced to play. There was resentment of the power and
wealth of the clergy. Explosions of rebellion broke out in various areas,
precursors of the final severing of ties with Spain; and, after declaring
itself independent in 1821, the Captaincy-General of Guatemala was beset
by a period of confusion over relationship with Mexico. But in 1823 the
United Central American Provinces was confirmed by a Central American constituent assembly.

This former kingdom of Guatemala, however, could not hold together. ". . . the provinces, inebriated with their newly acquired autonomy, were reluctant to accept a central authority and fell prey to disorders and rivalries which had been kept dormant by Spanish power."[38] There were disorders for the next two decades, and a last attempt in 1842 to achieve federation failed. "From then onwards, and in spite of many successive attempts to reestablish the Federation, the republics of Guatemala, El Salvador, Honduras, Nicaragua and Costa Rica took their separate courses."[39]

Franklin Parker indicates that there were some seeming paradoxes in these relationships, however, and that the sense of nationhood was not immediate. The first to call themselves republics were Guatemala, but not until 1847, and Costa Rica in 1848.

> Even then the republics continued to recognize a citizen of one as a citizen of another by simple change of residence, often giving political preference, even the presidency, to migrants of such status. Politicians thought nothing of using the territory and resources of a friendly one of the five in order to gain power in another. In fact the chief reason why several nineteenth-century attempts at reunion failed is that the politics of any one state were so intertwined with the affairs of the others that the slightest shift in power in one spot was often enough to shatter the entire construction.[40]

Each separate country had its own history of internal turbulence, each its succession of strong men, each its internal blood feuds and frequent blood lettings. The twentieth century differed from the nineteenth only on the calendar. Proclamations, elections, martyrs. Local loyalties hardened eventually into national loyalties, and political parties became in place after place not so much fortresses of ideologies as identification with family, town, tradition.[41]

The land and those who lived on it were changed in some ways after independence. Trade increased outward as commerce was no longer restricted by Spain. Between 1821 and 1825 the volume of exports doubled.[42] With the coming of coffee and bananas, agriculture was stimulated and commercialized, and a new group of powerful landowners arose. Economist Carlos Castillo's description of the consequences of the new wealth derived from the export of coffee and bananas is a case of change without change. True, a new infrastructure was created—the transportation, communication, credit system—necessary to the enterprise. Labor was shifted in large numbers from the haciendas to the commercial plantations, except for the continuity of the small landholders producing for domestic needs. National governments were strengthened over local ones. Some of the owners developed close ties with those of more advanced countries, and acquired their patterns of consumption, which they could afford in Central America because of low wages and the uneven income distribution. The result:

> This system of limited participation in the structure of ownership, where there remained large segments of landless people, was also a system of limited citizenship. The liberal constitutions of the period provided for universal suffrage and eligibility to public office, subject only to minimum requirements of age and place of birth. But, for the bulk of the population, real access to the political system and ability to act effectively before the governments were severely limited by weakness derived from lack of land or control over other resources.[43]

Inevitably, the United States took an interest, as the British had done earlier, backing this or that party or strong man as it suited their purposes. We mention here only some examples of interventions as they affected prospects for regional unity. Rodríguez calls the formative years of the republics "a violent period of ideological struggles and unadorned selfishness that the colonial past had almost institutionalized. Because of the machinations of aggressive British agents, the power of the world's leading nation worked against unionism and the establishment of liberal institutions; the traditional elements and centrifugal forces in the Central American environment did the rest."[44]

Bananas and boats dictated U.S. concern with the region. There were already canal treaties with Nicaragua before the U.S. helped carve Panama out of Colombia in 1903. Banana production took hold on a truly commercial scale around the turn of the century and only increased U.S. activity in Central America. Whether his speculation is valid no one can tell, but Parker says that had the first twentieth-century move toward unity ". . . come without the involvement of the United States in Central American politics it might have cut fifty years off the unification time table."[45]

One might speculate that were Central America one country or five, U.S. private investment would still have to some degree dictated U.S. government policy in the area. The twentieth-century period is replete with examples of U.S. concern with the separate countries. Whatever reforms might or might not have come about, for example, had the U.S. not accomplished the overthrow of elected President Jacobo Arbenz in Guatemala in 1954, one cannot say. The fear of communism had become in the fifties and sixties a pretext for action of many kinds. Much of it had been directed against needed reforms.

Even without foreign intervention, one cannot say that social change, peaceful or otherwise, could have been accomplished, given the power structure. There have been for well over a century repeated calls for reform in Central America to correct social and economic injustice, and more than once calls for revolution. If, for example, as we shall see, only a relatively small part of the people in Central America have had access to education—and that often only by accident of birth—there are inequities inherent in the social order which large numbers of people will continue to oppose. Access to education, or the lack of it, is only one index of the problem.

Rodolfo Stavenhagen points out, as indeed have many others, that external colonialism was supplanted by an internal colonialism, in which the underdeveloped rural areas still are at the mercy of the developed (generally urban) centers of power which drain wealth from them and put little back.[46] (Even without statistics this is clear to the unaided eye in Central America.) The society never was feudal, reciprocal, and closed, in the classical European tradition, but dedicated to extraction and export based on cheap labor.

Whether the calls for reform or revolution focus on the right problems or the right solutions cannot be assessed here, but education is part of either reform or revolution. The political battlefields which the universities have often been are only one manifestation of inquietudes which have a long history.

To see contemporary education in some meaningful context one must consider certain contemporary attitudes which have their logic in that past which has blended into a not-so-different present. To those who see education, along with industrialization, increased consumption of consumer goods, and the growth of a middle class, as a significant factor for change, some other of Stavenhagen's views are worth considering.

The belief, widely held and serving as a logic for certain kinds of policy making, that the development of a large middle class will alter basic institutions is one he challenges. He calls the grouping itself a merely statistical aggregate for those who do certain work or consume certain goods. He argues that those who see it as eventually filling the social universe and wiping out both power and numbers of elites and absorbing the lower strata are mistaken. The so-called middle class is, he says, "economically and socially dependent upon the upper strata; they are tied politically to the ruling class; they are conservative in their tastes and opinions, defenders of the status quo; and they search only for individual privileges."[47] Certainly the growth of that group between the power elite and the wretchedly poor, whatever its name, has not yet appreciably changed the face of Central America, and certainly the absolute numbers of the poor have been little diminished.

This Mexican social scientist argues that it is also a fallacy to look to industrializing urban sectors to change the economies. Indeed, although these sectors are growing in Central America, they have not voluntarily or through tax policies allocated the capital to develop the infrastructure, including educational systems, along other than colonial patterns. There is, Stavenhagen points out, no real conflict of interest between the industrial-business sector and the old agrarian sector. And the history of the Latin American town, as Hubert Herring says, is that the country population served it rather than the reverse, which happened in the growth of the town to meet the needs of the inhabitants of the country in England's American colonies.[48]

It would be surprising if educational goals and processes were greatly different from the pattern of other institutions of their societies. Educational systems in Central America, as the following chapters will clearly show, are strongly centralized in their control. Access to education is severely limited by factors of birth, residence, and public policy. Urban youth are better served than rural. Methods of instruction have been oriented toward dictation and memorization. Research and innovation are not characteristic of educational systems, on the whole. To all of these one may cite exceptions, and most often in Costa Rica, again a reflection of a society which has had a more democratic tradition.

There are also some of the elements which a UNESCO study commonly found in underdeveloped, tradition-bound societies world-wide:

1. A preference for programs leading to occupations which command relatively high income and have a high status.
2. An avoidance of occupations involving manual skills and the possibility of eventual employment in isolated localities.
3. Strong insistence upon specific, practical preparation for examinations and advanced study, and unwillingness to undertake studies beyond the stated requirement.[49]

After independence as before, the universities in Central America reflected the character of their societies. If higher education was, as we noted earlier, of more status value than practical, it was not destined to receive larger public or private investment. More important, it was not destined to command the attention of full-time professors, to be other than an elitist institution, or to look as much to a modern future as to a tradition-filled past.

Given the chaos of almost nonstop political strife in the nineteenth century, it is no surprise that universities in Central America had to struggle for existence itself, and were convenient rallying points for competing political factions. Their patterns of organization continued from the colonial past, although there was a more secular trend. Knowledge was arranged in categories of law, theology, and medicine most commonly;

and though the number of categories was later to be expanded to include such bodies of knowledge as engineering, dentistry, pharmacy, and economics, the character of the institution which bore the name "university" was little altered. It was from the beginning and until the recent past clusters of professors in separate *facultades* or schools imparting essentially vocational education.[50]

Traditionally the student arrived at the Latin American university with all his liberal, general education behind him. As will be evident in the pages to come, the level of formal preparation of those who taught him often went only a little beyond his own. What lay ahead was a program of studies designed only to prepare him as a professional person, and the career choice he was forced to make in his early or middle teens might be as little attuned to his capacities as the existing choices of professions were to national needs.

In Central America, as in the rest of Latin America, university teaching has been in the hands of the professional man who has come—or often failed to come—to lecture a few hours a week.

As one Honduran professor commented several years ago, somewhat cynically to be sure, "I am a lawyer first, a politician second, and a university professor third." If many do not or cannot claim a political vocation, practically all have given teaching duties a lower priority than their professions. It is prestige, not pay—often only a token sum—which has summoned the practicing engineer or pharmacist to lecture a few hours a week in mathematics or chemistry in his particular professional school. The *catedratico* or principal professor of a given subject, chosen originally in a competitive examination or *concurso*, holds his position for life, and he may if he chooses repeat forever what he learned as a student.

The few laboratories and libraries a university might boast served their separate proprietors, and, as with their separate courses, were often weak, duplicated, and costly.

Some critics, both within and without Central America, have attributed to student participation in university government the blame for certain deficiencies in quality of education and also for university involvement in politics. From the few descriptive statements above and the data in chapters to follow, it seems evident that who legally governs such an institution is not necessarily the unique and ultimate determinant of its nature. Neither the university nor the rest of education is a cultural isolate.

All of the Central American universities have achieved their autonomy, after sometimes bloody battles with repressive governments. This means that no longer can governments select administrative or teaching personnel, make policy, or dictate on academic matters. That autonomy has been used in a variety of ways, depending in part on the degree of social stability in the national environment. The University of Panama lost its autonomy with its takeover and closing by the Military Junta in 1968. By contrast, in the cooler political temperature of Costa Rica, the President of the Republic visits the university campus without so much as an accompanying policeman.

There has been for nearly twenty years a movement afoot in Central America, as well as in many countries in the rest of Latin America, toward modernizing the universities. *Reforma universitaria* is a phrase of both symbolic and operational significance in much of Latin America: a slogan to send students to the barricades, a plaything for politicians, a process for modernization of education. Reform may be all things at the same time in the same institution, and whether it is viewed as threat or promise depends in great part upon the nature of the society of which the university is a part.

Each of the Central American universities is in some stage along the road of modernization. The main reform features are toward development of full-time faculty whose main occupation is teaching and research, departmentalization of basic disciplines, university-wide physical facilities such as laboratories and libraries, and common programs for all students in the first year or two in good beginning courses in the sciences and humanities.

Slowly emerging out of and almost in spite of the weight of tradition, there is a new generation of educational philosophers and technicians. Their role in education is perhaps akin to that of those who labor to modernize economic and social aspects of Central America. Interestingly true with both groups, the greater scope of the region than the nation lends a certain leverage to their efforts.

Regional Cooperation

During the less than 150 years since independence, Central Americans have had to cooperate, if they were indeed able to do so, within a system of rather formidable class and special interest barriers as well as those of local identity and loyalty. As Rodrigo Facio points out, there was not even general unanimity over the blessings of independence. Guatemala's very potent oligarchy could hardly welcome a more democratic relationship with the economic classes and provinces over which she had long enjoyed distinct advantages. Certain of the artisans who enjoyed special protection for their budding industries saw threats in a system of free commerce.[51]

The common resentment among the provinces against Guatemala did not long hold them in any common cause; indeed, each had its own group, the conservative, which was usually pro-Guatemala, and which engaged in battles with the so-called liberals who wanted more local autonomy. These latter were scarcely infected seriously or for long by philosophical movements which went elsewhere by the same names. Facio describes the hardening of these allegiances even in the brief years of the post-Independence Federation,[52] and, as we have seen, these allegiances, tied to town or family, have shaped political life strongly ever since.

In 1824 the Political Constitution of Central America was adopted, creating a federal system. It was one which worked scarcely at all, and the years until it fell apart in 1839 were filled chiefly with internal and regional skirmishes and battles. There were intermittent movements in behalf of Central American union through the rest of the nineteenth century, and some treaties were signed in the twentieth century. Nothing more practical than hope resulted; but however small the spark, it remained. A more viable entity was finally brought into being in 1951 when a charter for a new organization was signed in El Salvador by the foreign ministers of the five republics.

After several postponements, the *Organización de Estados Centroamericanos,* known as ODECA, had its first meeting of foreign ministers in 1955. In the next few years it was to bear tangible fruits, among them several important ones affecting regional educational systems, as will be seen in later chapters. It has promoted regional meetings of such groups as cattlemen, investors, municipal leaders, ministers of public health, and university rectors.[53] Many have been the criticisms of ODECA, and several have been the hesitations about fully supporting it. But nothing perhaps speaks so eloquently as a recent critical editorial in a Guatemalan newspaper entitled "Decadence, Agony of ODECA."[54]

Here themes of regional jealousies, moves toward separation, seem subordinated: ODECA, in sum, is not strong enough.[55] Quoting and concurring with an editorial in *Diario Latino* of El Salvador, *El Imparcial* says, "ODECA is actually an indispensable organism for the progressive development of Central America in all its relations. It is indispensable in politics, in legal matters, in economics, in commerce and in matters cultural and social. In whatever field anything needs to be organized, the presence of ODECA is necessary, but it lacks authority . . . ."

Problems of administration, legal organization, and finance are mentioned. But ". . . ODECA comes to be the embryo, the nucleus, of the Central American superstate, the superstate for the direction and management of all those matters which go beyond the state jurisdiction of the five Central American parcels of land."

Central American political unification into a superstate may be a far-off dream. The Central American Common Market, however, is not. Even more than ODECA, it has had a catalytic effect on trade and the development of good working relations among economists and other technical specialists of the five member countries. (Panama has not joined, but does have special treaties with several individual countries. There are practical obstacles to Panamanian membership in the CACM: Panama's economic relations with the U.S., and its lack of a central bank, for example.)[56]

In 1950 trade amounted to $8,600,000 among the five members. By 1960 it had increased to $32,600,000, and in 1967 to $213,500,000. This 700 percent increase in seven years, or 2700 percent increase since 1950,[57] has not come without some difficulties, for the requisite ceding of sovereignty and subordination of national to regional goals touches sensitive financial and political nerves.

"Despite cries of 'crisis' in some quarters, the Central American Common Market (CACM) in 1968 registered the strongest advance in its seven-year history. Trade among the five CACM partners increased roughly 22 percent during the year, from $213 to $260 million . . ."; thus the *Miami Herald* began an article on February 25, 1969. Controversy makes headlines and political bonfires, but the technical competence in which the market had its beginnings has paid dividends.

The organization of the common market began with a request to the United Nations Economic Commission for Latin America (ECLA) in 1951 for help in developing agriculture, industry, and transportation systems, with a view to economic integration and the creation of larger markets for mutual exchange. This joint request was followed in 1952 with formation of the Economic Cooperation Committee, made up of the five economic ministers, under ECLA auspices. "It should be noted that in contrast with the legalistic Latin American tradition, and in contrast also with the European Common Market, the Central American programme was not derived from a fully comprehensive and logically consistent framework. It was, on the contrary, the result of a series of ad hoc decisions superimposed on one another."[58]

Economist Alberto Fuentes Mohr, closely associated with common-market development for over a decade, goes on to detail some of the network of early bilateral treaties which prevailed among members, and which even by 1960 had increased intraregional trade to 6.3 percent of all Central American imports.[59] After the General Treaty of Central American Integration, fully ratified in 1962, that trade continued to expand, and in 1965 made up 20 percent of total imports.[60]

Certain problems are inherent in cooperation simply because the five nations are in different stages of development. Honduras and Nicaragua are less industrialized than the other three, so that at once the problem of making uniform rules to foster industrial development, for example, causes certain inequities. El Salvador is suffering from intense population pressure on the land, while neighboring Honduras lacks needed manpower;

border frictions over migrants are smoldering.[61] Still heavily dependent on its agricultural export economy, the entire region suffers a chronic imbalance of payment.[62] Further, the machine tools to create industry are not available within the region, and their importation adds to the problem.[63] There are major policy questions to be resolved concerning the most just, acceptable, and practical ways both to develop agriculture and to industrialize.

"Free trade, tariff equalization, harmonization of fiscal systems, uniform social policies, regional development programs, and agreements to promote the free movement of factors of production are all measures requiring various degrees of political adjustment in each country to the larger interest of the region as a whole."[64] These words of the long-time general secretary of SIECA (Secretariat of the Economic Council of Central America) were a calm prediction of possible storms to come. One of the most potentially disruptive crises in CACM history, an example of problems of "political adjustment," is still unresolved.

In June 1, 1968, the Economic Council and the Executive Council of the Common Market met in San José and approved a protocol to impose a 30 percent tax on merchandise imported from outside the region, particularly nonessential goods. Nicaragua at once ratified the measure but it met resistance in the other countries. Political party divisions between President Trejos and the Legislative Assembly in Costa Rica left that country, for example, disunited on the subject. The outcry was general, however, that the consumers would bear the new tax burden. "Who will pay this new tax? Undoubtedly the working class, because in the end they always pay the taxes."[65] This letter from the Industrial Union of Textile Workers in San José, addressed to two members of the Legislative Assembly, was not untypical of the response.

There were other examples of "political adjustments."

> Nicaraguan guards delayed or turned back hundreds of trucks last week bearing products from Guatemala, El Salvador, Honduras and Costa Rica, insisting on the imposition of the protective levies. . . . General Anastasio Somoza, Nicaragua's president, has threatened to quit the common market unless his partners impose the tax. He has set a deadline of August 1, insisting that "they have got to play fair." The Nicaraguan government has accused El Salvador and Guatemala of obtaining duty-free rice from Mexico and obtaining precious dollars by exporting it to Nicaragua. Nicaragua hinted that Costa Rica was selling Nicaragua cheap shirts made in Hong Kong carrying Costa Rican labels. It also accused Honduras shirt makers of undercutting prices with tax free cloth imports. A similar assertion was made against Guatemala's soap. . . . Honduras struck back by rejecting 36 trucks carrying crackers from Nicaragua.[66]

This was prelude to the hastily convened summit meeting in San Salvador of all the Central American presidents and U.S. President Johnson, in which all signed on July 6, 1968, an accord looking forward toward co-operative action to solve mutual problems.

The problems, of course, persist, but progress is undeniable. One cannot help noting that alongside whatever story of political crisis in the press of any of the countries there is likely to be a news item about a regional meeting of some technical agency to confer on some aspect of a problem of common concern. One cannot assume that technicians alone can assure Central American unity, but the development of a cadre of national and regional people, well qualified in their respective fields, has without any doubt done much to facilitate cooperation. Indeed, the aims of all the protocols of joint action would come to little without technical implementation.

Under the direction of the permanent secretariat (SIECA) established by the Economic Council of Central America, work has gone forward on such necessary tasks as customs simplification, patents, and uniform mercantile law. There is a Central American Bank of Economic Integration, and a Central American Institute of Public Administration; agreements have been achieved on which countries will develop certain industries for the regional market, and new basic industries are being given special encouragement. Agriculture ministers have met to work out policies for price stabilization in basic grains and import quotas from outside the region.[67] Attention is being given to such urgent problems as the network of highways needed for development of the regional infrastructure, and the estimated completion date is 1972. Legal, technical, and commercial problems are being worked out to create and coordinate a system of telecommunications.[68]

Among the other regional agencies contributing at the technical level are the *Instituto Centroamericano de Investigación y Technología Industrial* (INCAITI); the *Consejo Monetario Centroamericano* which facilitates use of national currencies in regional transactions; the *Instituto de Nutrición de Centroamerica y Panama* (INCAP); the *Organismo Internacional Regional de Sanidad Agropecuaria* (OIRSA); the *Corporación Centroamericana de Servicios de Navegación Aerea* (COCESNA); and the *Federación de Cámara y Asociaciones Industriales Centroamericanas* (FECAICA). Oldest of all the regional organisms is the *Consejo Superior Universitario Centroamericano* (CSUCA),[69] whose contributions are discussed in chapter eight.

Still the required "political adjustments" of which Carlos Castillo wrote persist on a fundamental policy level. There is the continuing frustration felt by large numbers of Central Americans over the contradiction between professed values and the realities of daily living in their own environments. There are also honest differences of opinion on the uses of tariff, whether it is an income-producing device which may impede genuine tax reform, or whether it is a tool to protect developing industries. There is the very real question of whether industrialization will raise the living standards for a majority of the citizens.

Unity, cooperation, and integration are in some manner being realized. Yet population growth, a still ill-serving agricultural economy, migrations to cities with their scarcity of jobs and housing, and the insufficiencies of access to education all conduce to pressures against the old order. Castillo describes improved legislation on labor, housing, social security, public health, and land settlement of the last twenty years as too limited in character and scope to alter the politicoeconomic structure.[70] Whether the benefits of industrialization can be great enough and widespread enough to create a more equitable economic order is perhaps the most important question to be raised concerning the Common Market.

The poor are readily visible in Central America. So are glittering, costly kitchen gadgets and shiny plastic furniture in urban shop windows. Visible, too, are handsomely designed, rapidly growing, middle-class residential areas and private schools. Many—who can say how many—of the publicly supported school buildings are unbelievably bad: dirty, crowded, ill lighted or unlighted; rickety wooden fire traps, or crumbling adobe. Increase in number and quality of schools occurs, but the deficiencies in the systems are a mute challenge to a social order whose realities are not congruent with its rhetoric.

Whether the negative factors, so long lasting and so tightly woven into the fabric of daily relationships, can be countered or ameliorated through regional cooperation and integration remains to be seen. The chapters to come will show that some physical realities, and, even more, some aspirations, have changed as a result of regional cooperation in education. It is curious and heartening that frequently in times of internal political unheavals and external frictions of one government with another educators have traveled all through the isthmus to scheduled meetings and conferences almost as if politics did not exist, nor their quarreling national governments.

Viewed optimistically, as great numbers of technically capable people see it, the chances of a better life for all in Central America are greatly enhanced by cooperation, communication, and coordination. Real integration, economic and otherwise, will come only with the free movement of people, both workers and entrepreneurs. Real change will come when the traditionally dispossessed can make choices with their lives. Industrial development and political democracy are goals unrealizable without massive investments in education.

2
EDUCATION
IN
GUATEMALA

In all the history of Central America in colonial times, probably the most respected and loved figure is Francisco Marroquín, the first bishop of Guatemala. In the midst of the cruelties and repressions of the conquest, Marroquín and some of his fellow priests were not only concerned for the spiritual welfare of the Indians and of the *mestizo* offspring of Spanish soldiers and Indian women, but were interested in their education as well. These priests were the first promoters of literacy programs and they campaigned for higher levels of education as well. On March 15, 1545, Bishop Marroquín dispatched the first of a long series of messages to the Spanish crown, arguing that boys born in Guatemala were at an age when they were ready for humanistic studies and for Latin. From the beginning, priests offered some primary education; and by the end of the second decade of Spanish presence, there was some instruction at the secondary level. By the end of the sixteenth century there was a variety of schools, chiefly conducted by the Franciscans and the Dominicans. By the beginning of the seventeenth century the Jesuit Colegio de San Lucas was the most important of the secondary schools, and it had a library of more than 5,000 volumes, the best in Central America.[1]

The effects of these educational efforts in the sixteenth century can be seen, for example, in the quantity of important writings by Indians and *mestizos;* records of pre-Colombian culture, such as *El Popol Vuh, Anales de las Cakchiqueles,* and the drama *Rabinal Achí,* have been preserved.

There developed a considerable level of culture in the first century of Spanish life in Guatemala.[2]

When, after a century of planning and petitions, the University of San Carlos was founded in 1676, it is significant that one of the first five professorships established was a chair in a major Indian language, Cakchiquel. An account of the opening ceremony, December 18, 1680, describes the manner in which each of the new professors gave a brief lecture. The professor of Cakchiquel spoke in this Indian language and, the narrator adds, "it is presumed that he discussed art and grammar."[3]

Despite more than four centuries of educational history, however, Guatemala still suffers from acute weaknesses in its educational system and, above all, from the problem of incorporating the Indian population into the national life. Education must take a major responsibility for this process of assimilation.

Social, Economic, and Ethnic Background

The most striking statistic regarding Guatemalan education is the fact that, according to the latest census (1964), the average level of formal schooling of the Guatemalan people was 1.2 years.[4] The causes and consequences of this sad statistic ramify in many directions. According to the same 1964 census report, 63.3 percent of the population over seven years old was illiterate, the highest percentage in Central America and one of the highest in all Latin America. The illiteracy rate for the urban population is 36.2 percent; for the rural areas, 78.8 percent.[5]

If the people can neither read nor write, so do they likewise suffer short, hungry lives. For the period 1960-1965 life expectancy at birth was 47 years, the lowest in Central America and, with the exception of Haiti, the lowest in Latin America.[6] Half of the annual deaths are of children under age four.[7] There is endemic malnutrition. A 1965 survey showed a daily average intake of 1,994 calories. According to the United Nations organization for food and agriculture (FAO), 2,500 calories per day represents a minimum.[8] Another study for the period 1963-1965 indicates an average of 2,175 calories.[9]

The gross domestic product per capita in 1966 was $290. The average income per capita in 1964 was $360 and had risen only at the rate of 4.3 percent annually in the previous 14 years. The poor distribution of income is suggested by the fact that the average income of the rural population declined during the same period and was only $83 per capita in 1964.[10]

Economic, health, and educational problems are compounded by the explosive birthrate in Guatemala, estimated at 3.3 percent annually during the period 1964-1967. In the period between the 1950 and the 1964 census, the population increased 53.5 percent. This rate of growth represents a doubling of population in about 20 years. It is estimated that the 1967 population was 4,717,000 and that by 1980 the population may reach 7,191,000. In 1964 the urban population represented only one-third of the total. The population of the capital, the largest city in Central America, was over 570,000 in 1964 and represents almost half of the urban population.[11]

As would be expected in a country with Guatemala's high birth rate, the population is relatively young, and hence the burden of education is immense while, simultaneously, the economically active portion of the population is relatively small. The comparative figures for the last two censuses, shown in Table 1, illustrate the increasing problem.[12] Merely

TABLE 1. AGE GROUPS OF THE POPULATION

Census	Percentage Less than 15 Years of Age	Percentage Between 15 and 64	Percentage Over 65
1950	42.3	55.3	2.4
1964	47.0	50.3	2.7

to keep up with the rising numbers of youth represents a heavy investment in schools and teachers, let alone to reduce the immense, existing deficits. There is also an immense pressure upon the school-age youth to join the labor force rather than to attend school. When the only productive tool for human survival in many of the mountainous rural areas of Guatemala is the muscle power of the human body and when the level of subsistence is so marginal, one can understand the reluctance of many *campesino* families to defer their children's work in the field for some later, uncomprehended benefit of formal schooling.

Guatemala is still primarily rural. Migration from the country to the city is a characteristic of Guatemala, as it is in other Latin American countries. The growth rate of Guatemala City, almost twice that of the country as a whole, is an indication of this trend.[13] But the great majority of Guatemalans are still rural, living in some 7,000 villages, many of which have populations of less than 1,000 inhabitants.[14] The migration to the city will continue, but, unless economic growth is much more rapid than is anticipated, there will be an insufficiency of employment and housing, these newest migrants will live in unsatisfactory conditions, and the city will increasingly experience all of the social problems that accompany this type of migration; education will confront an additionally difficult task.

This migration from the rural area has some origins in the national pattern of land ownership and in the absence of any thoroughgoing program of land reform. The census of 1950 indicated that, on the one hand,

84.4 percent of landholders owned only 14.3 percent of the total land; and, on the other hand, only 2.1 percent of landowners possessed 72.5 percent of the total. Many rural families possess no land at all and work as hired laborers.[15]

At the root of many of these educational, health, economic, and agricultural problems in Guatemala are its ethnic characteristics. Bishop Marroquín and Father Bartolomé de las Casas (who lived in Guatemala from 1536 to 1539) were among many priests and some laymen who fought for the interests of the Indian; but four and a half centuries after the Spanish conquest many of the Indian peoples still remain within their traditional languages and cultures. Some scholars estimate that today at least three out of every five persons in Guatemala belong to the "unassimilated or partially assimilated indigenous population."[16]

The 1940 census in Guatemala attempted to classify the population as white, *mestizo* or mixed, indigenous, black, and yellow. Because these distinctions are most difficult to make and because of the large number of *mestizos,* the 1950 census used only the classification of *ladinos* and *indígenas. Ladinos* are those who dress and speak like Europeans; *indígenas* are those who speak and dress like Indians. (The term *ladino* was first applied at the end of the Middle Ages in Spain to Arabs who spoke Spanish; it means Latin or *latino.*)[17] In the 1950 Guatemalan census 54 percent of the population was officially classified as *indígena.* These indigenous peoples live chiefly in the highlands and in the sparsely settled northern part of Guatemala. They are principally rural, although they are much in evidence in the capital city. In the smallest rural communities up to 90 percent of the population may be Indian; the larger the city, the smaller the proportion.[18]

The Indians do not represent a homogeneous group, but rather a great variety of languages and cultures. Scholars identify some 23 distinct languages, classifiable into three language families. There are 1,294,376 speakers of Quiché languages; 199,933 speakers of Maya languages; and 10,230 speakers of Araguace.[19]

West and Augelli believe that the assimilation of the Indian communities into the national life will be difficult, much more difficult than the task of assimilation in Mexico.

> The Indian's principal social and political allegiance is to his *municipio*—to his *patria chica*—not to the nation. On the other hand, although many are illiterate and speak little Spanish, most Guatemalan Indians are successful farmers, craftsmen, or tradesmen within their own communities. They may be considered as an aboriginal peasantry, proud of their Indian heritage, rather than an abject and underdeveloped ethnic minority.[20]

That this preceding view is somewhat romantic is evidenced by the statistics already given regarding average daily caloric intake and by data on Indian farming which observes that methods are little changed from pre-Colombian times and that average production per acre of corn, the most important Indian crop, perhaps does not reach as much as 12 percent of the normal yields elsewhere.[21]

Some Guatemalan scholars take the rather different view that, in the absence of racial discrimination in Guatemala, the *indigenista* problem reduces itself almost completely to a problem of *campesinos:* i.e., to a problem of rural laborers and the need to modify the land tenure system. The economic aspect is the fundamental one, from this point of view. Increase in economic opportunity will result in greater mobility between country and city, and in greater educational opportunity, and assimilation and acculturation will occur rapidly.[22]

We think both views have some truth and some falsity. The Indian populations, as all of the national data show, live short and unproductive lives. Despite increased economic opportunity, centuries of cultural isolation will make assimilation difficult. The key factor is likely to be education, supplied more effectively by the state, both in quality and in quantity, than it has been supplied in the past.[23]

Regional efforts to improve the quality of education in Central America will be of benefit to Guatemala. Both Guatemala and her regional associates, however, are confronted with the lack of homogeneity of culture and tradition among them. Only Guatemala has the task of transforming an indigenous population from a national burden to a national asset, and only Guatemala has the tradition of political and educational dominance of the region from the colonial past. Both the present cultural realities and the remnant role from history could impede the progress of Central American unity, in which case both Guatemalan and Central American education will suffer.

Legal and Constitutional Bases of Education in Guatemala

The director of the educational planning commission of ODECA (the Organization of Central American States), Ovidio Soto Blanco, observes that the study of the constitutional provisions for education in Central America has a very special interest. Dull as the reading of national constitutions may be, constitutions do make statements of educational and cultural goals, and do provide the legal warrant for attempts to achieve them. On these legal bases are then erected the elaborate scaffolding of organic laws of education, as well as the proliferation of regulations emitted by the ministry of education.[24] If, as in Guatemala, for example, the constitution itself requires obligatory attendance in the primary school, visible failure to comply with the constitution is not necessarily an indictment of the constitution.

The Constitution of 1965 includes nineteen articles related to education.[25] According to Article 91 the stimulation and spreading of culture in all its aspects are essential responsibilities of the state. The goals of education are: the integrated development of the personality, physical and spiritual betterment, a sense of the individual responsibility of the citizen, the civic progress of the nation, the stimulation of patriotism, and the respect for human rights.

Parents, too, have a heavy responsibility and have the right to choose what will be taught to their younger children. The state must found and maintain schools, and has also the obligation to dignify the teacher economically, socially, and culturally. The education of teachers is a preferential function of the state (Art. 92). Academic freedom is guaranteed. Religious education is optional. Civic, moral, and religious education is declared to be in the interest of the state; and the state may support religious education, but without any discrimination (Art. 93). Primary education is obligatory for all inhabitants of the country between limits to be fixed by law. Primary education offered by the state is free (Art. 94). Private schools must be supervised by the state and, to offer valid certificates, they must at least fulfill official programs of study (Art. 95).

The constitution proclaims the national urgency of literacy and asserts that the state will organize and promote literacy programs with all necessary resources. Industrial and agricultural enterprises located outside of urban areas are obliged to organize and support primary schools in accordance with provisions of the law (Art. 97). Everyone has a right to education. Technical and professional education must be accessible to all on an equal basis (Art. 98).

Higher education, too, has its warrant from the constitution. The University of San Carlos is an autonomous institution and has the responsibility to organize, direct, and develop higher education in the nation. San Carlos will receive a minimum of 2.5 percent of the ordinary income of the state (Art. 99). The administration of the university will be in the hands of the University Council, made up of the rector, the deans of each school, a representative of each school drawn from the corresponding professional association, one professor from each school, and one student from each school (Art. 100). The only degrees and professional titles recognized in Guatemala will be those given or recognized by San Carlos and those issued by authorized private universities. Titles and degrees given by other Central American universities will be fully valid in Guatemala when there is a regional unification of basic plans of study (Art. 101).

Private universities now existing and those that may be created will be recognized as contributing to national development. The Council of Private Higher Education will approve the organization of private universities after an opinion has been received from San Carlos, and after approval has been received from the president of the republic, in consultation with the Council of Ministers. The Council of Private Higher Education will exercise supervision of the private universities and will be composed of the minister of education, two delegates from San Carlos, two delegates from the private universities, and two delegates who have no university responsibilities and who will be named by the presidents of the professional associations (Art. 102). When its means permit, the state may give financial aid to the private universities (Art. 103).

The law will regulate everything relative to the organization and functioning of the universities (Art. 104). The organization of professional associations is obligatory. These organizations will relate themselves to San Carlos, which must approve their statutes (Art. 105). Popular arts and industries, art and national folklore, will be protected and their cultivation encouraged in both public and private education (Art. 109). The state will work to achieve the socioeconomic improvement of the indigenous population and for its integration into the national culture (Art. 110).

These provisions in the constitution concerning education sometimes spell out details that might better have been left to the statutes. The organic law of national education under which the ministry operates was proclaimed in January, 1965, and includes 163 articles.[26]

Because of the autonomy of the National University established in the Constitution of 1945 and included in Article 100 of the Constitution of 1965 described above, a separate organic law is necessary for the university. San Carlos still functions under a law with 52 articles passed in 1947.[27] The provisions concerning private universities in the 1945 constitution and concerning the responsibilities of San Carlos to organize and direct higher education in the country (Arts. 99 and 102) seem somewhat contradictory.[28]

Because so much of the detail of structure of the Ministry of Education in the areas of primary and secondary education, as well as that of the public and private universities, is included in these organic laws, it appears best not to describe these statutes here, but to incorporate this material into the description of the administration and workings of the various levels and institutions of education.

Administration of the Educational System

Guatemala recognizes four levels of education: preprimary, primary, secondary, and higher,[29] with the Ministry of Education having responsibility for the first three levels, both public and private. The ministry is headed by a minister of education and a vice-minister. The minister has four principal advisory groups. The *Consejo Técnico de Educación* (Technical Council of Education) is the highest advisory group for the minister. The *Oficina de Planeamiento Integral de la Educación* (OPIE) is the planning office for the ministry, responsible to the minister for research, statistics, and planning; and obligated to maintain close relationships with the National Council of Economic Planning, with the planning group at San Carlos, and with educational planning offices in other countries, especially in Central America.[30] The minister also has a legal office and an office for the coordination of international matters, which, among other functions, has the responsibility for maintaining contact with international organizations which may offer assistance to Guatemala.[31]

At the operating level in education, the ministry includes two principal divisions, that of education and that of culture and fine arts, each headed by a general director. The *Dirección General de Educación* includes the offices for urban preprimary and primary education, rural socioeducational development, secondary education, literacy and adult education, esthetic education (for music, art, and dance), physical and health education, and student welfare and special education.

Urban and rural primary education are divided in the ministry. The Office of Socioeducational Rural Development includes departments for rural primary education, for community development, and for the professionalization of rural teachers, as well as the National Indigenous Institute. The Office of Secondary Education includes a department for basic education (the three-year program in general education for all secondary students), a department for the normal school and academic cycles which follow the basic three-year program, and a department for vocational and technical education.[32]

The General Office for Culture and Fine Arts has the responsibility for institutes, museums, libraries, and fine arts programs, including the National Institute of Fine Arts.[33]

Preprimary and Primary Education

The *Ley Orgánica* for Guatemalan education defines the objectives of primary education as follows:

(a) to promote the psycho-biological and social development of the child,

(b) to stimulate his moral and intellectual development,

(c) to develop in him the formation of habits and knowledge of hygiene as well as knowledge concerning adequate foods for the conservation of health,

(d) to encourage attitudes and to develop skills that favor a regard for productive activities,

(e) to cultivate the capacity to appreciate esthetic values and to develop artistic aptitudes,

(f) to prepare him for healthy recreation and the good use of free time,

(g) to strengthen family unity by the formation of individuals capable of recognizing and assuming family obligations,

(h) to inculcate and develop in the child necessary ideas concerning the fulfillment of his duties and the good use of his rights,

(i) to stimulate civic ideals and aspirations toward Central American unity,

(j) to harmonize the work of the primary school with the home and the community.[34]

Unfortunately, these fine goals reach few children. Although education is legally obligatory for all children between the ages of seven and fourteen, many in this age group never attend school at all, and, of those who do enter, most do not finish. Statistics reveal clearly the relationship between Guatemala's high rate of illiteracy and primary-school attendance. The 429,679 students enrolled in primary schools in 1966 represented only 49 percent of the age group.[35] The astonishing attrition rate is evident in a report by the Office of Educational Planning in the ministry (OPIE) in 1965. Following through the total number of students who entered the first grade of primary school in 1957 until 1962 (when this group would have finished the six-year program), one finds the data shown in Table 2.[36]

TABLE 2. PRIMARY-SCHOOL ATTENDANCE

Year	Grade	Enrollment	Percentage of 1957 Total
1957	First	110,843	100.0
1958	Second	49,899	45.0
1959	Third	33,501	30.2
1960	Fourth	24,524	22.1
1961	Fifth	19,135	17.3
1962	Sixth	16,954	15.3

The editors of this study comment that the percentage of survivors is "amazingly low." Other aspects of this study are significant. In the initial enrollment covered by this study 56,174 children enrolled in rural primary schools. Only 396, or less than 1 percent, were enrolled in the sixth grade in 1962! Taking into consideration that the birth rate is higher in the rural areas than in the city, it is distressing that during the period from 1950 to 1962 the average enrollment per urban primary school almost doubled, rising from 111 to 201, while the average size of rural primary schools increased only from 27.6 to 44 students.[37]

A later study by OPIE covering the period from 1960 to 1965 shows that the rate of attrition had declined very little. Less than 17 percent of the children entering primary school in 1960 finished the sixth grade in 1965. In the urban public schools the percentage was 24.9; in the rural public schools, 1.4. In urban private schools 56 percent graduated; in the rural private schools, 1.8 percent. Two explanations are offered for the low rate of success and for the differences between urban and rural schools. Only one-fifth of all primary schools offer a full program through the sixth grade. In addition, many children drop out at an early age in order to work. Frequently, too, in the rural areas poor families must migrate various times during the year to follow the seasonal opportunities for agricultural work.[38]

The *Ley Orgánica* (Art. 109) states that the school year may be adjusted according to the climatic and socioeconomic conditions of the country. In fact, however, the academic year (2 January–31 October) is uniform for the entire country and does not fit the seasonal activities of rural agriculture. Data show that in 1960, for example, 160,689 persons made a temporary move from the highlands to the coast, including 29,951 children, almost all of whom were of school age.[39]

It is estimated that a fourth of the elementary schools are private. In general the increase in the number of schools and teachers is slower than the increase in the primary school enrollment, increases which between 1960 and 1966 averaged 6.4 percent a year, double the rate of the general increase in population. In 1967 there were 4,608 elementary schools, 3,407 public, and 1,201 private. Public schools were served by 8,929 teachers; private schools by 3,224.[40]

Whatever the general level of the school system, teachers are important. Although two-thirds of the Guatemalan population is rural, the emphasis in primary education has always been urban. One-third of all primary teachers lack professional credentials, and most of these underprepared ones teach in the rural schools. Currently, only 24 percent of rural teachers have had training of a type specifically meant to prepare them for teaching in the rural areas.[41]

Primary teachers in Guatemala are trained at the secondary school level. After completing the six-year elementary school and the three-year basic program in secondary education, the prospective teacher enters a three-year, normal-school program, one of the diversified programs in the second cycle of secondary education. The 1967 statistics concerning graduates of the various types of normal-school programs, and from public and private normal schools, are shown in Table 3.[42] These statistics show

TABLE 3. DISTRIBUTION OF GRADUATES OF NORMAL-SCHOOL PROGRAMS

Types of Programs	Total	Men	Women	Total Public	Total Private
Urban primary teachers	1,540	649	891	822	718
Rural primary teachers	79	53	26	78	1
Preprimary teachers	42		42	29	13
Teachers of home economics	13		13	13	
Teachers of physical education	14	10	4	14	
Teachers of music education	7	3	4	7	

the importance of private secondary schools in the preparation of teachers and the extreme imbalance between the distribution of population and the preparation of teachers for urban and rural schools. This latter disproportion is a reflection of the fact that there are 27 public and 89 private normal schools, but only six concerned with the preparation of teachers for the rural schools, five public and one private.[43]

The plan of studies in the normal schools for the preparation of urban teachers is summarized in Table 4.[44]

TABLE 4. PLAN OF STUDIES FOR URBAN PRIMARY TEACHERS IN NORMAL SCHOOLS

Subjects	Number of Weekly Class Hours		
	1st Year	2nd Year	3rd Year
Mathematics	5		
Literature	5	4	3
Physics	5		
Social Studies	5		
General Pedagogy	4		
Psychology	4	4	
Teaching Methods	3	20	
Foundation of Ethics	4		
Chemistry		5	
Educational Organization		4	
Philosophy			4
Biology			4
History of Education			4
Educational Statistics			3
Evaluation			3
Seminar			4
Practice Teaching			10
Totals	35	37	35

The program for the preparation of rural primary teachers is different in some respects: it requires three hours weekly during the entire three-year program in an indigenous language, either Cakchiquel or Quiché; it assigns no specific period to science (though it includes science in the study of teaching methods); and it requires five or six more periods of study per week.[45]

The plan of study for the primary schools tends to be general for the entire country, to be taught in Spanish even in the indigenous areas, to be urban-oriented, and to lack relevance, particularly to the practical life of the agricultural rural population.[46] A general summary of the distribution of emphasis upon various subjects in terms of hours per year is the following: Spanish, mathematics, social studies, and science, 215 hours each; health and safety, and agriculture, 129 hours each; the arts, home economics (for girls), industrial arts (for boys), music, and physical education, 86 hours each; and religion, 43 hours.[47]

There is a scarcity of textbooks and libraries in the elementary schools and a tendency to rely upon memorization. The Regional Office for Central America and Panama of the U.S. Agency for International Development has been aiding in a regional textbook program for elementary schools. Between 1963 and 1968, 1,600,000 texts were printed in Guatemala.[48]

Cooperative plans between USAID, the Ministry of Education, and various international agencies propose a series of pilot elementary schools in rural areas with a goal of producing significant adaptation of elementary education to rural needs. There has been traditional support in the Ministry of Education for the concept of the one-room school; one effect of the careful work of the Office of Educational Planning (OPIE) has been to raise doubts concerning the efficiency of this pattern of school. Despite the obvious political advantages of placing a small school in each village, education which terminates after two or three grades is of little functional value and often is forgotten.[49]

The 1969 plan for the expansion and improvement of primary education gives hope for major changes, quantitatively and qualitatively, during the period 1969-1972. At a cost of $16,200,000, divided more or less equally between the government of Guatemala and USAID, four major steps are being taken:

(1) Four pilot schools are being established in typical areas of the country, two rural and two urban, to serve as centers of experimentation and demonstration, both in new methods of instruction and new teaching materials. It is recognized that many families in rural areas have not seen much value in the traditional primary schools in terms of the solution of practical problems.

(2) Around the pilot schools there will be developed fifty regional schools, all offering the full primary program of six grades. These regional schools will apply the new methods and materials of the pilot schools.

(3) Attached to each regional school will be four or five satellite schools. These schools will offer only the first three or four grades; they will both act as feeders of students to the regional schools and apply the new methods and materials received from the regional schools.

(4) The rural normal school in Chimaltenango will be improved and enlarged; a new rural normal school will be built in Santa Rosa.[50]

These plans will not solve all of the problems of primary education in Guatemala but should represent a great advance.

Secondary Education

The administration of secondary education falls within the office of secondary education in the ministry, an office which is divided into three sections: the Department of Basic Education, the Department of *Educación Normal y Bachillerato,* and the Department of Vocational and Technical Education. Secondary education in Guatemala has two major divisions: a first cycle of three years of basic or general cultural education, prerequisite to later study required for any professional certificate or diploma recognized by the state. The second cycle of two or three years is called a diversified or vocational cycle.[51] The Department of *Educación Normal y Bachillerato* is responsible for two of the programs in the diversified cycle—the normal school program for the preparation of urban primary teachers (already described) and the academic program leading to a bachelor's diploma in arts and sciences. This academic program requires two years above the three-year basic program, as does secretarial training; all of the other vocational programs require three years: industrial and technical training, elementary teaching, both urban and rural, physical education, music, bookkeeping, etc. Except for the addition of English, the three-year program in basic education is concerned with the same general distribution of materials as already outlined for the elementary schools. The courses have a traditional encyclopaedic quality and the emphasis is upon student memorization of materials directly presented by the teacher.

The goals of secondary education are defined in idealistic detail:
(a) to satisfy the educational needs of adolescents, guiding them

toward an affirmation of their personalities and toward the type of life which is vocationally appropriate and to which they are best adapted,

(b) to continue the integrated development initiated in the elementary school,

(c) to give the students general culture and a scientific-humanistic background,

(d) to form and develop a consciousness of Guatemalan nationality,

(e) to cultivate and develop ethical values which permit the youth to develop a balance between his own personality and the community,

(f) to stimulate the acquisition of attitudes and habits which promote health,

(g) to stimulate the creative imagination and the development of reflective thought,

(h) to enable the youth to understand the socio-economic development of Guatemala so that he can contribute toward its improvement,

(i) to prepare the youth to make good use of his leisure,

(j) to prepare the youth for civic and social life, for the responsible exercise of freedom, obtaining the basic knowledge of Guatemalan and Central American institutions within the democratic system,

(k) to form in the youth a moral consciousness which gives a basis to a sense of responsibility by means of a knowledge of his duties and rights—as a member of the family, as a future citizen, and as an effective factor in the material and spiritual progress of the community.[52]

These splendid objectives are frustrated by a series of fundamental problems: the low percentage of youth enrolled in secondary education, the poor geographic distribution of schools, the unbalanced distribution of students among the programs of the diversified second cycle of studies (especially in the industrial and agricultural programs), the shortage of buildings, laboratories, libraries, and equipment, and the very low percentage of qualified teachers.

Even though the percentage of youth between the ages of 15 and 20 enrolled in secondary education has risen somewhat in recent years, in 1967 still only 10 percent of this group were enrolled: of an estimated 600,190 adolescents in the age group, only 60,257 were in secondary school.[53] The concentration of secondary schools in the capital and the absence of opportunity in the rural areas are evident in the fact that, although 66 percent of the population in 1967 was rural, only 0.4 percent of secondary-school enrollment was rural; although the poulation of the capital was only 13.9 percent of the total for Guatemala, 44.3 percent of secondary enrollment was from the capital city.[54]

The data concerning secondary graduates indicate the lack of a desirable balance among fields and between public and private schools. In 1967, of a total of 3,607 secondary graduates, 1,650 received teachers' diplomas, 905 academic diplomas, 895 commercial diplomas, and 157 industrial-technical diplomas. Thus only 4 percent received diplomas in the technical field, clearly an inadequate number. In the academic secondary program, private schools carried 90 percent of the load, graduating 823 students by comparison to 82 graduates from public schools.[55] The problem here, of course, is that academic secondary education reaches chiefly those who can afford to pay and thus fosters class differences.

The major problem of secondary education in Guatemala, however, is not the small percentage of the age group in school; the major and key problem is the teaching staff, perhaps the most acute problem in all of Guatemalan education. The fact is that 99 percent of secondary teachers lack the educational background and professional qualifications for teaching at this level. In 1963 only 42 teachers possessed university degrees in secondary education; that is, degrees which combined training in secondary education and emphasis on the specialties taught at the secondary level; 360 teachers had only *bachilleratos,* that is, high-school diplomas in the academic curriculum; 238 were *peritos contadores,* graduates of the secondary-school program in accounting or bookkeeping; 750 teachers, many without any degree or diploma, were teaching physical education and music; 3,504 were graduates of the secondary-school level program for urban primary teachers; 43 had rural primary-school qualifications; and 261 had no formal educational title of any sort.[56]

The reasons for this extreme shortage of qualified secondary teachers are not difficult to pin down. In 1945 the School of Humanities was re-established in the University of San Carlos, having disappeared at the end of the nineteenth century; and in 1946 it began to offer programs for the formation of secondary-school teachers.[57] Within the next fifteen years, however, even though it offered the only program in the country, San Carlos graduated only about 60 teachers in secondary education. The reason for this small number of graduates may have been the absence of any formal agreement between San Carlos and the Ministry of Education to move toward a requirement of special training for secondary teachers.[58] Recent regulations have approached the statement of a requirement, even though the use of unqualified teachers is readily permitted.[59]

In 1964 the private university Rafael Landivar became the second university in Guatemala to prepare secondary teachers when it created, in the School of Humanities, departments of psychology and education. The

School of Humanities offers programs leading to the *licenciatura* in pedagogy (a five-year program with thesis) and to the preparation of secondary teachers with specializations in pedagogy and psychology, mathematics and physics, languages, and social sciences.[60] In the academic year 1968 there were approximately 28 students enrolled in the Department of Education (i.e., 12.6 percent of the total student body in Humanities).[61]

In the National University of San Carlos preparation of secondary teachers is in the hands of the School of Humanities. To receive a professional title as a secondary teacher, a student spends approximately three and a half years in the School of Humanities. The following specializations are offered: philosophy, language and literature, history and social studies, pedagogy, and the sciences of education, biology and chemistry, physics and mathematics, economics and accounting, and psychology.[62]

In the 1967 academic year, not including 116 students interested in education but enrolled in the general studies program of the first and second year, enrollment in programs leading to the title of professor of secondary education were as follows: biological sciences, 4; economics and accounting, 3; philosophy, 3; history, 26; literature, 7; pedagogy and sciences of education, 34; and psychology, 15. In the program leading to the *licenciatura* in pedagogy and sciences of education 93 additional students were enrolled. This more advanced program normally requires the completion of all of the requirements for the title of professor of secondary education. Further, in the branch of the university located in Quezaltenango 47 additional students were enrolled in programs of education.[63]

Notwithstanding the fact (as will be seen later) that the production of graduates in San Carlos is a low percentage of the number of enrolled students, it is clear that there is a sharp upturn of interest in San Carlos in secondary education as a career. There is a much higher degree of cooperation between the university and the Ministry of Education than in the past, and the high quality of planning in the university and the general consciousness of the role of the university in national development suggest some hope for the alleviation of the problems of secondary-school teachers in Guatemala. The constantly increasing demand for secondary education, both from the population growth and from the economic development of the nation, will continue to place both heavy quantitative and qualitative demands upon the secondary schools.

The immediate promise in 1969 for the dramatic improvement of secondary education rests in a very large cooperative project of the Ministry of Education, the University of San Carlos, and the World Bank. This project calls for the creation in San Carlos of a school for the preparation of secondary teachers with a capacity of 700 students, and the creation of 15 secondary schools located both in the capital and in strategic places throughout the country and with a capacity of 14,700 students. The project provides for adequate teaching material and equipment, and for a vigorous program for the improvement of instruction. There is also support for the expansion of the Institute of Agriculture.

The goals of this $12,000,000 project are to give educational opportunity to the less favored groups in the capital and in other parts of Guatemala, to improve the quality of instruction, and to increase the number of qualified secondary teachers.[64]

Technical Education

The 1964 census showed that, of the total working force in Guatemala, 440,529 or roughly one-third were below 20 years of age or above 55. Most of these, of course, fell into the group below 20 with the consequence that their productive skills had not been fully developed. It is thus not surprising that there are frequent complaints concerning the low quality of the worker and the lack of technicians, and concerning the necessity to import technicians.[65]

The Office of Vocational and Technical Education in the ministry has the responsibility in this field except in the area of agriculture. There are two technical schools at the secondary level. One is the Technical Vocational Institute in the capital. It was reorganized in 1958 in an agreement among the ministry, USAID, and certain industrialists. The enrollment has risen steadily from 22 in 1959, 73 in 1960, 341 in 1963, to 395 in 1965. The Industrial Technical Institute in Mazatenango was founded in 1964 under the auspices of the government of West Germany. In 1965 it enrolled 86 students.[66] During 1964 the Industrial Technical Institute in the capital graduated 42 students in various specialties, the most numerous being electricity and general mechanics. In 1965 a total of 54 students graduated from the two technical institutes.[67]

One of the major problems of technical education in Guatemala is the lack of programs for the training of teachers of vocational education. In 1965, for example, 22 of the 46 teachers in the two technical institutes were primary teachers.[68]

In agricultural education, Guatemala has two schools at the secondary level: the National School of Agriculture and the Central American Forestry School. Both are under the direction of the Ministry of Agriculture.[69]

Higher Education

Guatemala has the oldest and the newest universities in Central America, as well as the largest and the smallest. The University of San

Carlos was founded with the approval of Charles II in January 1676. The private universities, Doctor Mariano Gálvez and the University del Valle of Guatemala, were both founded in January 1966. In 1968 San Carlos had an enrollment of 9,585 and the University del Valle, 38. In addition to the three universities just mentioned, there is also the University Rafael Landivar, founded in 1961, the first private university in the country and named after the famous Guatemalan Jesuit priest of the eighteenth century.

Besides these four universities there are also several nonuniversity institutions of higher education. These include the School of Social Service under the Guatemalan Social Security Institute (118 students in 1966); the School of Dietetics and Nutrition under the Institute of Nutrition of Central America and Panama (INCAP, with 100 students in 1967-1968); the School of Nursing under the Ministry of Public Health (73 students in 1966); and the National Institute of Administration for Development, which is semi-autonomous (36 students in 1966). There is also the School of Rural Social Service in Quezaltenango attached to San Carlos (81 students in 1968).[70]

Even though the greatest responsibility for higher education falls upon the National University of San Carlos, we shall review the characteristics of the new private universities before turning to San Carlos.

The Jesuit university Rafael Landivar was founded in 1961 in accordance with the provisions of the National Constitution of 1956, and with those of the law for private universities of the University of San Carlos. As a private university it is now subject to the national law of January 27, 1966, which provides for supervision of all private universities by the *Consejo de Enseñanza Privada Superior* (the Council for Private Higher Education), composed of the minister of education, two representatives of San Carlos, two representatives of the private universities, and two nonuniversity representatives selected by the national professional associations.[71]

The governance of the university is in the hands of a directive council and a university council. The Directive Council, originally appointed by the Jesuit Order, is self-perpetuating, and includes thirteen members: the rector, the secretary-general, the general treasurer, and nine other members. In 1969 the council included seven Jesuits and six laymen. It has the responsibility for the property of the university, the budget, the organization of the university, the naming and removal when necessary of the rector, deans, and professors, for the fixing of admission quotas and student fees, and it is the court of last resort for all university problems. The University Council, made up of the rector, deans and vice-deans, directors of departments, the secretary-general, one elected professor for each school of the university, and one student, has the responsibility for setting the academic year and for approving plans of study.[72]

Rafael Landivar includes the Schools of Legal and Social Studies, Economic Sciences, and Humanities. The School of Legal and Social Studies offers only one program, a six-year program in law, and had an enrollment of 310 students in 1968. The School of Economic Sciences offers programs of six years in economics, accounting and business administration (with a total of 467 students in 1968). This school also includes a department of industrial engineering which offers two plans of study, a day program of five years and an evening program of six years, both leading to a degree in industrial engineering. There were 211 students in this degree program in 1968. In 1969 the Department of Food Marketing was opened. The School of Humanities has three departments. The Department of Philosophy and Letters offers a five-year program, as does the Department of Psychology. The Department of Education offers a five-year program in education, including a program for the preparation of secondary teachers in the areas of mathematics and physics, pedagogy and psychology, and language and social science. The three departments enrolled a total of 221 students in 1968. This school offers extension programs in Jalapa, San Marcos, and Quezaltenango for the preparation of secondary teachers in the three specialties listed just above. In 1968, 307 students were enrolled in these extension programs. In 1969 a similar program was opened in Antigua Guatemala for 345 primary teachers. In 1969 a program for secondary teachers was opened in the capital in the Colegio Belga with an enrollment of 145. Finally, the university conducts a short program for rural social workers in Quezaltenango, which enrolled 180 students in 1968, as well as a series of training programs in community and development. The total university enrollment in Rafael Landivar in the capital city was 1,282 in 1968, rising from 1,043 in 1967 and 981 in 1966.[73]

The total budget of the university in 1966 was $177,652, of which 70 percent was derived from student fees. In 1966-67 the university had 95 professors.[74]

The University Doctor Mariano Gálvez, named after the distinguished, early nineteenth-century intellectual and political liberal, is a private university founded in 1966 by the initiative of Guatemalan Protestant groups, and it was approved and is regulated by the same statutes as Rafael Landivar. The university is organized into departments which are grouped into schools. The outstanding characteristics of Doctor Mariano Gálvez are its departmentalization and its great emphasis upon the training of technicians. In various programs it offers training for medical visitors, management, business administration, law, civil engineering, and secondary education. In 1968 the general budget of the university was $62,418. There were 440 students enrolled in programs in the capital and 120 in the Regional Center of Chiquimula.[75]

The University del Valle is a private university created and regulated under the same statutes as the other private universities. It was established under the auspices of the American School of Guatemala, a well-known private elementary and secondary school of the U.S. type, founded in 1945. In 1968 the University del Valle was functioning in the buildings of the American School and 38 students were enrolled.[76]

Although this university is very new, it defines its plans as putting an emphasis on the liberal arts and sciences in a manner which will not duplicate that of any other institution in Guatemala. It plans to create a four-year program in the arts and sciences, uniting the last two years of secondary and the first two years of higher education. This four-year program will be followed by two or three additional years of more specialized programs in the arts and sciences. Overall, the principal emphasis may be in the social sciences.

The three private universities (half of the total existing in Central America and Panama) were all originally created under the Constitution of 1956 and hence under the regulations of the University of San Carlos. Relationships among the four universities are good, and both national planning and planning at San Carlos take account of the entire range of university activity. There is a satisfactory differentiation of role among the four universities: one is public; one functions under Catholic auspices; one is supported by Protestant groups; and one follows the distinctive pattern of an experimental U.S. liberal arts college.

The University of San Carlos bears the main brunt of responsibility, planning, and criticism of higher education in Guatemala. It also bears the principal responsibility for relating higher education in Guatemala to the broad regional Central American effort. In recent years there has been criticism of San Carlos, both from within and without the University.

In 1964 the planning office of the Ministry of Education complained in its general diagnosis of the needs of Guatemalan education that San Carlos had not defined its objectives in any precise manner, especially with reference to the needs of Guatemala in its stage of social and economic development.[77] In 1966 the planning office observed that the pattern of graduates from San Carlos in the period 1956-1965 did not fit the development needs of the country. In a country where 36 percent of the national product is agricultural, San Carlos graduated in ten years a total of only 30 agronomists and 23 veterinarians—1.8 and 1.4 percent respectively of the total number of graduates. By contrast, the planning office noted, in a country already "saturated professionally," 25.6 percent of the total number of graduates were lawyers.[78] The planning office argued that the university needs improvements in its programs, a lessening of the length of academic programs, the offering of more intermediate level technical and scientific programs, and a better vocational orientation of students.[79]

The planning office also blames the high level and the type of education students have received for their unwillingness to practice their professions in the rural areas where their services are most needed.[80]

The fact is that, though no university changes easily and centuries-old universities change even less easily, San Carlos has undergone a great deal of change during the last decade, has participated fully in the regional activities for educational improvement, and has done much planning on its own account, as is evidenced, for example, by the progressive development of a unified university campus, by the creation and effective functioning of a central registrar's office, and by the creation of an effective office of planning.

San Carlos includes schools of Medicine, Dentistry, Veterinary Medicine, Pharmacy, Engineering, Architecture, Agronomy, Law, Economics, and Humanities. There is also a center in Quezaltenango, including the schools of Law, Economics, and Humanities, which depend upon those in the capital, as well as the School of Rural Social Work. Admission is open to any student who has completed a five-year program of secondary education.

Table 5 includes enrollment data for 1968 for each school and also for each academic program.[81]

TABLE 5. STUDENT ENROLLMENT BY SCHOOL AND BY ACADEMIC
PROGRAM IN 1968

	School	*Academic Program*
School of General Studies	4,533	
Agriculture	89	
Agricultural Engineer		89
Architecture	188	
Architect		188
Economic Sciences	1,013	
Economist		440
Accountant		405
Business Administration		72
Career not specified		96
Law	1,279	
Lawyer and Notary		1,279
Medicine	583	
Doctor and Surgeon		583
Chemical Sciences and Pharmacy	127	
Biological Chemist		57
Pharmaceutical Chemist		43
Chemist		27
Humanities	661	
Librarian		26

TABLE 5—*Continued*

	School	Academic Program
Licenciados in		
Philosophy		22
History		43
Literature		33
Education		86
Psychology		123
Journalist		123
Secondary Teachers in		
Biology and Chemistry		1
Economics and Accounting		1
Philosophy		4
History and Social Studies		17
Literature		26
Mathematics and Physics		18
Education		64
Psychology		23
Humanistic Studies		10
Auditors		41
Engineering	751	
Civil Engineer		457
Chemical Engineer		120
Mechanical Engineer		16
Electrical Engineer		20
Industrial Engineer		76
Mechanical Industrial Engineer		40
Mechanical Electrical Engineer		20
Career not Specified		2
Dentistry	190	
Dental Surgeon		190
Veterinary Medicine	98	
Veterinary		98
Rural Social Service	81	
Social Worker		81

The dictatorship of Jorge Ubico in the 1930s was not friendly to San Carlos. The government exerted a direct control over the university and the president of the republic appointed university authorities. The university played a role in the overthrow of Ubico. After the Revolution of 1944, one of the first acts of the new government was to give the university its autonomy.[82] The Constitution of 1945 and the subsequent constitutions and university laws gave the university autonomy, a guaranteed assignment of funds from the state, and the election of its own officers by representatives of professors, students, and the national professional associations. The university is governed by the rector and by the Higher University Council (*Consejo Superior Universitario*), made up of the rector, all of the deans, the treasurer, the secretary, one professor from each school, one representative of each professional association, and one student from each school. The individual schools are governed by a dean and a council (*junta directiva*).[83]

The amount of data concerning programs, professors, methods of teaching, students, and university organization is quite astonishing, superior to that available in most U.S. universities and colleges. This quantity of data and studies developed in recent years is the result of the work of the Institute for Educational Research and Improvement (IIME), the various commissions of the Higher Council of Central American Universities (CSUCA), the office of the registrar in San Carlos, various studies by schools and commissions of San Carlos, and by the University Planning Commission.

Much of the important data accumulated in recent years is summarized in a statement concerning human resources in San Carlos through 1966, made by the University Planning Commission. Some of the major data and conclusions are the following:

(1) The student population of San Carlos shows a constant growth. Between 1957 and 1966 it increased from 4,336 students to 8,171, an increase of 88.4 percent. In 1968 the total was 9,585. The increase in total students, however, it should be noted, was due fundamentally to the accumulation of reenrolled students, since the annual number of graduates remained more or less unchanged.

(2) Of the total student body enrolled in 1965, only 45.8 percent came from public schools. Moreover, 78.5 percent of students came from schools in the capital, Quezaltenango, or from outside the country.

(3) The majority of students come from families with sufficient resources to have sent them to private secondary schools. Economic resources also influenced the choice of university program the students followed.

(4) The academic success of the students is less than 50 percent; i.e., the average student passed only half his courses each year and thus required an average of about 14 years to complete his degree. A recent evaluation of the School of Medicine confirms these generalizations, as well as citing the astonishing case of a student who graduated in 1968 at the age of 51 after studying medicine for 32 years.[84]

(5) Approximately half of the professors (49.8 percent) were teaching on an hourly basis. The remainder were divided between full time (20.5 percent), half time (25.0 percent), and teaching assistants (4.9 percent).[85]

(6) The majority of professors (87.6 percent) had received their own degrees from San Carlos. The remainder were graduates from various universities, particularly in Mexico and in the United States. Only 5 percent of the professors held graduate degrees, either master's or doctor's.

(7) The number of students per full-time professors or full-time equivalent (*profesor de tiempo completo equivalente*) is lowest in the schools of Medicine, Dentistry, and Veterinary Medicine: an average of 8.93 students; the number of students per professor falls in the intermediate range in the schools of Agronomy, Architecture, Chemistry and Pharmacy, and Engineering, with an average of 26.0; and it is highest—44.6 students —in the schools of Law, Economics, and Humanities. In the School of General Studies (which, until 1969, included all students during the first and second years in the university) the average was 46.8 students per professor or full-time equivalent.

(8) The production of university graduates is very low. During the period 1950-1965 an average of 143 students per year received their degrees. Thus the cost per graduate was very high.

(9) The production of graduates during this 15-year period was greatest in law and medicine (57.4 percent of the total). The professional schools in the sociohumanistic field produced 41.23 percent of the total number of graduates; those in the technical and engineering area produced 21.53 percent.

(10) The preparation of students in San Carlos is largely theoretical and the students have little direct contact with the national reality. This may be a reason why graduates are concentrated in the two major cities of the country. The education of students in the various schools of the university is also carried on in an isolated manner, and students in any one school receive a very incomplete view of the society which they will serve.

(11) It is estimated that the student body in San Carlos will increase from 8,171 in 1966 to a total in 1974 of perhaps as many as 14,070 (the maximum projection), or 12,564 (a medium projection), or 11,058 (the minimum projection). Probably there will need to be an increase of 104 professors during the same period. The university will need to make some investments in the preparation of professors in terms of the priorities of each of the schools.[86]

A major problem of the movement for reform in San Carlos in recent years has been its School of General Studies. Like the other national universities in Central America, San Carlos attempted to reduce the isolation of its professional schools by creating a two-year preprofessional program required of all entering students. The program proposed to give to the student an integrated view of the arts and sciences, to develop a university-level approach to his work, to offer vocational counseling, to eliminate duplication of offerings in the professional schools, and to remedy deficiencies of secondary education. After various studies beginning in 1959, the creation of the general studies program was approved in 1963 and it was inaugurated in February 1964. In 1968 the enrollment in the School of General Studies was 4,231, almost half of the total university enrollment.

On August 9, 1968, the Higher University Council voted to abolish the School of General Studies as of January 1, 1969. There had been opposition to aspects of the program and agreement that it required modification. The threat of a university-wide student strike precipitated the more drastic action.[87] The existence of this large school outside of the *facultad* pattern and as a direct dependency of the Higher University Council, the belief that it added at least a year to degree requirements, the dislike by many students of course requirements that did not appear to relate directly to their vocational aims, the erroneous belief of many students that the attrition rate was higher than under the old system of direct entry to a professional school, and the assertion by leftist groups that the basic concept of general studies was a North American, imperialist import—all of these factors contributed to the abandonment of the School of General Studies. Opinions differ as to the degree to which the professional schools will maintain significant aspects of the curriculum in general studies and to the degree that they will draw upon other schools for courses not related to their own professional discipline. As of 1969 there is a return to the traditional pattern of students entering directly the school they wish.

A second problem is that of the stimulation of research in the university. The School of Veterinary Medicine is the regional center for Central America and is active in research. The School of Chemistry and Pharmacy has a small research program. The postgraduate School of Sanitary Engineering has an international reputation; Agronomy carries out some studies. The School of Humanities also has some active scholars. The Planning Commission has analyzed needs and possible means for developing the research activity of the university, but at present there is no vigorous activity in research or serious emphasis upon it in San Carlos as a whole.[88] The only independent research institute in San Carlos is IIME (Institute for Research and Improvement of Education); but, for lack of funds, it maintains a relatively modest level of activity. There are research centers within several of the schools: the Institute of Economic and Social Research in the School of Economics; the Institute of Historical Research of the department of History in the School of Humanities; and the Calculation Center in the School of Engineering.[89] The shortage of professors with postgraduate training, the shortage of funds, and the lack of a traditional climate of research handicap San Carlos.

The budget of San Carlos for 1967 was $4,851,900, 70 percent of which came from the national budget. This represented a sharp increase over the $3,786,900 of 1966 and resulted from laws giving San Carlos 2.5

percent rather than 2.0 percent of the income of the government.[90] This budget represented an average of $517 per student, a per capita figure lower than that of the national universities of El Salvador, Honduras, Costa Rica, and Nicaragua, but higher than that of Panama.[91] The total budget for 1968 declined to $4,689,400.85.[92]

Overall, higher education in Guatemala faces some severe problems —the small percentage of the university-age population enrolled in higher education, the low efficiency in the production of graduates, the current lack of relationship between programs and the development needs of the country, and the absence of an ambience of research, either pure or applied. On the other hand, there is good cooperation among the four universities and between them and the state. Further, the program of planning and the vigorous participation in regional programs has led to educational innovation and progress in recent years and will continue to do so in the future.

In the total problem of education in Guatemala there is the heavy task of solving the problem of illiteracy and the assimilation of the indigenous groups. There is the crushing burden of the population explosion and the problem of providing adequate schooling. The upgrading of the quality of elementary and secondary teachers is an acute need, and the problem of qualified secondary teachers is particularly sharp. Teachers, physical facilities, better programs of study—all these problems confront Guatemala. The major new programs for the expansion and improvement of both primary and secondary education, and the cooperation of higher education in these programs, represent a hope for progress.

3

EDUCATION

IN

EL SALVADOR

Even in the nineteenth century at the time of
independence from Spain, El Salvador had not
yet developed into a separate entity within the
Isthmus. In the colonial period when political
and religious organizations were perhaps equally
important, El Salvador was late to develop a sense of identity in either
respect. Although the city of San Salvador was the second largest in
Central America after Guatemala, it was not until 1786 that San Salvador
was made an intendancy, putting it on a par with other units such as
Honduras and Nicaragua under the Captaincy-General of Guatemala. In
the ecclesiastical area, it was much later that El Salvador became a distinct
unit; it was almost two decades after independence before it received its
first bishop in 1842.[1]

At the time of independence most educated persons in the country
had studied at the University of San Carlos of Guatemala.[2] Without a
Bishop Marroquín, education developed more slowly in San Salvador
than it had in Guatemala, which remained the colonial center politically
and ecclesiastically. Despite the geographical proximity and historical
association, however, San Salvador exhibits sharp differences from Guatemala that affect its educational system.

Social, Economic, and Ethnic Background

Territorially, El Salvador is the smallest country in Central or South
America: 8,083 square miles. In 1958 it had a population density of 298

persons per square mile; in 1960 this figure had risen to 320; in 1967 to more than 400; and in 1980 it is estimated that the figure will exceed 600 persons per square mile. During the 1950s El Salvador had an annual population growth of 2.8 percent, but during the years from 1961 to 1967 it is estimated to have risen to 3.8 percent, which, like that of Costa Rica, is among the world's highest rates of increase. The total population in 1967 was estimated at 3,149,000.[3] These population densities are by far the highest in Central America, and, except for Haití, perhaps the highest in the hemisphere.

Combined with this population explosion is the fact that El Salvador is still primarily agricultural, and the percentage of its total territory in agricultural use is probably the highest in all Latin America. Since the end of the nineteenth century, El Salvador has imported basic foods from Honduras and Guatemala or overseas. Because there are no new lands to be settled in El Salvador (by contrast with Guatemala and other Central American countries), the only means to increase food production, relieve a difficult balance of payments problem, and increase the inadequate food supply for the population is through improved technology in agriculture and in industrialization, both of which require the increased human skills and capabilities that come from education.[4] Thousands of Salvadorans have migrated legally and illegally to less populous Honduras, creating growing political tensions between the two countries.

If the average *Guatemalteco* lives in a state of hunger, so does the average *Salvadoreño,* both in a chronic condition of malnutrition. The average per capita daily intake of calories in Guatemala is estimated at 1,994. In El Salvador the average is even lower, only 1,975, the lowest figure in Central America, and well below the minimum standard for health of 2,500.[5]

Even though San Salvador, the capital, increased in population by 57.9 percent during the period between 1950 and the last census of 1961, the urban migration had been a generally moderate one during the past two decades. The rural population in 1965 represented 60.7 percent of the total.

There are essentially two types of agriculture in El Salvador. One type, a kind of subsistence farm on tiny tracts, produces much of the country's food. *Campesinos* own, squat on, or rent these small farms. The best land, however, held by a wealthy elite, is in large tracts, the ownership of which in many cases goes back to colonial days; and these large farms are the principal traditional producers of coffee and, more recently, of cotton. The owners usually do not live on the farms but turn the management over to an overseer or *mayordomo.* This second type of agriculture, primarily for export, brings in most of the country's foreign exchange. The most productive coffee estates, for example, are large tracts of 3,000 to

4,000 acres. Eighty percent of coffee land is owned by 15 principal Salvadoran families, families who not only have the major economic power in the country but, traditionally, much of the social and political control as well.[6]

By contrast, 40 percent of the farms of El Salvador are smaller than 2.5 acres and make up only 2 percent of total farm land. These small farms are scattered in all parts of the country, but many of them are concentrated on poor, eroded, hillside land. Many of these poor farmers perform the role of migratory workers as well, especially during harvest seasons. As in Guatemala, these small farmers are scattered in little villages throughout the country.[7] An educational consequence of this heavy population, its relatively even distribution throughout this small country, and the fact that there is no language problem are reasons for the current interest of Salvadoran educators in the use of educational television.

Other aspects of the Salvadoran population need to be included in the background of the problem of education. In sharp contrast to Guatemala, there is no problem of indigenous peoples unassimilated to the national life and culture. The great majority of the people are *mestizos,* mixtures of white, Indian, and perhaps traces of Negro. Probably less than 3 percent of the population maintain a semi-indigenous culture, even though those of Indian blood may be a considerably higher percentage.[8]

Like Guatemala, the population of El Salvador is relatively young. With a very high birth rate and with a life expectancy at birth (based on the period 1961-1966) of only 52 years, the percentage of the total population under 20 years of age in 1965 was 56.5.[9] In 1966 the portion of the population in the working force was 31.6 percent, a small fraction to carry on its back the entire economic burden of the whole population. This group, according to a study of 1963, can be classified in the following categories: managers 0.3 percent, professional men 2.5 percent, semiskilled employees 3.3 percent, salesmen 5.2 percent, farmers 59.9 percent, and workers 28.8 percent. A study made in 1966 indicates that the rate of illiteracy in El Salvador was 51 percent, much higher than that in Costa Rica and Panama, but somewhat lower than the high percentage in Guatemala and Honduras.[10] Gross national product per capita in 1966 was $270.[11]

Something needs to be said about the political background, the context in which education exists. The stereotype in widest circulation is that an elite of 14 or 15 families controls the wealth and political power in El Salvador. No doubt this common saying is an exaggeration. On the other hand, by contrast to Guatemala, where in the twentieth century most of the large landholdings fell into the hands of foreigners or persons of foreign extraction, in El Salvador the coffee *fincas* or plantations remained under traditional Salvadoran family ownership.[12]

Franklin Parker, the author of a recent historical analysis of Central America, comments that the government of El Salvador has given considerable attention to public works and economic development in recent years. During the rule by the *Consejo Revolucionario de Gobierno* in 1949, El Salvador received its first social security law, and during the presidency of Colonel Oscar Osorio between 1950 and 1956, a number of social and developmental programs were instituted, but there was no land reform and little democracy. Parker comments: "Every chief executive of El Salvador since 1931 has been an army officer. The 1950 charter says, 'The Armed Forces are non-political and essentially obedient . . . .' Yet nothing is plainer about the politics of the country since 1948 than that the army retains control, regardless of the means through which manipulation takes place, and that whatever obedience it has rendered has been to the interests of El Salvador's aristocratic society rather than to the country at large."[13]

Parker may be a little unfair when he evaluates the policies of the six political parties involved in the elections of Osorio's successor, the candidate of the government party being Lt. Colonel José María Lemus. "Lemus and his opponents all planned a continuation of Osorio's social welfare program. They were also all agreed not to rock very violently the mid-twentieth century structure of Salvadoran society, not greatly changed from the nineteenth. One might say they all stood for what a fairly progressive aristocracy believed correctly 'modern' for the six years ahead. (Under such reasoning, for example, social security is approved not because of the plight of the people but because it is embarrassing to be listed in world reports as one of the few countries on the globe which do not have it.)"[14]

In the presidential elections of 1955-1956, Lemus, who was finally the only active candidate, was elected. By 1960 there was heavy resistance to Lemus. "Street demonstrations against Lemus grew in volume and violence after May 1960, with university students playing the most active role but carrying with them the sympathy of many parties." Although government repression was heavy, Lemus was deposed in October and was replaced by a *Junta de Gobierno* of three military men and three intellectuals closely tied to the National University. Although the goals of this group, except for a stated emphasis on education, seemed merely an attempt to create a democratic system in place of an arbitrary one, in January 1961, a new military junta violently overthrew the civilian-military group before the new elections could be carried out, asserting the need to protect the country against communism.[15]

In more recent years the emphasis on social services and economic development has continued. The fact that El Salvador spent 22.9 percent of its national budget on education in 1966, a much higher percentage than

Nicaragua and Guatemala, and only slightly less than Costa Rica, Panama, and Honduras, is an evidence of this continuing concern.[16] We hope that Professor Parker is correct in the following prediction:

> El Salvador has a tradition of public works expenditures extending back into the earlier years of this country. Her willingness to spend for social services in the years since Hernández Martínez, despite the lack of democratic controls over the government, is an indication of her aristocracy's understanding of the nation's sad economic realities. Increased outlays for education, as in many other lands, will sooner or later force radical revisions in the economic world as well.[17]

Legal and Constitutional Bases of Education in El Salvador

The 1950 Constitution of El Salvador includes nine articles concerning education and culture, articles in many ways similar to those in the Guatemalan constitution, but perhaps preferable in the fact that the focus is upon principles rather than detailed prescriptions.

Education, says the constitution, is an essential attribute of the state, which will organize the educational system and the services that are necessary (Art. 197). Education should work toward the full development of the personality of the students in order that they cooperate constructively with their society; it should inculcate a respect for man's rights and duties; it should combat the spirit of intolerance and hate; and it should promote the ideal of the unity of the peoples of Central America (Art. 198). All inhabitants of the Republic have the right and duty to receive a basic education which will make them capable of carrying out their roles as workers, parents, and citizens. Basic education includes primary education and that imparted by the state will be free (Art. 199). Literacy is of public concern. All of the people of the country will contribute to this goal in the manner determined by law (Art. 200).

Education in the public schools will be secular. Private schools will be subject to the regulations and inspection of the state. The state may take exclusive responsibility for the education of teachers (Art. 200). No school can deny admission to students because of the nature of the union of their parents or guardians or for social, racial, or political differences (Art. 202).[18] Teachers must have the qualifications which the law will specify. In all educational centers the teaching of history, civics, and the constitution will be imparted by Salvadorans by birth. Academic freedom is guaranteed (Art. 203).

The University of El Salvador is autonomous with regard to teaching, administration, and finance, and is obliged to render social service. It is governed by statutes based on a law which establishes general principles for its organization and functioning. The state will contribute toward assuring and increasing the property of the university and will consign annually in the budget funds destined for the maintaining of the university (Art. 205).[19]

In general, there are no sharp differences between these constitutional provisions for education and those of the other Central American countries. El Salvador and Panama differ from the other four in not fixing the specific percentage of the national budget, or that of the Ministry of Education, that is to go to the national university.

Administration of the Educational System

By contrast to Guatemala, El Salvador does not have any organic law of education. In addition to the constitutional provisions just described, there are many laws concerning different aspects of education, ranging from laws defining the conditions of service of secondary teachers to laws creating various medals of honor. There are also many treaties, agreements, and conventions concerning education, ranging from the recognition of educational titles and degrees from certain other countries to the creation of three scholarships funded by the United States. There are many individual regulations promulgated by the executive power of the state, some of which are elaborate and of great importance in providing the operating basis for secondary, or normal, or technical education; there are others which regulate excursions by school children. Another national rule specifies that a kindergarten class must not have more than 40 pupils and the school hours must be from 9-11 A.M.

In its *Diagnóstico de la Educación, Septiembre de 1964* (not published until 1967) the Department of Planning of the Ministry of Education summarizes all of the laws, international agreements, and regulations mentioned above. The department then describes the tangled web which all of these legally valid laws and regulations form. The department points out the disorganized manner in which these laws and regulations touch on various levels and aspects of the educational system and the very diverse criteria on which they are based. The department rightly and forcefully asserts that the putting of the laws and regulations in order is indispensable to education in El Salvador. It recommends two steps in this difficult task: compiling all the laws, agreements, regulations, and executive decrees, and organizing the necessary ones in a logical and harmonious way.

The department acknowledges that the need for a code for education or an organic law is most acute and has long been felt. "The defects and disorder in this area can leave us groping because in some cases there exist up to three different rules on a problem and in other cases (in special circumstances that should be regulated) there are no rules or they are deficient." The Department lists six previous unsuccessful efforts to codify the regulations: 1916, 1919, 1933, 1941, 1948, and 1953.[20]

Until 1968 the administrative organization of the ministry was almost as chaotic as its laws and regulations. According to the organizational chart of the ministry, all of the principal offices (24 of them) reported directly to the minister, and these offices were physically located in more than 20 different parts of the capital. These major offices included two planning groups attached to the minister: the Department of Planning and an office for cooperation with international agencies, especially the very active UNESCO group. Then the chart shows four categories of offices, none subordinate to the other: first, eight *direcciones generales,* or general offices, responsible for primary education, secondary education, normal school education, physical education, educational experimentation, publications, library and archives, and fine arts; second, six departments, including school supplies and lodgings, fundamental education (responsible for literacy and for community education), audiovisual aids, school construction, and music (the administration of the national symphony); third, four *jefaturas* (or bureaus), responsible for agricultural education, home economics, music education, and educational television; fourth, five other institutions: the Higher Normal School, the School of Social Work, the Museum, the Reform School, and the Zoo.[21]

The new minister of education, appointed in 1967, has made some fundamental changes. In January 1968 branches of the ministry reporting directly to the minister were reduced to four, and the various offices were grouped in a systematic way. An independent office of school supervision was established, no longer responsible to the division of elementary education, secondary education, and technical services. All of the offices of the ministry except engineering were brought together physically and located in one center in the building of the National Library. A second stage of reform was scheduled for 1969, in which new or improved systems of personnel and finance were instituted. Further rationalization and coordination of divisions of the ministry are scheduled to follow.[22] Despite the reorganizations many observers feel that both external and internal communications remain inefficient.

Preprimary and Primary Education

Preprimary education is optional for children from ages four to six. In 1966 there were 195 kindergartens in El Salvador with a total enrollment of 20,025 children. By contrast to Guatemala, 153 of these programs were public and only 42 private. More than one-half of these schools are located in the capital, but some exist in each province of the country.[23] The Office of Planning in the ministry has commented that El Salvador cannot afford the luxury of public kindergartens at a time where there is still too great a shortage of funds and facilities to take care of the entire primary-school population and that it would be preferable to leave the kindergarten program to private schools and for the ministry merely to give supervisory and technical services.[24]

Because there is no uniform organic law covering primary education or a codification of the regulations, it is difficult to state exactly what goals the ministry has in this field. The annual report of the minister for 1966-1967 states that primary education is the most important level of education and should receive first priority in the ministry's activities. The budget for 1966-1967 in primary education was about $14,900,000 (U.S.), of which 80 percent went for salaries. There were 3,511 primary schools and 13,164 teachers. Of the 640,700 children of primary-school age (7-14 years), only 465,394 were enrolled, leaving 32 percent of the age group outside of school, even though primary-school attendance is presumably compulsory in El Salvador.[25] Data concerning schools and students are somewhat contradictory, however. One report shows 1967 enrollment as 475,365 students in a total of 2,675 school plants, fewer schools than, according to another report, existed in 1964.[26] In any event, there can be no doubt of the greatly increased primary enrollments in recent years.

The dropout rate is high; perhaps only one of each five children entering the first year goes on through the sixth grade. Something of the seriousness of the overall problem and of the acute situation in the rural areas is evident in the statistics for the whole of primary education and for the rural sector shown in Table 6.[27]

TABLE 6. PRIMARY ENROLLMENT AND DISTRIBUTION BY GRADES IN
FEBRUARY 1967

Enrollment	Total	First	Second	Third	Fourth	Fifth	Sixth
All Primary Schools	475,365	160,726	103,355	73,357	58,797	43,797	35,887
Rural Primary Schools	172,198	80,470	44,442	23,293	12,293	6,668	4,402

If two-thirds of the population is rural, it is clear that the plight of the rural population, even in a small country with a common language and culture, is almost as serious as that of Guatemala.

Overall, some progress may be occurring. Taking 1957 enrollments in the first and sixth grades as a base, by 1963 first-grade enrollments had risen to 134.5 percent of the base, while sixth-grade enrollments reached 154.6 percent. By 1967 first-grade enrollments were 157 percent of the 1957 base and sixth-grade enrollments had reached 247 percent.[28]

The root of the problem does not rest in the absence of legally qualified teachers. From 1960 on, a great effort was made to remedy the deficit of qualified primary teachers. Fifteen normal schools had graduated only 234 teachers in 1959. The number of normal schools increased to 65 in 1964, of which 25 were night schools aimed at primary teachers who lacked professional qualifications. The number of graduates shot up to 2,616 in 1965 and dropped back only to 2,026 in 1966. There is almost nowhere in the Americas such a paradox as the fact that, with the estimated need for new graduates of 1,165 per year, there is now a major problem of unemployment among these newly graduated primary teachers; perhaps 3,000 graduates were without a position in 1967. In 1968-1969 all normal schools were closed, and a plan was developing to convert some primary teachers into secondary teachers.[29] The lack of long-range planning reflected in the opening and closing of normal schools suggests that poor training of teachers may be a major problem.

One factor in the rate of attrition in the primary schools is the low rate of academic promotion from one grade to another. Traditionally in many Latin American countries, the academic failure rate is high, even in the primary schools. In 1962, out of a total matriculation of 338,314 students, only 197,119 were promoted to the next higher grade. In 1966, however, out of a matriculation of 393,083, 315,245 were promoted. The rise from 58 percent to 80 percent is an extraordinary one, perhaps resulting from a decision of the ministry to give automatic promotion in the first, third, and fifth grades.[30]

A striking analysis of the 1967 primary-school enrollment made by Mr. Theodore Foley of USAID, El Salvador, indicates that even though the dropout rate is high, over 20 percent of the students enrolled in the primary schools are repeating grades. Mr. Foley estimates that the wastage and inefficiency represented by both dropouts and repeaters in 1967 were equivalent to $5,869,000 or 26.1 percent of the national budget for education.

In 1963, of 2,621 primary schools, only 803 offered the full six grades; of 1,678 rural schools, only 91.[31] In 1968 more than 1,000 primary schools still offered less than six years.[32] The perennial frustration for the individual and the eternal loss to national development in El Salvador, as in Guatemala, is the lack of schooling beyond the merest reading and writing level. There is no guaranteed magic in six years of schooling in even the best of schools. There is little social utility in less.

The other factors underlying the high rate of attrition are those common to developing countries: socioeconomic and health and nutritional problems, as well as the seasonal movements of large numbers of agricultural laborers.

There is an official curriculum for the elementary schools. The hours per year in the various subjects are distributed as follows: Spanish, mathematics, social studies, and science (180 hours each); agriculture, fine arts, music, physical education, home economics for girls, and industrial arts for boys (72 hours each).[33] Various attempts have been made in recent years to modernize the curriculum, but without notable success. In 1968 a national curriculum commission, aided by a technical staff, was working to revise the whole elementary and secondary program. There are many problems in this process apart from the natural conservatism of most educational systems. In addition to the problems of coordination among the Department of Planning of the ministry, the National Planning Council, the Office for Primary Education, the new Office of Educational Supervision, the Office of Educational Experimentaton, the Office of Fundamental Education (literacy and community development), and the normal schools, there is the problem of cooperation at the Central American regional level, especially in the regional program for textbooks and in the regional planning efforts in technical aid supplied by USAID and by UNESCO.

Literacy and Community Development

The Office for Fundamental Education of the ministry is active, both in literacy campaigns and community development. It had a budget in 1966-1967 of $270,000 (U.S.), and it acted as a coordinating body for all national and international agencies active in these areas in El Salvador. During 1966-1967 this office maintained 1,246 literacy centers, 270 in urban and 977 in rural areas. It employed 410 paid teachers and 836 unpaid volunteers. During the year it involved 27,610 students, formally evaluating the progress of 21,684 of them. Of the latter 15,538 were evaluated as having reached the literate level.

Various centers for the stimulation of cooperative community development were maintained, as well as several centers for training workers in such skills as carpentry and dressmaking. Many radio stations cooperated in programs of literacy and community development. There were also cooperative programs among this office, the armed forces, and USAID in literacy and development projects.[34]

Secondary Education

Secondary education has developed slowly in El Salvador and has never received the major attention that primary education has received, even in recent decades. Various church-related schools operated in the first half of the nineteenth century. When the national university was established in 1841, a secondary school, the Colegio de La Asunción, was included. When the National Institute, an academic secondary school, was established in 1885, it was the only public high school, though two others were created by the end of the century. The movement for educational reform of 1940 focused almost entirely on primary education. After the long dictatorships of General Hernández in El Salvador and Jorge Ubico in Guatemala ended in 1944, there was a new stimulus to educational reform. The Convention of Santa Ana in 1945 (called as a result of President Arévalo's desire to create uniformity between the educational systems of Guatemala and El Salvador) again concentrated upon primary education, but it did take the steps that led to the present basic pattern of secondary education: a basic three-year program of general studies (*plan básico* in El Salvador) followed by a diversified cycle of academic and vocational programs.[35]

Table 7 indicates how a student in El Salvador in the three-year common plan, *plan básico* (four years in the evening school), must spend his time.[36]

TABLE 7. CURRICULUM REQUIREMENTS FOR A BASIC PROGRAM OF GENERAL STUDIES

| | Number of Hours per Week | | |
Subjects	1st Year	2nd Year	3rd Year
Mathematics	5	5	5
Spanish	5	4	
Spanish Literature			3
Physics		4	
Chemistry			3
Geography	3	3	3
History	3	3	3
Biology	4	3	3
English	3	3	3
Ethics and Civics	3	3	3
Drawing	2	2	2
Music	2	2	2
Manual Arts	2	2	2
Physical Education	2	2	2
Total Hours per Week	34	36	34

A student might choose the *plan básico industrial,* which includes some special subjects relevant to industrial-technical education, or the *plan básico de orientación,* which puts emphasis on vocational orientation but includes essentially the same curriculum as the common plan. Some secondary programs—e.g., bookkeeping, office work, and certain technical programs—may be entered directly from primary school. Completion of *plan básico* is required for the secondary-school technical diploma, for accounting, and for the diploma in sciences and letters, in agriculture, and in teaching. These last programs require three years, except for accounting, which takes four.[37]

In 1966 there were 728 secondary schools, including 318 offering the three years of basic studies, 132 offering the academic program leading to the diploma in sciences and letters, 54 normal schools, and 224 offering various forms of commercial subjects: accounting, bookkeeping, stenography, etc. In addition, there were two schools of nursing, a school of agriculture, a school of social service, an institute of graphic arts, several schools of fine arts, and a half dozen technical schools.[38] A World Bank loan calls for the expansion of the second cycle of secondary education in 1970 by the addition of five technical institutes, four commercial schools, one school of hotel management and tourism, one school of fishing and seamanship, and three schools of agriculture.

In 1965 approximately 14 percent of the secondary-school age group was enrolled, an increase from 11 percent in 1960. In 1967 secondary enrollment was as follows: *plan básico,* 40,123; the academic program, 9,263; accounting, 4,194; commercial secretaries, 2,995; bookkeeping, 4,277; office workers, 3,756; stenography, 656; typing, 374; teaching, 3,352; *plan básico industrial,* 501; industrial diploma program, 373; *plan básico* in art, 453; and diploma in art, 33. The total enrolled in February 1967 was 70,300.[39]

By contrast to primary teachers, who receive salaries of about $85 per month, secondary teachers have no fixed salary scale and most of them teach part-time in one or more schools. As in Guatemala, there is a severe shortage of teachers prepared for the secondary level. The Higher Normal School and the national university are the sources of trained secondary teachers, but the production of teachers is low. The ministry believes that the normal school and the university will hardly be able to prepare teachers for the diversified level and hence plans to upgrade some of the surplus primary teachers to supply the *plan básico* schools. A major goal in the new program of television in *plan básico* is the upgrading of teaching.

A study of the educational background of the 1,211 teachers at the secondary level in 1963 gave the following data: teachers with secondary credentials (usually graduates of the Higher Normal School), 14 percent; university graduates in such professions as medicine, law, engineering, or pharmacy who teach in addition to practicing their profession, 4.8 percent; primary-school teachers graduated from a normal school at the secondary level, 32.5 percent; high-school graduates in the academic curriculum, perhaps university students, 26.2 percent; others, such as accountants and bookkeepers, 11.9 percent; and those without any secondary-school or university credentials—perhaps teachers of foreign language, 10.7 percent.[40]

The children who somehow made it to the secondary level, by 1963 figures, were under the tutelage of those who in almost eight cases out of ten had themselves only 12 years or less of schooling.

Everyone believes that the greatest problem in education in El Salvador is *plan básico*. Its enrollments have remained fairly constant during recent years from lack of facilities, lack of teachers, and lack of a sound course of study.[41] Other educational specialists would argue that there are three major problems of secondary education: the lack of articulation and coordination between primary and secondary education and between secondary and higher education (the surplus of primary teachers and the shortage of secondary teachers are examples); the lack of adequate diversification of programs following the basic three years in some coordination with national needs; and the problem of well-prepared secondary teachers. The lack of close cooperation between the national university and the ministry has deprived secondary education of the kind of teacher who can best be prepared in the university, especially in scientific fields.[42]

The major experimental project in secondary education in El Salvador in 1968 was the effort to set up a large educational television program at the level of *plan básico*. This program was inaugurated February 17, 1969. By 1972 it is expected that there will be 1,400 day-session TV classrooms serving 49,000 *plan básico* students and that 700 of the classrooms will also serve 26,000 night-session students.[43] The small geographical size of El Salvador and the acute need at the lower secondary level suggest the feasibility of this TV approach. Doubts concerning the project stem from the difficulties of reforming the curriculum while simultaneously going into TV, the relative lack of success in the ministry in the handling of the regional textbook program, the traditional lack of adequate supervisory programs, the immense technical problems, the inflexibility of the TV system confronted by the sharply different rural and urban needs, and the problem of coordinating the TV program with the efforts at Central American regional cooperation through ODECA. There has been considerable privately expressed skepticism over the U.S. role in pushing this program hastily. Said one long-time observer, "It was designed for its impact value more than its educational worth."

Higher Education

Higher education in El Salvador is represented by four institutions: the national university, the University of El Salvador; a new private university, José Simeón Cañas, founded under the auspices of the Society of

Jesus; the Higher Normal School; and the School of Social Work. An institute of technology was under construction in 1968 with the goal of offering two- or three-year postsecondary programs.

The Higher Normal School was created in 1952 to provide training for directors and teachers in secondary education.[44] It is under the direction and control of the Ministry of Education. Originally located in the capital, this school was transferred to San Andrés in early 1968. In 1969 it was returned to the capital city, but it is believed that it may shift again to San Andrés. The enrollment in 1968 was 175 students.[45] The requirement for admission is either an academic high-school diploma or graduation as a primary teacher. The three-year program of studies includes specialization in one of eight secondary-school subject areas: biology and chemistry, mathematics and physics, social sciences, Spanish language and literature, educational sciences, English, special education, and music education.[46] The major problem of the Higher Normal School has been its limited number of graduates in the face of the tremendous shortage of secondary teachers.

Like the Higher Normal School, the School of Social Work also is dependent upon the Ministry of Education and represents a postsecondary, nonuniversity type of institution. It offers a three-year program, open to students who have an academic high-school diploma or one in primary education.[47] In 1966 there were 61 enrolled students.[48]

The University José Simeón Cañas began its first academic year in February 1966. Under the law for private universities, passed in March 1965, the statutes of this first private university were approved in September 1965.[49] The university states its objectives as the social and economic betterment of the country through higher education, through pure and applied research, and through the integrated education of the student, especially in professional fields. The university includes professional schools in industrial engineering and economics, and offers degrees in chemical, mechanical, and electrical engineering, and in business administration, economics, and accounting. The engineering programs and the day-time program in business administration require five years. The evening programs of the School of Economics in all three of its professional areas require six years.[50]

The university is operated by the Jesuit order, and the basic powers of budget and faculty and administrative appointments are held by the rector and the *Junta de Directores* (Board of Directors). The University Council is primarily concerned with matters of teaching.[51]

In 1968 José Simeón Cañas had 719 students (plus 100 in an institute of theology), 322 day students and 387 evening students. The School of Economics enrolled 509 students; Engineering, 210. In 1969 enrollment totaled 1,030 students, including 180 students in a new School of Sciences of Man and of Nature which emphasizes philosophy, psychology, counseling, and secondary teaching.[52] There were 40 professors, 12 of them full-time. The university budget for 1968 was 391,480 colones or $156,592.[53] In February 1969 this university moved to a new campus made possible by private contributions even though, perhaps, the number of private contributions has not been as high as university officials had earlier hoped.

The major institution of higher education in El Salvador, of course, is the National University of El Salvador. In February 1841, in the same month that a constitutional assembly created a new constitution, it also enacted a decree providing for the establishment of a secondary school and a university. The secondary school, the Colegio de La Asunción, was begun eight months later in August 1841. Emphasizing Latin in its program, the Colegio de La Asunción graduated 22 students two years later, all prepared to enter the university for a three-year course in philosophy. The formal opening of the university took place in 1843.[54] Salvadoran youth seeking higher education had previously studied either at San Carlos in Guatemala or at the University of León in Nicaragua.

The university functioned during its first hundred years with many political and physical setbacks. In 1854 the entire city of San Salvador was destroyed by an earthquake and the university had to be transferred temporarily to San Vicente. In 1873 an earthquake shook its buildings apart a second time. Simultaneously, the university suffered from the vagaries of chaotic national politics with frequent governmental intervention. Even in recent years both physical disasters and conflict with government have continued to plague the university. In 1955 a fire destroyed a great part of the physical plant of the university, and in 1965 an earthquake so severely damaged the new multistory administration building, as well as other physical facilities, that it has not been usable since and may have to be torn down.[55]

In recent years, as in the nineteenth century, the university has struggled to maintain or establish its autonomy. In 1927 the students forced the lifting of the state of siege that had existed during much of the presidency of Quiñonez and brought about the reestablishment of the autonomy that had been denied for 20 years. By 1931 there was conflict again, and in 1932 General Maximiliano Hernández Martínez suspended university autonomy. In the Constitution of 1939, promulgated directly by General Hernández Martínez, university autonomy was abolished and the dictator took control of the university. In constant conflict with the dictator, the university was an important force in the bloody efforts leading to his overthrow in 1949. As has already been noted, university students and university professors were important in the overthrow of Lt. Colonel Lemus in 1960.[56] Today the University of El Salvador is fiercely independent of the government and very vigorous in the defense of its autonomy.[57]

Neither the goals nor the government of the University of El Salvador are significantly different from those of San Carlos in Guatemala. There is a General University Assembly which elects the rector, vice-rector, deans, vice-deans, and the legal officer *(fiscal)* of the university. This assembly is composed of two professors, two students, and two representatives of the professional association of each school of the university. The rector is the principal administrative officer of the university. The Higher University Council *(Consejo Superior Universitario)* is the highest decision-making body. It is made up of the rector, the legal officer, the secretary-general, the deans, a representative of the professors of each school, and a representative of the students of each school. Each school has a dean and an administrative council *(junta directiva)*. There are three major central administrative offices that assist the rector: the Office for Business Affairs and Budget, the Office for Student Affairs, and the Department of Publications. There is also the Office of Admissions and the Office of the Registrar.[58]

Administrative leaders in the university would assert, and we believe they are correct, that there have been two clear-cut stages in the vigorous reform movement in the university during the last 15 or 20 years. Later than many Latin American universities, the University of El Salvador arrived by 1950 at a well-defined autonomy and at full participation of students in the government of the university.[59]

In 1963, with the election of Dr. Fabio Castillo Figueroa as rector (a professor of medicine who had been a member of the junta that replaced President Lemus), the second stage of university reform began in a vigorous manner through the organization of a university reform commission. This movement for reform continued during the rectorship of Castillo's successor, Dr. Angel Gochez Marín. There were three basic areas of change: teaching, student welfare, and the physical plant of the university.[60]

In the area of teaching there was emphasis upon the replacement of part-time by full-time professors. In 1962 there were only 45 full-time professors among a total of 508, and 38 of these were in the School of Medicine.[61] In 1966 the University of El Salvador had the highest percentage of full-time professors in Central America, 52.8 percent, with 237 full-time professors in a total of 449.[62]

Within this same area of university instruction, there was a new concern for general education, a move toward departmentalization, the establishment of a common admission examination, the creation and strengthening of a central university library, an attempt to emphasize active student participation in the learning process rather than the traditional emphasis upon lectures and memorization, and a new sense of the need in university teaching for relevance to national problems and national development.[63]

In the area of student welfare there were many changes. As late as 1963 there were no student scholarships; by 1966 there were 278.[64] In 1967, 384 scholarships were granted of a type that covered all student expenses; 483 scholarships covering fees were also granted.[65] The scholarship program has been developed vigorously, both with the aim of democratizing the university and also with the goal of influencing students to enter such priority areas as the basic sciences.

The unification of the physical facilities of the university in a single campus has been a major goal in the second movement of reform. By 1968 all schools were located on the campus or the necessary buildings were under construction.

The university includes eight professional schools: Agriculture, Economics, Chemistry and Pharmacy, Humanities, Engineering and Architecture, Law, Medicine, and Dentistry. In addition, there are three university-wide science departments: Biological Sciences, Physics, and Mathematics. In addition to these science departments, all of the professional schools are departmentalized. In 1967-1968 the university offered degree or diploma programs in the following fields: medicine, medical technology, food technology, veterinary medicine, dentistry, civil engineering, electrical engineering, mechanical engineering, agriculture, industrial engineering, pharmacy, chemistry, biology, physics, mathematics, industrial production, philosophy, letters, the sciences of education, secondary education, journalism, psychology, archaeology, sociology, business administration, economics, history, languages, law, and architecture.[66]

Two important changes in the academic programs of the university represent recent major accomplishments of the second period of reform. One is the requirement of a year or two of preprofessional education in a fashion somewhat less rigid than the controversial general studies program in San Carlos in Guatemala. These preprofessional programs are called *areas comunes*. The second recent change, which puts some flexibility into the programs of students, is the introduction of a system of credit hours and grade points.[67]

In 1968 Dr. Angel Gochez Marín, the rector, pushed hard for another major reform, the creation of a school of sciences and humanities, a change which he described as undoubtedly the most important of his term as rector. The creation of this central school of arts and sciences has several purposes: to create a unified academic structure to serve all of the professional schools of the university in the basic disciplines; to offer nonprofessional, academic programs which the nation needs in the sciences and humanities; to achieve a proper balance between sciences and humanities; to avoid proliferation of schools; and to enable the student enrolled in the *areas comunes* legally to participate in university life and government.[68] This new School of Sciences and Humanities was approved in late 1968 and went into operation in March 1970. It will be made up of two institutes, the Institute of Sciences and Mathematics and the Institute of Humanities and Social Sciences. Both of the institutes will be made up of departments.[69]

In some respects it is ironic that the University of El Salvador, the fiercest defender of its autonomy in Central America and in many respects the most suspicious of U.S. technical aid, moves very rapidly to an academic reform which in its major aspects is very similar to the pattern of the U.S. university. San Carlos in Guatemala, on the other hand, cooperative in many ways with U.S. aid programs, disbands its general studies department at the same moment that the University of El Salvador moves even farther toward the U.S. pattern. The establishment of the School of Sciences and Humanities in El Salvador represents the third Central American national university to adopt this pattern; Costa Rica and Nicaragua did so earlier.

As shown in Table 8, the budget of the university, despite the university's frequent conflicts with the national government, has increased sharply in recent years.[70]

TABLE 8. ANNUAL BUDGET OF THE UNIVERSITY OF EL SALVADOR, 1963-1968

Year	Colones *
1963	3,636,960
1964	4,691,362
1965	6,518,725
1966	7,315,940
1967	10,871,825
1968	12,613,409

* 2.5 colones = $1.00 U.S.

Student enrollment as shown in Table 9, has also increased rapidly during the same period.[71]

One of the persistent problems of the university, as in San Carlos of Guatemala, is the small production of graduates. During the years 1953-1962 there was a total of only 570 graduates, only 3 percent of the number of entering students, and the lowest percentage among the Central American national universities.[72] The statistics for 1967 seem more favorable (287 students received their degrees) but the percentage of the student body is still small.[73]

Probably the most dynamic educational activity in El Salvador is the National University. The private university Simeón Cañas moves effi-

TABLE 9. STUDENT ENROLLMENT IN THE UNIVERSITY OF EL SALVADOR, 1962-1969

Academic Year	Students
1962-1963	2,961
1963-1964	3,236
1964-1965	3,514
1965-1966	3,690
1966-1967	4,818
1967-1968	5,460
1968-1969	6,036

ciently but slowly in its limited area, handicapped greatly by lack of adequate support from the private sector. Public primary education shows the good effects of the priority placed upon it in the past; secondary education is now the first priority of the ministry because it is the major bottleneck in the entire system. Major attempts at reform were occurring in the Ministry of Education in 1968-1969, both in administrative reorganization and in commissions for the revision of both the primary and the secondary programs. The most dramatic experiment in 1969 is the major effort to use television in *plan básico*.

4

EDUCATION
IN
HONDURAS

Honduras is the most completely rural of
the Central American countries.[1] For ten
years in the early sixteenth century the
gold and silver production of Honduras
made her seem the likely leader of the
isthmus;[2] but mineral production, though it continues on a small scale
even today, did not achieve the importance of agricultural production in
the other countries and today Honduras is the least developed country in
Central America with the lowest domestic production per capita.[3] West
and Augelli comment that Honduras has often been considered the prime
example of the "banana republics," with "commercial economies based on
a single export crop under the complete control of large North American
companies." They go on to comment, however, that, especially since
World War II, the economy has become more diversified.[4] Though there
are similarities to both Guatemala and El Salvador in political, economic,
and social development in Honduras, there are also striking and interesting
differences.

Social, Economic, and Ethnic Background

The most vivid concept of Honduran geography can perhaps be
derived from comment concerning the transportation system. The capital
Tegucigalpa is the only national capital in Central America (and perhaps
one of the few in the world) that lacks a railroad; and in 1968 it was still

not accessible to the larger jet airplanes. Most of the population lives in the mountainous western and southern highlands. The Caribbean coastlands around San Pedro Sula, the country's second city, are a second concentration of population, especially after the expansion of the banana industry in recent decades.[5] Until the late 1950s there were no paved roads in Honduras, and today there are still very few. Even though since the 1940s the government has constructed many truck routes in rugged mountainous areas, it is estimated that 50 percent of the population must travel by horseback or on foot to reach their markets.[6] Even in the 1960s there were all-weather roads connecting only nine of the country's 18 departmental capitals.[7]

Describing major problems of Honduran education, a USAID expert writes:

> Some of the gravest problems stem from the extremely difficult terrain. The land is largely mountainous, with a network of unbridged rivers. Travelling 30 miles from one location to another on a road often entails fording several streams. If a river or stream is flooded, the traveler must often wait until it goes down before continuing his journey. All-weather roads, with one exception, are non-existent. Commercial plane travel to the urban centers is usually feasible, but again, dependent on the rains and the condition of the grass landing strip. Supervision of primary schools is carried out under great handicaps, many being visited only once a year. This is due to the total inaccessibility by road, which means using burros or horses for a day's journey to one school. The majority of Departmental Supervisors have jeeps to assist them in their work, but many schools are not accessible by any type of vehicle.[8]

In an area of 43,277 square miles, Honduras had an estimated population in 1967 of 2,455,000.[9] The contrast in population density between Honduras and El Salvador is very sharp. In overcrowded El Salvador it exceeded 400 per square mile in 1967; in Honduras it was only 53.[10] According to the most recent census (1961), 58 percent of the population was under 20 years of age and more than 75 percent was rural. Life expectancy was only 49 years, and illiteracy, according to the 1961 census, was 55 percent.[11] Most Hondurans depend upon agriculture for a livelihood; bananas and coffee are the principal exports.

Racially, 90 percent of the population is a mixture of white and Indian, with some Negro; 7 percent of the population is Indian, 2 percent Negro, and 1 percent white. In terms of culture almost the entire population is *ladino;* i.e., Spanish-speaking and accustomed to wearing European style clothing. In this respect, Honduras is similar to El Salvador and very different from Guatemala.[12] Even the tiny elite in Tegucigalpa refers complacently to its *mestizo* heritage.

In 1966 Honduras spent 23.0 percent of government tax revenue on education, very slightly more than El Salvador (22.9 percent) and a sharply higher percentage than Guatemala (14.5 percent).[13]

The history of Honduras has been roughly parallel to that of Guatemala. Under colonial rule it became an intendancy in 1786 with something like its present geographical area, although it had had for many years an ecclesiastical unity under the bishopric of Comayagua. From independence until 1839, there was constant political turbulence.[14] The U.S. scholar who has most thoroughly studied the government of Honduras writes: "Frequently violence has led to political power in Honduras, and unrestrained executive authority sanctioned by force has been more the rule than the exception. However the subject is examined, by the microscope or the telescope, the result is the same. Government in action is government by *caudillo, él que manda* (the one who commands). . . ."

Since the national constitution of 1894, this same scholar continues, most Hondurans have accepted democratic political principles, but the government institutions necessary to make these principles operative have not yet developed. "For practical purposes, therefore, the 'principles' represent at best long-term objectives, at worst, window-dressing for dictatorship. . . ."[15] At the same time, it must be noted that authoritarian government has, on the whole, limited itself to such fields as police, education, health, sanitation, and the courts; in other areas Hondurans have maintained a remarkably whole humanistic and independent system of values, a certain simplicity, naturalness, and sense of human quality; a spirit that seems less aggressive than, for example, that of the Guatemalans.[16]

Some Historical Background of Education in Honduras

As in Guatemala and El Salvador, education in colonial Honduras was principally private or religious. Only a small minority received education, usually the children of the elite. In spite of the Laws of the Indies, a recent Honduran writer says that education was limited to Spaniards and *criollos,* and even children of Spanish fathers and Indian mothers were excluded. The curriculum was little more than reading and writing, and Christian doctrine. Even after Independence education remained chiefly in the hands of the church until the middle of the nineteenth century. The violent years of the Federation of Central America and the chaos of the early years of the republic—with constant changes in rulers and interventions by Guatemala, El Salvador, and Nicaragua—kept educational progress to a minimum.[17] Lic. Ardon reports that the first elementary schools in Honduras were opened in Camayagüela in 1820 and in Tegucigalpa in 1822.[18] The first simple laws governing education were passed in 1830, chiefly stating the importance of elementary education and the necessity of data concerning existing schools. A decree of President Juan Lindo in 1847 established somewhat more detailed regulations, including a requirement that students be examined every four months before the local authorities and the priest. If the examinations were not held or if the pupils did not show some progress, the law stated that the teacher would lose one-third of his salary during the ensuing four months. There is little reference to curriculum, but considerable comment on cleanliness, discipline, and religious observances.[19]

Despite the issuance of these early regulations, in 1855 the Secretary-General of Government reported to the National Congress that the regulations were so neglected as hardly to be known to exist. This official blamed the neglect of public schools on war and promised renewed efforts.[20]

A third set of regulations was passed by the National Congress in 1866. For the first time, there is the statement that primary education is required of boys between 6 and 18 and of girls between 6 and 12. It is to be free for those whose parents are completely poor (but the poverty line is not defined). There is a compulsory curriculum which includes: Christian doctrine, ethics and manners, reading and writing, the first rules of arithmetic, and, for girls, instruction in the occupations of their sex, such as sewing, embroidery, and making flowers. There will be monthly examinations attended by local authorities and the parish priest or their representatives. Reprimands, fines, and dismissal will penalize poor teaching.[21]

The first code of public instruction appeared in 1881 and was revised in 1893.[22] Secondary schools were established during the second half of the nineteenth century, reaching a total of 15 in 1900. The first normal schools for the preparation of primary teachers appeared in 1900.[23] The shaky basis of the economy and of the school system well into the twentieth century is illustrated by "El Hambre" of 1915, a year of food shortage in which almost half of the schools did not open.[24]

As the educational system slowly developed there were frequent revisions of educational regulations. In the new regulations of 1923 and those for elementary education of 1928, for example, there is a classification of elementary teachers. In view of the high attrition rate of elementary students in all Central American countries, a problem with which Honduras still struggles, it is interesting to note the three categories of teachers and the qualification required: first, those who have normal-school degrees, 10 or more years of service, and 75 percent or more of whose students pass their courses; second, those with normal-school degrees, 7 to

10 years of service, and 70-75 percent of whose students have passed; third, teachers with degrees or certificates of aptitude or those not falling into categories one and two.[25]

Also interesting are some of the activities prohibited to teachers by these regulations:

1. To receive any emoluments from parents or to accept fiestas or gifts that may affect the impartiality of teaching.
2. To teach with a dependence upon the teacher's own open book or notebook.
3. To give private lessons to students in the same school.
4. To call students by nicknames.
5. To ask for subscriptions or to incite students to draw up petitions, whatever be their objects.[26]

The primary curriculum has not been thoroughly revised since 1938. The secondary and normal school curricula were revised in 1966, but lack coordination with the curriculum of the primary school, the University of Honduras, and the development needs of Honduras.[27]

Legal and Constitutional Bases of Education in Honduras

The preceding notes on the history of education refer to some of the statutes concerning education. The constitutional bases of the system, however, are contained in the Constitution of 1965. Despite the fact that the constitution represents the ideal more than the reality, the 18 articles are worth attention. Like the constitution of El Salvador, and unlike that of Guatemala, the constitution of Honduras avoids detailed specification of structure and operation.

In addition to the usual statement of the special responsibility of the state for education and the diffusion of culture (Art. 147), the constitution specifies that the state carry out a policy of planning and coordination for community development (Art. 148). There are provisions for the various levels of education, including the preprimary level, vocational education, and special education (Arts. 149, 160). The state will supervise public and private education; public elementary and secondary education will be free and primary education will be obligatory (Art. 150). The preparation of teachers is a preferential function of the state (Art. 151). Teachers have the right to adequate salaries and retirement; primary teachers are exempt from taxes on their salaries (Art. 152). Private education is subject to regulation and supervision by the state (Art. 154), and the state will prescribe qualifications for teachers (Art. 155). In both public and private education, teachers of the constitution, civics, and Honduran geography and history must be Hondurans by birth (Art. 156).

The National University of Honduras is autonomous and is guaranteed a minimum of 3 percent of the national budget; it is also exempt from all taxes. The state may authorize the creation of private universities, hearing first the opinion of the national university (Arts. 157-158).[28] Detailed prescriptions and procedures are given by the *Ley Orgánica de Educación*.

Administration of the Educational System

As in other Latin American countries, public education is highly centralized in the Ministry of Education. Among the offices reporting directly to the minister are the General Office for Primary Education; the General Office for Secondary, Normal School, and Commercial Education; the General Office for Vocational Education; the General Office for Cultural and Artistic Activities (including libraries and museums); the Higher Normal School for Secondary Teachers; and the Department of Fundamental Education (literacy and community development). Among the other offices reporting directly to the minister is the active and efficient Office of Planning.[29]

The director of the educational division of the U.S. Agency for International Development in Honduras and his colleagues recently made an evaluation of the principal characteristics of the organization and administration of education in Honduras, one which merits quotation at length:

(1) Administration and control are centralized in the national government ministry; (2) Financing is a national government responsibility; (3) The curriculum and courses of study are dictated by the central government; (4) There is very little delegation of authority by the minister or his two or three ... deputies; (5) People at the local level have very little voice in the conduct of public education, and, consequently, feel very little responsibility for its success or failure; (6) The wealthy, the politically and economically powerful families send their children to private schools, thus draining off the influence, the concern, and the potential financial support that is needed by all sectors of public education; (7) Elaborate policies with regard to testing, grouping, and promotion are rigidly enforced with little concern for the extremely different cultural and social influences experienced by children in the various sections of the country; (8) There are no enforceable

tenure or civil service laws to protect the efficient incumbent against displacement by less capable political friends of the administration; (9) Salaries are too low to demand and enforce adequate teacher training, or to attract the best qualified teachers after the training has been completed; (10) Unequal distribution of adequate transportation, communication, health, and leisure-time facilities makes it practically impossible to attract qualified teachers to some of the more remote rural areas of the country; (11) The limitations of physical facilities and personnel dictate against the enforcement of the compulsory school attendance laws; (12) National revenues are such that in the absence of other sources of support even the most efficient organization with the most effective administration could not adequately provide for the educational needs of Honduras.

Acknowledging the negative implications of many of the preceding generalizations, the AID analyst goes on to list factors favorable to educational improvement in the current administrative and governmental environment. The ministry searches vigorously for new methods and new ideas and is open to change; the efficient planning office of the ministry supplies, quantitatively and qualitatively, educational data never before available in Honduras; the government has greatly raised its level of support of public education, providing currently almost 25 percent of the total governmental budget; there is close cooperation between the ministry and the National Planning Council, which gives a high priority to education; school building and maintenance are efficiently organized; Honduras supports and participates in the Central American regional organization for education; teaching materials are being improved and distributed very rapidly; the reduction of the bottleneck of secondary education is given a high priority, and the national university is attempting a rapid modernization and has been granted sharp increases in funding through the 1965 constitutional provisions. Even vocational education, which has been traditionally very weak, has been reorganized and offers promise now.[30]

Preprimary and Primary Education

Preprimary education is a three-year program for children from four to seven years of age and is not obligatory. It has the usual objectives of the kindergarten and is administratively under the supervision of the General Office of Primary Education in the ministry. In 1966 there were 77 kindergartens in Honduras: 44 public, 33 private; 75 urban, 2 rural. Enrollment was 6,153 children and there were 151 teachers.

A somewhat different organization of data for 1967 shows a total of 83 kindergartens, including those operated by the National Council of Social Welfare: public, 9; semipublic (i.e., receiving some support from the government), 44; and private, 30. There was an enrollment of 7,119 and a teaching staff of 167.[31] In 1968 the total enrollment was 7,102.[32]

Primary education has grown rapidly in recent years as the result of heavy emphasis on this field by the government of Honduras. Until 1957 primary education depended financially upon municipal governments, which had the responsibility for building and repairing schools and for payment of teachers. The municipalities drew their income from merchandise taxes. As means of transport and communication improved, economists asserted that these municipal sales taxes were a deterrent to commercial development and they were abolished. The resulting diminution in municipal tax income resulted in the transfer of the financial responsibility for primary education to the national government.[33]

Between 1950 and 1955 the enrollment in primary education rose 4.2 percent per year, 3.7 percent in public elementary schools and 9.5 percent in private schools. Between 1955 and 1961 enrollment rose 9.5 percent a year, 10.2 percent in public schools and 4.0 percent in private schools. Although one may agree with the generalization made earlier by AID-Honduras that centralization of control in the national government reduces the sense of responsibility of the local community, nevertheless at this particular period the taking of financial responsibility by the ministry clearly resulted in more rapid expansion of elementary education.[34]

The growth of elementary education continued in the 1960s. In 1966 the enrollment in primary schools was more than double that of 1960.[35] Between 1966 and 1967 enrollment rose by more than 11 percent to a total of 370,462.[36] The real difficulty of reducing deficiencies while trying to keep up with the birth rate is vividly clear in another set of statistics: the overall percentage of the primary-school age group enrolled in school according to the 1961 census was 46 percent; in 1966 this percentage had risen to only 50 percent.[37]

In his annual report for 1967 the minister of education, Rafael Bardales Bueso, speaks with some pride of the reduction of the attrition rate among students in primary education. Some progress is occurring, but Table 10 indicates how severe the problem still is.[38]

Of 100 students who entered the first grade in 1957, 13 reached the sixth grade in 1962; of 100 children who began the first grade in 1961, 17 reached the sixth grade in 1966. Not all of these students who reached the sixth grade in 1966, however, graduated. The total number of students completing primary education in 1966, including those in primary schools for adults, was only 14,134.[39]

In 1966 there were 4,119 elementary schools in Honduras, of which all but 137 were public schools. There were 482 schools in urban areas;

TABLE 10. NUMBERS OF STUDENTS ENROLLED BY GRADE IN PRIMARY SCHOOLS (PUBLIC AND PRIVATE) AND PERCENTAGES OF FIRST GRADE STUDENTS CONTINUING TOWARD SIXTH GRADE

Years	First		Second		Third		Fourth		Fifth		Sixth	
1957	72,942	100										
1958	93,287	100	32,869	45								
1959	95,372	100	44,948	48	23,099	31						
1960	95,372	100	48,108	50	28,612	31	15,358	21				
1961	100,110	100	50,994	53	32,458	34	18,655	20	11,880	16		
1962			53,846	54	34,867	37	21,357	22	14,390	15	9,988	13
1963					37,099	37	23,384	25	16,710	18	12,065	13
1964							24,452	24	17,791	19	13,923	15
1965									19,045	19	14,677	15
1966											16,600	17

3,637 in the rural areas. A principal reason for the high student attrition rate is evident in the data concerning schools offering the complete six-year elementary program. Only 734 schools were complete; 3,385 were incomplete.[40]

Another aspect of student attrition is evident in statistics concerning examinations in the elementary schools. In 1966 there were 333,301 matriculated students. Of these, 278,844 completed the year and took examinations. Of this number, 238,962 students passed the examinations and were eligible to move forward in 1967.[41] The percentage of students completing the year in terms of the total matriculated was 71 percent in comparison with a percentage for 1959 of 60 percent, an evidence of slow progress during recent years.[42]

Between 1957 and 1966 the number of elementary teachers increased from 4,574 to 9,965. The number of students per teacher increased from 32.0 in 1957 to 36.7 in 1966. The problem of the qualifications of teachers has been as severe in Honduras as in Guatemala. In 1957 only 45 percent of elementary teachers had normal-school degrees. With the increases in numbers of students after 1957, the percentage of qualified teachers dropped to 43.4 percent. By 1967 there was improvement: 53.3 percent of teachers had normal-school preparation; 11.84 percent were undergoing in-service training; and 34.8 percent lacked qualifications.[43]

The ministry has initiated a number of experimental programs. One is the program of *nucleos escolares* (educational centers), eight centers with affiliated elementary schools, adult education and literacy projects, and activities in community development. A second program of *escuelas de guía técnica* has somewhat similar goals. The experimental school Dionisio de Herrera in Camayagüela was trying team teaching in the upper elementary grade in 1967.[44]

The curriculum of the primary schools, unrevised since 1938, is badly in need of renovation. In general, distribution of materials is not very different from that of El Salvador. There is less science, mathematics, and social sciences, and more home economics and industrial arts.[45] The great success in Honduras of the Central American textbook program (under the auspices of ODECA and AID), by contrast to the very slow distribution of books in El Salvador, has made even more imperative a modernizing of the curriculum, since the textbooks are based on modern concepts of curriculum and teaching method. The old curriculum is based on student listening, copying, and memorizing. The new materials, in the use of which many teachers have had some training, demands a more active approach by students.[46] More than a million copies of these books had been distributed by February 1967, and there is evidence that the use of these teaching materials has increased student retention in the primary schools.[47]

The national budget of Honduras, the budget of the Ministry of Education, and the costs of primary education have all risen considerably in recent years, but expenditures on primary education have increased more rapidly than either of the other budgets. The average cost per matriculated student in primary education in 1959 was 41.83 lempiras; in 1965, 72.15 lempiras (2 lempiras equal $1.00 U.S.).[48]

Secondary Education

The purposes of secondary education are described as the continuation and broadening of the formative process of the elementary schools, the integrated educational development of the adolescent, the preparation of the student for middle-level jobs, and the preparation for university studies. As in Guatemala and El Salvador, there exists a three-year cycle of general studies followed by diversified programs of two or three years. Some secondary areas, however, do not require the common cycle of general culture.

The various programs of secondary education are as follows:

(1) an academic program of two years above the three year general cycle and leading to the university,

(2) a program of commercial studies lasting three years above the general cycle and giving a diploma in bookkeeping or accounting,

(3) the normal school program for elementary teachers of three years above the first cycle,

(4) a program in secretarial training of two years above the first cycle,

(5) a program of military education of three years above the first cycle,

(6) a program of technical and vocational education of four years above the elementary school,

(7) a program in the National School of Fine Arts of five years above primary school,

(8) a program of three years above elementary school in the demonstration farm school and giving access to the Pan American School of Agriculture, which teaches at the level of higher education,

(9) a four year program above elementary education in the National School of Music.[49]

Perhaps the most significant statistic with reference to the secondary schools is the fact that less than 7 percent of the population in the ages between 13 and 18 are attending secondary schools.[50] Enrollment is growing, however: in 1950 there were 3,674 students; in 1955, 6,842; in 1960, 10,211; in 1966, 28,092; and in 1967, 32,337.

In 1967 secondary students were distributed among the various programs as shown in Table 11.[51]

TABLE 11. DISTRIBUTION OF SECONDARY-SCHOOL STUDENTS

Program	Enrollment
Common Cycle of General Culture	20,436
Normal School Education	4,615
Academic Program: Arts and Sciences	2,254
Commercial Education, Bookkeeping	1,950
Secretarial Education	513
Vocational Education	2,349
Art and Music	220
Total	32,337

Secondary-school graduates in 1966 were distributed as shown in Table 12.[52] The statistics in tables 11 and 12 concerning enrollment in technical schools and numbers of graduates in technical fields, are somewhat deceptive. In Honduras there were seven technical or vocational schools in 1965: three for nursing, one in agriculture, one vocational school for boys, one for girls, and one in industrial arts. Omitting the nursing schools, there was an enrollment of only about 650 students in secondary-level vocational schools, or less than 3 percent of the total secondary enrollment.[53]

TABLE 12. DISTRIBUTION OF SECONDARY-SCHOOL GRADUATES

Program	Number
Primary teachers	1,127
Diplomas in Arts and Sciences	796
Business and Accounting	739
Secretaries	148
Technical Fields	989
Teaching of Art	7
Total	3,315

Altogether in Honduras in 1967 there were 112 secondary schools, 15 public, 25 semipublic (i.e., with some financial support from the government), and 72 private. In 1967 there were 2,275 teachers.[54]

There is no good recent data concerning attrition in the secondary schools. In 1956, 2,420 students passed the first year of secondary school. Five years later in 1960, 1,658 students passed the fifth year. It appears that the attrition rate is somewhat lower than in the elementary schools.[55]

Less is known about secondary-school teachers than about elementary teachers, perhaps because so great a part of education at this level is carried on in private schools. Even the data concerning numbers of teachers is very contradictory, doubtless because secondary teachers are usually paid by the hour or by the course and most teach in more than one school. Little more is known about the level of qualifications of teachers. Up until 1957 there were almost no properly qualified secondary teachers. The creation of the *Escuela Superior del Profesorado Francisco Morazán* by a decree of December 1956 has undoubtedly been of great benefit to secondary education. By 1968 this school had graduated 325 secondary teachers, and it reported that all of them were teaching in Honduras at an average salary of 300 lempiras per month ($150.00 U.S.).[56]

The curriculum in the academic, the vocational, and the commercial programs is very similar to that in El Salvador.[57] The greatest weaknesses are probably to be found in the vocational programs, both in terms of quality of instruction and equipment and in terms of response to the needs of national development. In spite of the heavily agricultural economy of Honduras, there are very small enrollments in agriculture. By contrast to other countries, the National School of Agriculture falls under the authority of the Ministry of Education. Numbers of graduates in recent years were as follows:[58] 26 graduates in 1961, 34 in 1962, 28 in 1963, 31 in 1964, 30 in 1965, and 36 in 1966. Since the National University did not found a school of agriculture until 1968 and since the Pan American School of Agriculture in El Zamorano is international, clearly the needs for education in agriculture have not been met.

The problems of public education in Honduras, like those in El Salvador and in Guatemala, are immense. Since the development of public education depends upon adequate public funds, these problems will not be readily solved. The availability of public funds depends upon economic development; and, even though in recent years the government has placed a high priority upon education, lack of funds will retard development. Despite the problems of finances, of politics, of theoretical rather than practical methods of teaching educational material, of social attitudes which minimize the importance of mass education, and of transportation and communication, all of the statistical data presented above suggest improvement, specially since 1957. Some credit must be given to outside agencies such as UNESCO and AID. AID has worked with the ministry since 1951, with an emphasis on primary education in earlier years and, since 1967, with a concern for the immense problems of secondary and vocational education.[59] Despite the crises and changes in the political situation in Honduras, public elementary and secondary education is moving forward.

Higher Education

By contrast to all of the other countries in Central America, except Costa Rica, there is no serious movement to create private universities in Honduras. The Pan American School of Agriculture, the School of Social Service, the Higher School for Secondary Teachers, the School of Nursing, and the National University are the only institutions of higher education in Honduras. The first four are classified as postsecondary institutions but nonuniversity.[60]

The Pan American School of Agriculture was established in Zamorano in 1941 by an agreement between the United Fruit Company and the Honduran government. The program requires 33 months of study; it is open to students with secondary diplomas from some 16 Latin American countries. The school accepts about 70 new students each year. Of the 574 graduates between 1950 and 1961, only 113 were Hondurans. The school cannot serve all of the needs of Honduran agriculture; hence, as will be described a little later, the University of Honduras established its School of Agriculture in 1968.[61]

The School of Social Service, established in 1957 by the Military Junta, was placed under the supervision of the Ministry of Labor and Social Security. It offers a three-year program opened to secondary-school graduates from the academic or normal-school curriculum. The enrollment is small (61 students in 1961) and the total number of graduates through 1962 was only 35.[62]

The *Escuela Superior del Profesorado Francisco Morazán* (for secondary teachers) was founded by decree of the Military Junta in December 1956. Until 1956 there was no formal preparation of secondary teachers in Honduras; until 1968 the *Escuela Superior* was the only source. In 1968 the university began the preparation of science teachers. According to the *Catálogo de Estudios* (p. 136), in 1962 the university authorized a program leading to degrees in pedagogy and psychology under the direction of the University Center of General Studies, but this program did not begin to function until 1968.[63]

Francisco Morazán has been performing two major roles: the preparation of secondary-school teachers and in-service programs for primary teachers. In 1965 it worked with 1,009 primary teachers; in 1966 with 838; in 1967, 1,392 were enrolled. In 1967, 194 students were enrolled in the regular secondary program, and 74 in in-service programs. In 1967 the faculty consisted of 56 teachers, 29 of whom were regular members and 27 of whom were temporary teachers used in vacation programs.[64]

The administration of the school is energetic and innovative. The major problem is the low enrollment and the small number of graduates and hence the impossibility of supplying the demand for qualified teachers in the secondary schools. Until 1966 or 1967 there was close cooperation between the school and the science departments of the national university, but it is reported that this cooperation has ceased. Currently, the *Escuela Superior* graduates about 40 students per year, although the estimated need of Honduras is approximately 150.[65] The expansion of secondary education being carried out by the Ministry of Public Education with the assistance of the Agency for International Development provides for expansion and improvement of the facilities of the school.

The major institution of higher education in Honduras is the National University. The immediate predecessors of the university were a literary society *(La Sociedad del Genio Emprendedor y del Buen Gusto)* and an academy *(La Academia Literaria de Tegucigalpa),* both founded in 1845 by the Nicaragua-educated Honduran priest José Trinidad Reyes. In 1847 Juan Lindo (educated in Mexico and president of El Salvador in 1841) began a period as president of Honduras. During his first year he raised the academy to the university level, establishing the public University of Honduras. Until 1881 the curriculum was largely focused upon philosophy, theology, and liberal arts. In the positivistic spirit of the time and under the new educational laws of 1881, the university was professionalized, offering programs in medicine, law, and engineering, and it lost its autonomy. In 1957 university autonomy was reestablished and a fixed proportion of the national budget was assigned to the university, 2 percent originally, but raised to 3 percent in 1966 in the new national constitution. By 1960, as in other Central American universities, an academic reform movement had begun, a principal first step being the creation of the University Center of General Studies.[66] A second important step is the building of the new university campus outside Tegucigalpa, centralizing all of the previously dispersed parts of the university except for the Center of General Studies and Economics in San Pedro Sula and the new School of Agriculture which is being built in La Ceiba.

The university includes the following professional schools: Engineering, Medicine, Chemistry and Pharmacy, Economic Sciences, Law, Dentistry, and Agriculture. In addition there are the School of Economic Sciences in San Pedro Sula and the University Center of General Studies. On the whole, the university is organized in much the same fashion as the national universities in El Salvador and in Guatemala. One striking aspect of university government is that student participation in the *Claustro Plena* (the body which elects the rector), the *Consejo Universitario* (the administrative and policy making body), and the *junta directiva* of each professional school, is exactly equal to that of the professors. This 50 percent participation of students compares with the approximately one-third student membership in El Salvador and Guatemala.[67]

The academic year in the university runs from February to November 30.[68] There is no admission examination, as there is in El Salvador and Guatemala; but all students are required to take a preparatory course in the University Center of General Studies. In 1968 this course extended from the fourth to the twenty-fifth of January; the only requirment for passing preparatory courses is attendance at 80 percent of the classes.[69]

This preparatory course should not be confused with the preprofessional requirements of work in the University Center of General Studies (CUEG), which are usually two semesters (as in law, nursing, or economic sciences), but four semesters in medicine.

Table 13 shows the enrollment by professional school for the years 1965, 1966, and 1967, and the number of graduates of each school (studies in CUEG are allocated to their prospective professional school).[70]

Of the 2,465 students enrolled in the university in 1967, 1,037 were enrolled in the University Center of General Studies in Tegucigalpa; 242 in General Studies in San Pedro Sula. In 1968 the total enrollment was 2,883.[71]

The bottleneck that secondary education represents for Honduran education is shockingly visible in the fact that in 1966 there were only 3,315 secondary-school graduates. According to university regulations only graduates from secondary academic programs may pursue studies in law, medicine, engineering, pharmacy, and dentistry; graduates in accounting and business and academic graduates may enter economic sciences; and both of these plus normal-school graduates may enter the new programs for secondary teachers. Since there were only 40 students in CUEG in the

Schools		1967	1966	1965
Total University	Enrolled	2,465	2,551	2,217
	Graduated	213	170	126
Law	Enrolled	608	682	566
	Graduated	59	67	64
Medicine	Enrolled	455	480	394
	Graduated	78	36	25
Engineering	Enrolled	346	333	339
	Graduated	26	37	17
Economic Sciences	Enrolled	289	259	363
(Tegucigalpa)	Graduated	22	11	5
Dentistry	Enrolled	52	62	77
	Graduated	9	6	4
Chemistry-Pharmacy	Enrolled	94	100	124
	Graduated	16	13	9
Economic Sciences	Enrolled	285	210	114
(San Pedro Sula)	Graduated	3		

first year preparing for education, then all of the other first-year students had to come from the academic and business programs. There were only 1,135 of these. A comparison of these data with the statistics regarding CUEG shows clearly the dependence of the university upon expansion of the secondary schools for its own future growth.[72] One may even speculate that the university must be flexible in these admission requirements; and one can readily understand the university's effort not to eliminate students through an admission examination but to repair some of the deficiencies of the weaker students through the preparatory course that precedes the first year program.

A major problem of the university is the teaching staff. Until 1960 all professors taught by the hour. With the creation of CUEG and the reform movement, there was intense effort to add full-time and half-time professors, particularly in general studies, medicine, and dentistry. By 1966 there was a total of 286 professors; 41 taught full time (14.3 percent), 74 taught half time (25.9 percent), and 171 (59.8 percent) were still teaching by the hour.[73] The shortage of highly trained people in Honduras, especially in the basic sciences, and the problems of budget have made it difficult for the university to solve the problem of staff. The university, like the other national universities in Central America, has struggled hard in this area, and has committed a heavy proportion of its budget to salaries and to scholarship programs for the faculty.

Budgets have risen substantially in recent years. The problem is the low base from which they began. Table 14 shows budget figures for recent years and per capita student expenditures in U.S. dollars.[74]

TABLE 14. BUDGETS AND PER CAPITA STUDENT EXPENDITURES

Year	Total Budget	Per Capita Student Cost
1963	$ 992,940	$661
1964	1,415,096	851
1965	1,347,518	607
1966	1,841,217	721
1967	2,336,806	948

In recent years the university has received some funds from the Ford Foundation and from the Inter-American Development Bank. A major step forward was the granting of a $2,800,000 loan by BID for the purpose of supporting a broad university-development plan during the period 1968-1972. The emphasis of the plan is upon the basic, engineering, and agricultural sciences. The loan will assist the university in building academic buildings, buying laboratory equipment, and supplying advanced training for staff.[75]

The National University of Honduras has shared in the movement toward modernization of the Central American universities during the past eight to ten years. Like the Ministry of Education, and perhaps more rapidly, it is moving away from traditional educational patterns toward modern systems. Elementary education has the great problem of including all of the youth of primary-school age in its programs; secondary education is the real bottleneck of the educational system in Honduras and needs expansion in both quality and quantity; higher education is taking vigorous steps in appropriate directions, but lacks funds and, particularly, well-prepared university teachers who are willing to devote full time to teaching and research in the new university campus.

5
EDUCATION
IN
NICARAGUA

In his recent history of Central America, Professor Mario Rodríguez speaks of contemporary Nicaragua as "Somozaland," referring to the tight control exerted by the late General Anastasio Somoza and his family over the military, political, and economic life of Nicaragua from 1936 to the present.[1] The maldistribution of wealth and power in Nicaragua parallels the maldistribution of educational opportunity. In 1963 (the last census) it was estimated that the average years of formal schooling of the general population was 2.5 in urban areas and only 1.5 in rural areas. These figures are almost as low as those for Guatemala, even though Nicaragua does not confront the immense linguistic and cultural problem of the indigenous peoples.[2]

Within the vast range of educational needs, the preparation of teachers and the development of vocational programs probably represent the highest current priorities.

Political, Economic, and Social Background

In the eighteenth century Nicaragua was, second to Guatemala, a principal center of power in the Central American region. Even before independence, however, conflict developed between the leading families of two small cities, León and Granada. When Guatemala declared its independence from Spain in September 1821, León almost immediately declared its separation from Guatemala. Granada then proclaimed its adherence to Guatemala. For a time it was not clear who governed Nicaragua. During the years of the Central American Federation conflict continued. With the establishment of a separate government in 1838, the focus of the Liberal party developed and remained in León and that of the Conservative party in Granada. Even the placing of the capital in Managua, midway between the two cities, did not mitigate the conflict, very strong remnants of which still characterize the politics of today.[3] Political party labels *Liberal* and *Conservative* are in no way philosophically descriptive, and party affiliation comes generally by the accident of birthplace.

With the aid of Honduran and Salvadoran soldiers, the Conservatives captured and nearly destroyed León in 1845; in 1855, with the aid of a group of U.S. soldiers of fortune led by William Walker of Tennessee, the Liberals captured Granada. In 1856 Walker made himself president of Nicaragua. All groups opposed him, and, with the help of Costa Rica and other Central American governments, the Nicaraguans deposed Walker.

During the mid-century period there was competition between Great Britain and the United States for transit rights across Nicaragua. The Conservatives controlled the presidency through most of the second half of the nineteenth century. From 1893 to 1903 a Liberal ruled. From the time of his overthrow in 1909 until 1933 the United States intervened almost constantly in Nicaraguan affairs, often at the request of one Nicaraguan faction or other. A Nicaraguan National Guard trained by U.S. Marines was headed by Anastasio Somoza at the time the Marines left Nicaragua in January 1933. Ousting the president in 1936, the Somozas have controlled Nicaragua to the present day.[4] Probably more than any other Central American country except Panama, Nicaragua in this century has been influenced by the United States, both politically and economically. The possibility of an interocean canal across Nicaragua has undoubtedly maintained this high level of U.S. interest. From the point of view of many Latin Americans and certainly from that of all anti-Somoza Nicaraguans, the policy of the U.S. government a great part of the time since 1900 has been imperialistic.[5]

Geographically, Nicaragua is the largest of the Central American countries and the one with the lowest population density. Its area, not including the surface of the lakes, is 53,668 square miles. The estimated population in 1967 was 1,800,000.[6] By contrast to El Salvador but like Guatemala and Honduras, the population is not distributed at all evenly. Almost half the population is located in the region of Lakes Managua and Nicaragua and the Pacific coast. The climate in this coastal area is tropical. Like Salvador, Nicaragua is crossed by a chain of volcanoes which have often been destructive. One favorable result, however, of the frequent eruptions is a rich, volcanic soil, highly productive of cotton, coffee, and sugar.[7]

The capital, Managua, has more than 300,000 population, and there are nine other cities of above 10,000. Nicaragua's population grows at the same extremely high rate as El Salvador's, 3.8 percent per year. More than 57 percent of the population is under 20 years of age. The urban population (40.9 percent in 1963) is higher than that of El Salvador and much higher than that of Guatemala.[8] Racially, the population is estimated to be 75 percent *mestizo,* or mixed Indian-white ancestry. There are few Indians left; perhaps 10 percent of the population is Negro, living on the Caribbean coast; 10 percent of the people are classified as white, "mainly descendants of colonial families who live in urban centers and form the upper landholding class."[9]

With annual gross domestic product per capita of only $330, with farm products representing 70 percent of the total value of exports,[10] and with half its population illiterate, Nicaragua clearly confronts all of the problems of economic underdevelopment. As one turns directly to the field of education, one expects to find, and does find, the same degree of underdevelopment.

Legal and Constitutional Bases of Education in Nicaragua

The constitutional basis of Nicaraguan education rests on the Constitution of 1950, which includes provisions for education similar to those in Guatemala, El Salvador, and Honduras. Parents have the basic obligation for the education of their children; needy families may ask economic aid from the government for their children's education; the state will provide special subsidies for families with numerous children; archaeological and historical treasures, regardless of their owners, are part of the cultural heritage of the nation and cannot be exported; public education is a preferential obligation of the state; elementary and secondary education are supervised by the state; elementary education is obligatory, and both public primary and secondary education are free; religion may be taught by teachers approved by appropriate religious authorities, but courses in religion may not be obligatory; the state will promote secondary and higher education, as well as vocational and agricultural education; all educational centers will concern themselves with moral and civic education; the state will control the licensing of professionals; foreign professionals will be approved by the state after advice from the national university; the national university is autonomous and will receive a minimum of 2 percent of national tax income; academic freedom is guaranteed as long as it does not contravene public order and *buenas costumbres* (good customs); various rights are guaranteed to primary and secondary teachers; teaching must be nonpolitical; agricultural or industrial enterprises outside of the radius of public schools must maintain an elementary school when there are more than 30 children of school age.[11]

Administration of the Public Educational System

A minister and a vice-minister of public education have the responsibility for elementary and secondary education in Nicaragua. Reporting directly to the minister are the Budget Office, the Technical Council, the Office of Planning, the Office for Primary Education (including sections for the primary schools and for adult education), the Office for Secondary Education (including sections for academic, normal, and vocational schools), the Office of Administrative Services, and the Office of Cultural Extension.[12]

The administrative personnel of the ministry is small in number (perhaps one hundred persons), and the physical quarters are noisy and small. It is reported that even the minister shares his office. Educational statistics are collected more slowly and less adequately than in other Central American countries. School construction is not under control of the Ministry of Public Education, but is a function of the Ministry of Public Works.[13]

As in other Central American countries, the educational system is highly centralized. In 1965 the expenditure per student both in primary education and in academic secondary education was the lowest in Central America.[14] The total budget of the ministry in 1965 was 72,651,000 córdobas or approximately $10,378,000 U.S.[15]

The School Calendar

Traditionally, in the primary schools there have been two calendars, a general calendar from the first of May to the end of February and a second calendar for coffee and cotton-growing areas from the first of February to the end of November. In 1968, however, a new unified calendar was put into effect, running from mid-February to the end of November. Thus the months of heaviest agricultural activity fall during the period of vacations.[16]

Primary Education

In 1966-1967 there were 2,238 elementary schools, 6,630 teachers, and 234,685 students. Public education included 89.9 percent of the schools, 80.8 percent of the teachers, and 82.4 percent of the pupils.[17] The Statistical Section of the Office of Planning of the ministry estimates that in 1964-1965, 62.3 percent of the children between ages 7 and 12 were enrolled in school.[18] The constant improvement in this percentage, despite the constant increase in numbers, is evident in the data for recent years: 1959-60, 44.2 percent; 1960-1961, 48.5 percent; 1961-1962, 51.0 percent; 1962-1963, 53.6 percent; 1963-1964, 55.8 percent.[19]

In the 1964-1965 year only 172 of the 1,793 primary schools offered the full six-year program; 624 offered only the first grade and 497 only the first two grades.[20] For the same year there are significant data (see Table 15) concerning the distribution of students through the six elemen-

TABLE 15. DISTRIBUTION OF STUDENTS IN ELEMENTARY GRADES AND PERCENTAGE OF DROPOUT

Grade	Initial Enrollment	Final Enrollment	Percentage of Dropout
1	89,059	59,038	33.7
2	26,063	19,644	24.6
3	14,893	11,994	19.6
4	9,006	7,654	15.0
5	5,778	5,151	10.8
6	4,258	3,887	8.7

tary grades, both at the beginning of the year and at the end.[21] Almost half the total primary enrollment is in the first grade. In addition to the high percentage of incomplete schools, there is also the traditional requirement that students pass an examination at the end of the year before moving to the next grade. It is likely that many students drop out at some point during the year and then return the following year to the same grade.

The program of studies in the primary schools includes 266 hours annually in Spanish, 152 hours in mathematics, 114 hours in social studies, 76 hours in both art and music, 76 hours in both physical education and religion, and 76 hours in home economics for girls.[22]

In 1965 the average number of students per teacher in elementary education was 42, roughly the same as in the four preceding years.[23] The standard preparation of elementary teachers in Nicaragua, as in all of the other Central American countries except Costa Rica, is graduation from a normal school at the secondary level. Until 1967 the normal-school program included only five years of study above a primary-school diploma; now six years are required.[24] A major problem in elementary education, in addition to the lack of complete six-year schools, the high attrition rate, and the large number of children who do not obtain any elementary education, is that of the qualifications of teachers. In the year 1964-1965 there were 4,362 primary teachers in public schools. Of these only 1,521 (34.9 percent) had normal-school diplomas; 704 (16.1 percent) had an academic high-school diploma or some type of preparation beyond the elementary school; but 2,137 (49 percent) were *empiricas,* that is, self-taught and without any formal qualifications.[25]

Secondary Education

In 1966-1967 there were 146 secondary schools in Nicaragua, 1,858 teachers, and 29,642 students. Statistics on secondary schools are shown in Table 16.[26] Approximately 70 percent of the students were enrolled in academic secondary schools; the others attended normal schools for the preparation of primary teachers, commercial schools for secretaries and bookkeepers, and agricultural, technical, and military schools. The increasing interest in technical education is indicated by the growth of enrollment in the Technical Vocational Institute from 528 students in 1965-1966 to 950 in 1966-1967.

TABLE 16. NUMBERS OF SCHOOLS, TEACHERS, AND STUDENTS IN PUBLIC AND PRIVATE SECONDARY SCHOOLS IN 1966-1967

Type of Instruction	Schools	Teachers	Students
Academic	94	1,269	20,661
Normal School	28	333	4,774
Business	15	163	2,122
Agriculture	4	30	303
Vocational	1	33	950
Others	4	30	832
Totals	146	1,858	29,642

Secondary education in Nicaragua includes at least six patterns:[27] (1) Secondary or academic education, chosen by more than two-thirds of the students: a five-year program above six years of elementary education. (2) Normal-school preparation of primary teachers: five years of study above the primary school. (3) Military education: five years above the sixth grade and leading to a commission in the army. (4) Accounting or bookkeeping: four years of study above the sixth grade. (5) Secretarial training: three years above elementary education.

In 1965 the population between the ages of 14 and 19 numbered 209,880. Only 23,362 were enrolled in secondary schools. The rate of attrition in secondary is lower than that in elementary education, but it is still high. Of students, for example, entering the academic secondary schools in 1960 only 54 percent graduated.[28]

Approximately 40 percent of students at the secondary level are enrolled in private schools.[29] In 1965 there were 9,519 students in private schools, more than half of the students in the secondary program leading to higher education.[30] Programs of study are identical with those of public schools, since all of secondary education conforms to patterns set by the ministry and all schools are under the supervision of the ministry.[31]

During the first three years of the basic cycle of secondary education the program follows the pattern shown in Table 17.[32]

TABLE 17. DISTRIBUTION OF SUBJECTS IN BASIC CYCLE OF SECONDARY EDUCATION

	Number of Periods per Week		
Subjects	1st Year	2nd Year	3rd Year
Spanish	5	2	5
Sciences	4	5	7
Social Studies	6	6	6
Foreign Language	4	4	4
Mathematics	5	5	5
Physical Education	–	–	–
Introduction to Art	2	2	2
Industrial Arts or			
Home Economics	1	1	1
Total Periods per Week	27	28	30

The preparation of secondary teachers is as great a problem as it is in Guatemala or El Salvador. In 1964-1965, for example, only 6.9 percent of the teachers in the public secondary schools (the schools offering the academic, preuniversity program) were qualified as secondary teachers.[33] The standard is a university degree (four years beyond eleven years of elementary and secondary school) in a specialty in education in the university.[34]

The School of Education, a part of the Faculty of Humanities of the National University, was not established until 1960. It graduated its first students in the four-year program for teachers in 1964 and its first *licenciados* in education (a six-year program) in 1966. The numbers of graduates through 1967 are shown in Table 18.[35]

TABLE 18. GRADUATES OF THE SCHOOL OF EDUCATION

Type of Degree	1964	1965	1966	1967	Total
Teachers of Secondary Education	31	18	11	30	90
Licenciados			2	6	8

Many of these graduates represent veteran teachers completing their work through the evening courses offered by the School of Education. Among all of the Central American countries, Nicaragua was the last to give formal attention to the preparation of secondary teachers. The explanation for this delay goes beyond the usual reasons for the neglect of the preparation of secondary teachers in Central America: the tradition of part-time teachers, the inadequate salaries, the lack of clearly defined policies concerning the secondary teaching career, etc.[36] The Ministry of Education in the late 1950s and early 1960s was underfinanced, understaffed, and inefficient. The National University, where the desire for reform was intense, lived with an incredibly low budget. In the year 1954-1955, for example, the total university budget was 570,000 córdobas, or $81,430 U.S., for an enrollment of 1,002 students. When the rector and the dean of Humanities established the School of Education in Managua in 1960, the budget had risen to 1,605,000 córdobas, or $229,000 U.S., for 1,199 students.[37] Despite the lack of an atmosphere of cooperation between the university and the ministry, the School of Education met a great need. It used classrooms that hardly deserved the name and teachers who volunteered their services; and yet it managed to teach and to grow.[38] The program for the preparation of secondary-school teachers in the National University is one of the most striking examples in Central America of the effects of devoted and competent administrative leadership.

As in other secondary-school programs in most parts of Central America, where the teaching staff is largely made up of part-time, unqualified teachers, the teaching method is chiefly that of lecture by the teacher and note-taking and memorization by the students. A survey of libraries in the public, academic secondary schools in 1964 gave the data in Table 19.[39]

TABLE 19. BOOK COLLECTIONS OF LIBRARIES IN PUBLIC, ACADEMIC SECONDARY SCHOOLS

Number of Books	Number of Schools
0— 200	5
201— 500	6
501—1000	4
1001—2000	1
2001—3000	2

"The total number of books in all of the libraries of public secondary schools was 11,882, which represented an average for the year 1964 of 1.34 books per matriculated student with the extreme situation of two schools which had not a single book." A survey of laboratories made at the same time indicated that only six of the 18 schools had science laboratories, and "it may be supposed, furthermore, that the existing teaching equipment was not efficient in that its total value was estimated at approximately 100,000 córdobas [$14,200 U.S.]."[40]

Normal, Technical, and Vocational Schools

The statistics concerning normal schools are somewhat confusing. The ministry operates eight schools, but there are normal-school programs in other secondary schools, both public and private.[41] According to the most recent data, there were 28 programs, 333 teachers, and 4,774 students in 1966-1967.[42] Two-thirds of the students are women; Nicaraguans comment that the policy of paying low salaries in the elementary schools discourages men from entering the field.[43] Not much is known about the qualifications of teachers of the normal-school programs. The generalization has been made that most are either university graduates in various professions or primary-school teachers who have supplemented their own normal-school diplomas by studies outside the country.[44]

In the plan of studies during the five-year program the distribution by percentages of the various subjects is as follows: educational sciences, 20.11 percent; practice teaching, 9.19 percent; social studies, 15.51 percent; Spanish, 12.06 percent; mathematics, 9.77 percent; natural sciences, 8.62 percent; music and art, 6.89 percent; foreign language (English or French), 6.32 percent; physical education, 5.74 percent; education for the community and the home, 5.74 percent.[45]

Commercial education also presents its problems in terms of statistics. The programs in accounting-bookkeeping (five years) and secretarial training (four years) are legally controlled by the ministry and require graduation from primary school for admission. There are private commercial schools, however, that often do not require even the completion of elementary school. The opening in 1966 of a program of accounting in the National University has also affected enrollments in commercial secondary schools.[46]

The Military Academy of Nicaragua was established in 1939 with the aid of the U.S. Army, and both its director and the teaching staff during its first years were U.S. officers. The program was originally based on that of West Point, although it has always been at the secondary-school level. Entering students are required to have completed the first two years of the academic secondary program. During their first three years in the academy, students complete both their military studies and the requirements for an academic diploma and graduate with army commissions. In their fourth year they are sent for 40 weeks of training in U.S. military programs in the Canal Zone.

The total enrollment in 1967-1968 was 94 students; the total budget was 1,338,400 córdobas ($192,258), or an average of $2,045 per student. Through 1965-1966 the academy graduated 468 army officers. It is reported that the physical facilities of the academy are excellent. The academy is maintained by the Ministry of Defense.[47]

In the field of vocational education there are two principal schools, the Technical Vocational Institute in Managua and the International School of Agriculture located in Rivas. The institute was opened in 1951 under an agreement between the governments of Nicaragua and the United States, and up to 1961 it was directed by personnel from the *Servicio Cooperativo Interamericano*. Since 1961 it has been under the control and responsibility of the Ministry of Public Education. The enrollment has steadily increased, reaching 950 in 1966-1967. Graduates in 1964 numbered 134. The programs vary from three to four years above the six-year primary-school requirement for entrance. There is a wide variety of technical specialties, such as electricity, welding, metal-working, auto and diesel mechanics, radio and television repair, and mechanical drawing. In 1965 programs were opened for girls in hairdressing, dressmaking, and architectural drawing. The growing industrialization of Nicaragua clearly indicates that this one school cannot be adequate to national needs.[48]

The International School of Agriculture, a private school, was opened in 1951. Boys who have completed primary school are eligible for admission. Graduates of the three-year program receive diplomas as agricultural or veterinary technicians. In 1965-1966 there was an enrollment of 128 students. Perhaps one-fourth of the enrollment comes from outside Nicaragua, chiefly from El Salvador. The Nicaraguan Ministry of Agriculture supplies 25 resident scholarships, since this private school requires the payment of tuition fees. In 1966 there were 49 graduates.[49]

Higher Education: Nonuniversity

The only institutions of higher education of a nonuniversity type are the National School of Agriculture and Animal Husbandry (ENAG), and four hospital schools of nursing, the National School of Nursing and three private schools. Located in Managua, ENAG was for many years an agricultural school producing technicians at the secondary level. In 1956 it was raised to the postsecondary level and attached to the Ministry of Agriculture and Animal Husbandry. An academic high-school diploma is a requisite for admission; the program requires five years and leads to the degree of agricultural engineer. The school accepts both resident students (who receive scholarships from the ministry) and day students.

In 1965-1966 there was an enrollment of 158 students and there were 20 graduates.[50] Some observers have commented that the school is well organized and relatively well equipped and that, on the whole, it meets the needs of Nicaragua for higher level agricultural personnel.[51]

The situation in nursing is different from that in agriculture. Although it is said that a country should have a minimum of 3.5 trained nurses per 10,000 population, in 1964 Nicaragua had 1.8 per 10,000. Not only is the average low, but the distribution is very uneven; Managua has 6.93 nurses per 10,000 population; three other provinces have more than 1.0 per 10,000; 13 provinces have fewer than 1.0 per 10,000, including one province on the border of Costa Rica that has no nurses at all.[52]

Of the four nursing schools in Nicaragua, the National School of Nursing is public. It is located in Managua, and 85 students were enrolled there in 1965. The three private schools had a total enrollment of 50. Three of the four schools require a secondary-school diploma for admission; the nursing program is three years.[53] The only medical school in Nicaragua is a part of the National University and is located in León, but, despite some discussion in the past in the university, there is still no school of nursing directly associated with the medical school.

Higher Education: Universities

The creation of the private University of Central America in 1960 provoked vigorous controversy, just as did the creation of the University José Simeón Cañas in El Salvador several years later. Even though the problem originated in Nicaragua, we will postpone the discussion of the relationship between public and private education until chapter eight.

The National University of Nicaragua has had a long history, full of many problems, but with some moments of major creative activity. A somewhat detailed account of this history may be valuable, not only in terms of the development of the university itself, but also as illustrative of the difficulties of most Central American universities during the past century and a half.

In the late seventeenth century the Seminary of San Ramón was authorized by Charles II of Spain. Through the eighteenth century it offered courses in Latin, religion, and philosophy, but was not entitled to confer degrees. During this period only the University of San Carlos of Guatemala had this authorization. In 1802 the rector began a campaign in the court of Spain to obtain for San Ramón the power to confer degrees. After consultation with San Carlos, Charles IV acceded in 1806 to the request that it be entitled to give some types of degrees. In the period between 1812 and 1815, after some controversy between the king and the

Cortes (Parliament), approval was given for the conversion of San Ramón into the University of León with the requirement that it observe the statutes of San Carlos. In 1816 the university was formally opened, thus becoming the second of the universities of Central America founded during the colonial period. After independence in 1822, the first layman became rector. Although the university was sustained principally by its own small funds, and though handicapped by the violent political changes taking place in Nicaragua, the university was a major educational center, attended not only by many of those who were to be leaders in Nicaragua but also by other Central Americans, including the later founders of the University of Honduras and the University of Costa Rica.

Between 1869 and 1887 the university was closed by the government. In 1888 the university was divided into sections in León, Granada, and Managua. In 1893 the government eliminated the central administration of the university and managed the various professional schools directly. In 1946 General Somoza closed the section of the National University in Managua; in 1947 the university section in León was made *the* National University and the rectorship was reestablished. In 1957 the university center in Granada was closed. Between 1953 and 1956, led by students and professors from the School of Law in León, there was great pressure for university autonomy. In 1957 two leaders of the law-school group became rector and general secretary of the university, Dr. Mariano Fiallos Gil and Dr. Carlos Tünnermann Bernheim. In 1958 President Luis Somoza granted the university its autonomy and the university quickly reformed its structure, providing for the election of the rector and the deans and adding students to the various governing groups of the university. In the following year the Higher Council of Central American Universities met in León, reorganizing its structure with Dr. Fiallos as president and Dr. Tünnermann as general secretary. From 1959 there followed a general movement for educational reform in the university, aided by the efforts of CSUCA.[54]

In the late 1950s and early 1960s relationships between the university and the government and between the university and the U.S. Embassy (with its powerful influence over the government) were sometimes very difficult. The reform movement, the miniscule budget, and the anti-Somoza and the anti-U.S. sentiment in the university led to conflicts. Especially difficult moments were the massacre of university students in 1959 by the National Guard and the cancellation of medical scholarships in 1960 by the U.S. Embassy.[55] The lack of interest in the university during the periods of U.S. ambassadors Thomas Whelan and Aaron Brown was both complete and regrettable. In any event, the university progressed enormously during these years.

The current statement of the goals of the university is brief but probably represents more accurately the actual efforts of the university in recent years than is true of most such catalogue statements:

(1) To prepare students scientifically and morally for the exercise of the liberal professions and to prepare researchers and technicians for the cultivation of the sciences, the humanities, and the fine arts,

(2) To support the formation of a body of university professors who are dedicated exclusively to the scholarly life and to university teaching, converting the traditional university chair into a profession,

(3) To collaborate with governmental and private agencies in the study of cultural, scientific, social, and economic problems, but without the loss of university autonomy,

(4) To complete the integrated education of students, stimulating in them an ample sense of social responsibility and preparing them to exercise the rights and fulfill the duties of free men in a democratic society,

(5) To serve the interests of Central America and to strengthen the bonds with the other countries of the isthmus by means of interchanges of professors and students and by collaboration with universities and organizations which pursue the same goals,

(6) To contribute to the development of the national culture, organizing university extension in behalf of the people.[56]

The university has worked toward goals similar to those of the national universities in Honduras and El Salvador: the emphasis on curricular reform, especially in the basic disciplines, the effort to improve laboratories, the creation of a central library, the difficult financial task of raising the number of full-time professors and of sending them outside the country for training, the efforts to stimulate research, the creation of a general studies program and of the School of Arts and Sciences, the very active participation in CSUCA, and the efforts to develop a modern extension program.

The government of the UNAN is very similar in form to those of other national universities in Central America. There is a General Assembly made up of the central administrative officers and the members of the administrative councils of all the schools of the university. Its powers are primarily advisory. The *Junta Universitaria* is the highest council of the university and is made up of the rector, the vice-rector, the general secretary, a representative of the Ministry of Public Education, all of the deans, and one student. The student representation is very much reduced from that in El Salvador or San Carlos and very different from the 50 percent participation in Honduras. The rector is the principal administrative officer and is elected for four years (with the possibility of reelection) by a special commission made up of the members of the administrative councils of all the schools. These administrative councils (*juntas directivas*) in each school are made up of the dean, the vice-dean, the secretary, three professors, and one student. It is interesting to note the qualifications required of the student; he must have completed his third year of studies with a grade average of at least 9 during the previous year (on a scale of 10 where 8 is passing).[57]

The university has an unusual organization in terms of Central America. The traditional location of the university has been León and hence the university is the only Central American national university in which the administrative center has been located away from the capital and largest city. It is sometimes said that the reason for the closing of the University in Managua by the government in 1946 was to locate the student body a safe distance from the center of government. As was indicated earlier, the Somozas perhaps did not completely succeed in their goal, although Professor Kalman Silvert commented in 1964 that "the location of the national university in Nicaragua outside Managua, the capital city, certainly has something to do with the relatively little one hears of Nicaraguan students."[58]

Actually the School of Engineering, a part of the university in Managua, did not cease to function when the university was closed in 1946 but in 1947 attached itself to the university in León when the latter was raised to the status of the National University. When the university received its autonomy in 1958, the authorities in León began to name the leadership of the school, taking over this function from the Ministry of Public Education.[59] The enrollments in engineering remained small for many years and the number of graduates ranged from three to six per year.[60] In 1959 the School of Economics was opened in Managua and in 1960 the schools of Education and Journalism.

Currently, the university has two centers. In León there are the School of Sciences and Letters; the School of Law; the School of Medicine; the School of Chemical Sciences, including divisions of pharmacy and chemistry; and the School of Dentistry.

In Managua, there is the School of Sciences and Letters, with departments of biology, social sciences, philosophy and letters, mathematics and physics, and chemistry. In the School of Economic Sciences, there are divisions of economics and business administration, and departments of mathematics, economics, accounting, and administration. In the School of Physical-Mathematical Sciences, there are divisions of civil engineering, architecture, and surveying. In the School of Humanities there are divisions of education (both for Managua and for Jinotepe), journalism, and social service. The academic programs offered by the university include all of the specialties implied by the academic organization.[61]

Between 1960-1961 and 1968-1969 university enrollment rose from 1,267 to 3,188, an increase of 151 percent during eight years. The distribution of student enrollment in the year 1968-1969 is very significantly different from that of nine years before, as Table 20 shows.[62]

TABLE 20. DISTRIBUTION OF STUDENT ENROLLMENT IN UNIVERSITIES

Divisions	Enrollments 1960-1961	Enrollments 1968-1969
In Leon:		
Medicine—total	341	296
Medicine	341	259
Medical Technology	–	37
Law	308	131
Pharmacy	83	43
Dentistry	90	57
Sciences and Letters	–	462
General Studies (1st year)	–	368
Chemistry	–	62
Biology	–	19
Physics-Mathematics	–	13
Total in León	822	929
In Managua:		
School of Physical-Mathematical Sciences	121	498
Civil Engineering	121	325
Architecture	–	150
Surveying	–	23
School of Economics	181	760
First Year	–	229
Economics	181	291
Business Administration	–	231
Public Accounting	–	9
School of Humanities	89	505
Education	89	411
Journalism	–	51
Social Service	–	43
Sciences and Letters	–	314
Total in Managua	391	2,077
In Carazo:		
General Studies	–	87
In Jinotepe:		
Education	54	35

A good many generalizations can be drawn from these statistics, generalizations many of which are also applicable to other Central American universities:

(1) In less than ten years the total enrollment has increased two and one-half times, an astonishingly high rate of increase.

(2) The number of blanks in the table in the column for 1960-1961 vividly shows the rapid diversification of programs offered by the university.

(3) The rapidly growing interest in careers in pure science in the university represents an advance of the greatest significance for education at all levels and for professional and technical education in particular.

(4) The development of schools of sciences and letters in both León and Managua offers a real basis for the stimulus of the university teaching and research career as a profession, rather than as a part-time activity, and a real opportunity by means of the preprofessional programs of general studies for the orientation of students and the counseling of students into fields which national development requires.

(5) The absolute declines in numbers of students in law, medicine, and pharmacy represent a modernizing trend in the university with causes that go far beyond the development of new programs in Managua which permit students to work full time while living at home and the establishment of a new law school in the new private university.

(6) The much higher increases in enrollment in the schools of the university located in Managua than in those located in León signify major problems and crises in university planning and development, problems and crises which were very evident in 1968 and 1969. The plans of the university necessarily call for the full development of campuses in both León and Managua as well as the expansion of centers in other cities, as in the new university center in Carazo.[63]

A major problem of the Managua campus, one of great concern for the university, is the high percentage of students who work and hence expect the programs in education, economics, and engineering to be offered at night. A recent study offers these data concerning the percentage of students who work: in economics, 61.98 percent; in engineering, 45.92 percent; in humanities and education, 78.41 percent; and in Sciences and Letters, 61.73 percent.[64] The percentages who work in León are much smaller; the percentage of students who live in university residences there is considerable. Overall, the León campus is unique in Central America in being located away from the capital and major center of population and, from our subjective point of view, it would appear that the León campus represents the most closely knit university community in the region, an impression the validity of which needs to be studied. By contrast to the university made up of commuting students, a high percentage of whom work while living at home, the León campus deserves attention as representing a special kind of university environment.

The statistics concerning university graduates are somewhat sur prising since there seems to be little relationship between these figures and the number of students enrolled. During the period between 1960-1961 and 1966-1967, there were 822 graduates. Of these 622 graduated in León, 49 received degrees in Managua, and 151 received teachers' diplomas in education in Jinotepe and Managua. In Managua in 1966 in the schools of engineering and economics there was a total of six graduates. In León there was a total of 119. Sociologist Ronald Fundis draws the following inferences from these data: "(1) León, with more professors of half-time and full-time, has succeeded in a higher productivity; (2) León, with the university leadership, or rather possessing the central administration, shows a more efficient system; and (3) León, with day-time classes has more full-time students; i.e., students with sufficient time to study."[65]

In 1967-1968 there were 402 professors, 79 (19.6 percent) full time, 52 (13 percent) half time, and 271 (67 percent) part time. It is estimated that the total represents 173 full-time equivalent professors and hence that there are 15.8 students per full-time equivalent.[66] From an absolute point of view the percentage of full-time professors does not seem high. In terms of great change over a relatively brief period, however, one notes that the percentage of full-time professors was 5.0 in 1962 and the percentage of half-time profesors was 5.5.[67] In 1957 every professor taught part time.[68] The great problem of the university, like that in Honduras and in El Salvador, is the absence of adequate numbers of qualified professors, particularly in view of the great expansion both of total numbers of students and number of university programs.

Many of the problems of the university reduce themselves to the problem of finances. The total budget and the portion coming from the government during a five-year period are shown in Table 21.[69] When

TABLE 21. UNIVERSITY BUDGETS AND GOVERNMENT GRANTS

Year	Grant by Government	Total Budget
1964-1965	$ 515,000 U.S.	$ 859,000
1965-1966	616,000	976,000
1966-1967	673,000	1,299,000
1967-1968	1,272,000	1,741,000
1968-1969	1,317,000	

we remember that the budget includes not only operating expenses but capital expenditures as well, the hard problem of building the two campuses, improving equipment and the central library, and increasing the number of full-time professors reveals itself very clearly.

Though still very young, the Central American University (UCA) was the first private university founded in Central America. When the government closed the university in Granada in 1951, leaving only the university in León, the citizens of Granada and others struggled for a second university. Because there was a Jesuit secondary school in Granada, there was pressure for the order to establish a private university there and a committee was created and some funds raised. Eventually, the Jesuit order decided to establish a university but chose Managua for its site. In July 1960, the National Congress passed a law authorizing the establishment of a university, and in March 1961 the minister of government approved its statutes.[70]

The UCA declares its purposes as the integrated education of its students in the Christian concept of life and their preparation for the various professions in a scientific-technical, social, and patriotic manner. The university includes the School of Law; the School of Engineering, offering programs in civil, electro-mechanical, and industrial engineering; the School of Business Administration; the School of Education; the Institute of Languages, offering programs in French and English; and the School of Veterinary Medicine. The matriculation fee is $21 U.S. and the tuition approximately $192 U.S. per year.[71]

In 1967-1968 there was an enrollment of 1,787 students, divided as follows: in business administration, 621; law, 514; engineering, 262; veterinary medicine, 211; and education, 179. There were 100 professors, 28 full time, 15 half time, and 57 part time. The budget for 1966-1967 totaled $315,000 U.S. The UCA has a scholarship fund of $28,900 U.S. and reports that 6.2 percent of the student body held scholarships in 1966-1967. A study of the background of the student body indicates that 11.9 percent were children of workers, 18.2 percent were married, 21.1 percent were women.[72]

The University Centroamericana has grown rapidly since its founding in 1960 and thus undoubtedly meets a need. A major criticism has been the considerable duplication of programs of the National University.

Overall, both in the area of higher education as well as in elementary and secondary education, there has been progress in recent years in Nicaragua. The progress has been more rapid in the area of higher education than in the other levels; the degree of innovation and imagination has also been correspondingly greater. The shortage of funds at all levels is the most important limiting factor; the 16.5 percent of the national budget devoted to education in 1966 cannot support a major advance in education.

Recently an officer of a U.S. foundation commented that change in the National University of Nicaragua seemed more in form than in reality. The statistics recited here concerning the last decade of the history of the university clearly show that the change has been a major one and that one must judge the progress of universities in their own real terms, rather than in some kind of absolute terms. A decade is not a long time in the history of a university. The same comment applies to ministries of education and to national systems of education.

6

EDUCATION
IN
COSTA RICA

When one turns from Nicaragua and Honduras to Costa Rica, one enters a different world of education, not an ideal world to be sure, but one in which, both quantitatively and qualitatively, educational institutions are different from those of her northern neighbors. When K. H. Silvert compares Latin American countries in terms of institutional complexity and degree of modernization, Costa Rica is placed with such countries as Mexico, Argentina, and Chile. When he discusses the level of economic planning, he again places Costa Rica with Uruguay, Mexico, and Chile.[1] When Aldo Solari classifies systems of secondary education in terms of the proportion of the age group enrolled in school, he too places Costa Rica in the top group along with Argentina, Uruguay, and Panama. Nicaragua and Honduras, on the other hand, fall in the lowest group.[2]

Something more is involved than the traditional boast of Costa Rica that she has more schoolteachers than soldiers. In the 1830s John Lloyd Stephens, a U.S. diplomat in Central America, wrote that Costa Rica was "not like the rest of Central America, retrograding and going to ruin, but smiling as [sic] the reward of industry."[3] Costa Rica, despite Stephens' optimism, has always had problems. It may be that the base of Costa Rican progress, however, is expressed by Carlos Monge Alfaro (former rector of the University of Costa Rica) in the introduction to the twelfth edition of his high-school textbook on the history of Costa Rica. The purpose of his book and of the study of Costa Rican history, he says, is "the development in youth of a vigilant civic spirit, as an expression of the highest values of national democracy; to interpret . . . the attitude of constant loyalty to republican values of the Costa Rican people."[4] A factor that differentiates Costa Rica from other Central American countries, as well as most of those of South America, has been its almost constant holding to the values of constitutional government.

Geographic, Historical, Social, Political, and Economic Background

Costa Rica was slow to be colonized, for there was neither an alluring quantity of gold or silver, nor Indian labor to work the land. The city of Cartágo was not founded until 1564. The colony grew very slowly and was undoubtedly the least prosperous and most unhappy of the Central American colonies throughout the seventeenth and eighteenth centuries. The colonists worked their own subsistence farms on small holdings; there were few large holdings in the *meseta central* where the population was concentrated, and there were few important centers of population. Carlos Monge describes the development of a kind of independent-minded rural democracy—without slaves and without aristocracy, without schools and with little learning.[5]

At the time of independence Costa Rica was still the poorest and weakest of the provinces, isolated from the others in most respects. It even received news of independence late, by correspondence, and without really expecting it.[6] There were some local conflicts among the small cities of the *meseta central* over such matters as the location of the national capital, but, on the whole, Costa Rica remained relatively isolated from the swirling conflicts in Central America from independence until the breakup of the Federated States of Central America.[7]

There was confusion and there were occasional dictators in the middle of the nineteenth century. From 1859 on, however, "each step backward . . . carried with it some gain in the breaking of the pattern." There were some presidents in the second half of the century who one way or another generated material progress. Tomás Guardia, for example, succeeded in getting railroads built; Bernard Soto, a liberal, with his Minister of Education Mauro Fernández, gave the real base to the development of primary education. It was in 1889 that "Costa Rica experienced her first genuine election in which the people at large took part and her first peaceful transition from a group in power to the opposition. Only Honduras of the other Central American countries has ever experienced the latter phenomenon in her history."[8]

Education continued to expand, even though government was usually in the hands of the wealthy. Some social legislation began to develop between 1924 and 1936, and, except for the revolution of 1948, when the election of Ulate was rejected by the Calderón forces in the Congress, there was the steady increase in social legislation through a democratic process. Since 1948 there have been four peaceful elections in which one party or the other turned over the executive authority.[9]

Despite economic crises and natural disasters, Costa Rica has maintained the social and political stability necessary for cultural, economic, and educational progress. Costa Rica, like her neighbors to the north, has had to live with earthquakes and volcanic eruptions. Tons of grey ash poured out on farms and towns from Irazu volcano in 1963 and 1964, for example, and in 1968 a hitherto quiet mountain exploded destructive ash and lava on thousands of *hectares* of Guanacaste province.

Costa Rica had an estimated population of 1,594,000 in 1967, up one-quarter million since the census of 1963. In recent years Costa Rica has had an annual growth of population of 3.6 percent, an extremely high rate and one which has limited educational and economic progress. The gross domestic product per capita in 1965 was $415, much the highest in Central America except for Panama. The population is young; even in 1963, 57.4 percent were under 20. Life expectancy is 66 years; the literacy rate was 84.4 percent in 1963 and has undoubtedly risen in the past half decade. Only 34.5 percent of the population is urban, and there is only a mild movement of the rural population toward the cities. Between 1950 and 1965 the urban population rose only 90 percent while the country as a whole increased 82 percent. Most of the urban population is concentrated in the metropolitan area of San José.[10]

By contrast to a great part of Latin America, even rural housing has been evaluated by BID as adequate. There are extensive housing developments, both urban and rural. Public health programs are vigorous; piped water was available in 1965 to 61.3 percent of the population, including 89.9 percent of urban residents.[11]

Racially, Costa Rica is estimated to be 80 percent white, made up of descendants of Spanish settlers (90 percent in the *meseta central*); 17 percent are *mestizos*, chiefly in the northwest province of Guanacaste (long a part of Nicaragua) and along the Pacific coast; 2 percent are English-speaking Negro descendants of Jamaicans who live in the former banana areas of the Caribbean; fewer than 1 percent are Indians living in very isolated mountainous areas.[12]

The way in which land settlement has developed in Costa Rica is different from that in other Central American countries. "This outward movement has taken place without a decrease in the population of the Meseta Central, the core area. Moreover, the settlers have come almost solely from the natural increase of the Costa Rican population. The national government has not controlled this expansion; it has been a spontaneous, unplanned movement of surplus peasants who were seeking new lands for subsistence and commercial farming. Generally, the more important movements have followed new lines of communication." About 60 percent of the Costa Rican land is settled, but good land is still available and settlement continues as roads are developed.[13]

Coffee, bananas, and cacao are the principal means of livelihood for most farmers and on them the national economy has been overdependent, though manufactured products have increased rapidly since the development of the Central American Common Market. There is much less problem of unbalanced land tenure in Costa Rica than in most Latin American countries; 94 percent of farmland in 1963 was operated by its owners.[14]

The historical development of Costa Rica and the politicoeconomic-cultural environment are favorable for educational development; this development occurs and in turn reinforces the other factors.

Legal and Constitutional Bases of Education in Costa Rica

The Constitution of 1949, approved after the Revolution of 1948, has 13 brief articles relating to education. Similar to other Central American constitutions in its treatment of education, it has, however, several significant variations.

Public education will be organized as an integrated process, correlated in its various cycles from the preschool to the university. Primary education is obligatory; primary and secondary education are free and paid for by the nation. The state will provide scholarships for higher education for those who lack resources. The adjudication of these scholarships and financial aids will fall under the responsibility of the Minister of Education.

Academic freedom is guaranteed. Notwithstanding, private schools will be subject to supervision by the state. Private initiative in the educaional field merits stimulation by the state.

The general direction of public education is the responsibility of the Higher Council of Education, presided over by the minister of education. This is a point in which all of the other countries differ in that they give this responsibility directly to the minister of education.

The state will provide food and clothing to needy students and will sponsor and organize adult education, both to combat illiteracy and to provide cultural opportunities for those who wish to improve their intellectual, social, and economic situation.

The University of Costa Rica is a cultural institution which enjoys independence in carrying out its functions, and it will receive support from the state in a sum no less than 10 percent of the budget of the Ministry of Education, a sum to be paid in monthly quotas. The state will educate teachers both in specialized institutes and in the University of Costa Rica. Academic freedom is a fundamental principle of university teaching. The Legislative Assembly will not enact laws relative to any matters placed under the responsibility of the university, or related directly to them, without first hearing the views of the University Council.

A final article covers the protection of national treasures and assistance to private initiative in scientific and cultural progress.[15]

In addition to these constitutional provisions, the organic law of 1965 provides the basis for the organization and administration of education in Costa Rica.

Administration of the Educational System in Costa Rica

Although it can be said of Costa Rica as of other Central American countries that the administration is heavily centralized,[16] there are some significant differences in the organization of education in Costa Rica and that in Nicaragua and the other countries to the north. Rather than giving to the minister his traditional power, Costa Rica provides for the Higher Council of Education of 10 members, presided over by the minister, a council which is given the responsibility for the general direction of education. It is then the function of the minister to execute these policies.[17] There is hence an effort to shift the power over education from a single official to a conciliar system. Within the ministry, too, there have been not always successful efforts to delegate authority. A recent minister has commented on this problem, saying that the ministry "must overcome its paternalistic administrative system in which each subordinate solves his problems in private conversation with the Minister. The growth of enrollment does not permit this method of behavior . . . the Minister of Education has been engaging himself, especially with the school supervision, in the process of forming a new sense of responsibility and the consequent possibility of complete delegation of functions. This problem will take some time, because it goes counter to established paternalistic practices."[18]

The ministry itself is organized in a somewhat different fashion from that of other countries. The minister is appointed by the president and is both head of the ministry and president of the Higher Council of Education. There is no vice-minister, but there is an *oficial mayor,* appointed jointly by the president and the minister, who serves as deputy minister. "All other employees of the educational system, including ministry department heads, school administrators, teachers, and janitors, are civil servants."[19]

There is an attempt at decentralization within the ministry. The *oficial mayor* is responsible for the housekeeping functions within the ministry itself. There are departments of finance, of teacher preparation (including the normal schools and in-service programs), of personnel and of cultural extension and the national library. A central department serves for the general administration of instruction, including advisory technical commissions for each level of instruction, a division of supervision, and a division for the provincial administration of instruction. Each of the seven provinces of Costa Rica has its provincial administration, depending upon the Department of General Administration of Instruction in the ministry. The provincial administrations have the responsibility of coordinating administrative and educational functions at the provincial level, taking account both of special sociocultural conditions of the province and of the policies of the ministry. As director of the Planning Office of the ministry, Licenciado Ovidio Soto Blanco comments on these provincial coordinating offices that "doubtless it should be made clear that, even though these functions are announced in the organic law for the Ministry, the truth is that this administrative organization does not operate fully in the reality."[20] Overall, however, despite this last comment, there is clearly an effort in Costa Rica toward a measure of decentralization and respect for regional differences not evident in other Central American countries.

The educational system in Costa Rica follows the general Central American pattern of four levels: preschool (for children between ages four and six), primary education (six years), secondary education (five or six years), and higher education. After the extensive reform of secondary education in 1964, Costa Rica required a common three-year program of general cultural education, followed by several diversified programs. In Costa Rica the normal-school programs fall at the level of higher education since a high-school diploma is a requisite for admission. There is also a nursing program at the same level. The only university is the University of Costa Rica, a national university supported by the state.[21]

The School Calendar

Schools for both primary and secondary education begin the first Monday of March and end on the last Saturday of November. There are 36 weeks of classes per year and a total of 210 teaching days. The class period is 40 minutes. The University of Costa Rica follows a similar schedule, classwork beginning on the first Monday of March and ending the second of December. There are 35 weeks of classes and 164 teaching days.

The Financing of Public Education

In its most recent report the Inter-American Development Bank comments: "Costa Rica's outlays for education are about 4 percent of the Gross Domestic Product, comparable to ratios in the industrialized nations. Nearly a fourth of government expenditures goes to education, one of the highest ratios in Latin America." According to the Bank, 25.8 percent of total governmental expenditures in 1966 were for education.[22] The report of the ministry for 1966 gives somewhat more detail. The actual expenditures of the national government in 1966 were higher than those laid out in the regular budget. Using these expenditures as a base and including all of the expenditures directly or indirectly related to education (such a support for cultural and educational activities, school construction, and teachers' pensions), the educational percentage was 28.71.[23] In recent years educational expenditure in Costa Rica has increased at an average annual rate of 9.4 percent.[24]

Preprimary and Primary Education

In 1969 Costa Rica celebrated the hundredth anniversary of the establishment of the principle of free, compulsory primary education in the Constitution of 1869.[25] Costa Rica has not yet fully reached this goal of universal primary education, but it has come far closer than its neighbors. In 1967, of the 317,751 children between 6 and 12 years of age, 277,756 or 87.69 percent were enrolled in school.[26]

A recent ten-year study of Costa Rican education offers much useful data concerning the progress of elementary education between 1957 and 1967.[27] Table 22 gives the numbers of schools, public and private, and the numbers of teachers and students, public and private, during the decade.[28] These data permit some conclusions. The growth in primary-school enrollment has been rapid, in the public schools averaging 9.06 percent per year between 1957 and 1967. On the whole, private primary schools have not played a significant role; in 1967 they carried only 3.1 percent of the total enrollment, and during the 11-year period they increased only 3.2 percent per year, little more than a third the rate of the public schools. During the same period the number of public schools increased sharply (65 percent), while the number of private schools decreased 15 percent. During the decade the number of primary teachers increased in a proportion very nearly equal to the enrollment increase.

Although some of the data conflict, in the supremely important matter of obligatory school attendance at the primary level it appears that Costa

	Number of Schools			Number of Teachers			Number of Students		
Year	Total	Public	Private	Total	Public	Private	Total	Public	Private
1967	2,300	2,232	68	9,446	9,047	399	315,343	305,277	10,066
1966	2,235	2,165	70	9,354	8,942	412	296,058	286,307	9,751
1965	2,080	2,004	76	8,854	8,557	297	283,210	272,666	10,544
1964	1,978	1,901	77	8,157	7,953	204	267,702	254,510	9,192
1963	1,875	1,796	79	7,934	7,593	341	249,346	239,464	9,882
1962	1,805	1,730	75	7,557	7,208	349	230,620	221,074	9,546
1961	1,691	1,618	73	6,701	6,567	134	212,349	203,146	9,203
1960	1,634	1,561	73	6,334	6,076	258	202,801	193,679	9,122
1959	1,568	1,494	74	5,930	5,752	178	188,764	180,642	8,122
1958	1,512	1,432	80	5,668	5,302	366	180,887	172,531	8,356
1957	1,461	1,381	80	5,319	5,019	33	168,122	160,226	7,896

Rica has practically succeeded in fulfilling the constitutional requirement of compulsory attendance of all children between the ages of 7 and 14. The report of the minister of education for 1966 declares that 96.1 percent of all children between 7 and 14 were enrolled in school and that only 11,808 children of this age, scattered throughout the country, were not enrolled.[29]

There are interesting statistics available for Costa Rica on the problem of attrition during the school years and the results of year-end examinations. These figures also indicate one of the reasons for the difficulties of establishing exact enrollment figures, since the numbers change considerably during the year. Table 23 gives data for 1957, 1962, and 1967

TABLE 23. INITIAL AND FINAL ENROLLMENT IN ELEMENTARY SCHOOLS
AND PERCENTAGE OF RETENTION

Year	Initial Enrollment	Final Enrollment	Percentage of Retention
1957	160,226	148,177	92.90
1962	221,074	207,063	92.98
1967	305,481	291,403	95.46

concerning initial enrollment and final enrollment.[30] Progress was made during these years and the high retention rate is in sharp contrast with the statistics for Nicaragua or Honduras.

Concerning final examinations, even in the primary school the rate of failure has traditionally been high in Central America. Results are expressed in three categories: *aprobado,* or passed; *reprobado,* or failed; and *aplazado,* or permitted to take a second examination, sometimes with required make-up courses. The data in Table 24 for 1957, 1962, and 1967 for Costa Rica show important improvements in this key problem area.[31]

TABLE 24. RESULTS OF FINAL EXAMINATIONS IN PRIMARY SCHOOLS

Year	Percentage Passed	Percentage to be Reexamined	Percentage Failed
1957	75.82	14.37	9.81
1962	79.47	14.19	6.34
1967	87.70	9.69	2.61

Both student dropouts during the school year and the academic results of the year affect the productivity of the primary-school system. In all Central American countries the productivity of the system is a major problem. In Costa Rica, although there has been progress in the past ten years, the problem is still a major one. Taking the numbers of students in the first grade in 1957 and following the statistics for succeeding grades through 1962, and the statistics for the first grade in 1962 and the parallel enrollments through 1967, we see both the progress that has been made and the problem that remains (see Table 25).[32]

TABLE 25. ATTRITION OF STUDENTS, GRADES ONE THROUGH SIX

Year	Grade	Absolute Numbers		Percentages	
		Retention	Loss	Retention	Loss
			(over previous year)		(over previous year)
1957	1st	57,627		100.00	
1958	2nd	39,379	12,248	76.28	23.72
1959	3rd	31,766	7,613	61.53	14.75
1960	4th	24,928	6,838	48.29	13.24
1961	5th	19,295	5,633	37.38	10.91
1962	6th	16,019	3,276	31.03	6.34
1962	1st	66,613		100.00	
1963	2nd	52,437	14,176	78.72	21.28
1964	3rd	45,947	6,490	68.98	9.74
1965	4th	39,370	6,577	59.10	9.88
1966	5th	33,664	5,706	50.54	8.56
1967	6th	30,162	3,502	45.28	5.26

Although this set of statistics does not follow exactly the same pupils through the elementary school (students repeat years, for example), it does imply that there has been slow improvement during the ten-year period, since the sixth-grade group in 1967 represents 45 percent of the first-grade group of 1962 by contrast to 31 percent for the 1957-1962 group. Nevertheless, the fact that the sixth year numbers less than half in 1967 of the first grade of 1962 indicates that a most serious problem remains. It is obvious, too, that, as in other countries, the highest dropout comes between the first and second years.

Recent data concerning the numbers of "complete" and "incomplete" schools are difficult to obtain, partly because the situation is changing very rapidly and partly because it is sometimes difficult to define the terms. In 1965, in Central America as a whole, 27 percent of primary schools were classified as complete. In the same year 57 percent of Costa Rican schools offered all six years of primary instruction, the highest percentage in Central America. In Table 26, the Costa Rican statistics for 1963-1965

TABLE 26. CLASSIFICATION OF PRIMARY SCHOOLS AS COMPLETE OR INCOMPLETE

Years	Total Number of Schools	Complete	Incomplete
1963	1,774	660	1,114
1964	1,874	804	1,070
1965	1,974	1,113	861

show the rapidity of the change.[33] This change continued during 1966-1967 at an even more rapid pace as is shown by the fact that during these two years 262 first-grade classes or sections were added by comparison with 631 sixth-grade classes or sections.[34]

The problem here is that, even though Costa Rica aims at the offering of the complete six grades of primary school to all children by 1974,[35] the dispersion of population in Costa Rica and the problem of roads and transportation as agriculture expands into new geographical areas make the task very difficult. One solution, where student numbers are small and where it is not yet possible to transport them to larger centers for lack of adequate roads, is the creation of one-teacher schools, not as incomplete schools offering only two or three grades but as schools offering the entire primary program with one teacher. This one-room school will probably be necessary for some years, but it requires a teacher with special qualifications and preparations.[36] In 1966, for example, there were 723 primary teachers in one-room schools, but 225 of them were offering the full six-year program. Various training programs aided by foreign experts were attempting to make it possible for a child to find the full elementary program in any elementary school in Costa Rica.[37]

The qualifications required of the primary teacher in Costa Rica are higher than those in the countries to the north where teachers are prepared in normal schools at the secondary level. The standard requirement is a degree from a normal school, which requires a high-school diploma for admission, or a degree as primary teacher from the School of Education of the University of Costa Rica, a program requiring one year of preprofessional studies and two years in the School of Education.

There are five categories of primary and preprimary teachers in Costa Rica:

Group A: those teachers who have a teaching degree from the University of Costa Rica or from one of the three normal schools which prepare elementary teachers. Also included in this group are teachers who received in-service training degrees from the very successful IFPM, the Institute for the Professional Training of Teachers, which was run by the ministry from 1955 to 1965.

Group D: teachers holding a *certificate* from the IFPM; because they did not have a secondary-school diploma, they were not eligible for the IFPM degree program.

Group C: teachers holding a Superior Aptitude Certificate, mostly older teachers who had not completed secondary school but who obtained certain certificates from institutes and summer courses.

Group D: teachers holding the Elementary Aptitude Certificate, very similar to those in Group C.

The Group of *Aspirantes:* "aspiring teachers," who hold no teaching degrees or certificates, often secondary-school graduates with no further training.

In 1965 the numbers and percentages of public school teachers in the various categories were as shown in Table 27.[38]

TABLE 27. DISTRIBUTION OF TEACHERS BY CATEGORIES OF QUALIFICATIONS

	Group A	Group B	Group C	Group D	Aspirantes	Total
Total	6,164	1,288	1,200	304	1,299	10,235
Percentage of Total	60.1	12.6	11.7	2.9	12.7	100.0

A study carried out in 1966 of a representative sample of Costa Rican teachers showed that only 30 percent of them lacked degrees. A high proportion of the teachers with degrees were located in the metropolitan area. "Indeed, it seemed that the level of preparation of teachers continually diminished the further one travelled in any direction" from the center.[39] Primary teachers in Group A receive salaries of about $100 per month, but there are some favorable fringe benefits. Salaries are not only paid for 12 months but there is also the *aguinaldo,* a thirteenth monthly payment at Christmas. To induce teachers to work in the rural areas, there are also "Zone" payments, additional salary ranging from 25 to 100 percent of the regular salary and depending upon location, health conditions, and problems of transportation. Retirement after 30 years is possible at the average salary paid during the teacher's last ten years of service.

As an added inducement to teachers in less favorable geographic areas, retirement is sometimes possible after 25 years.[40]

Teachers' associations are well organized and strong. In 1968-1969 they fought vigorously against plans of the minister to extend the minimum age for retirement to age 60 or 65.

The programs of study in the elementary schools are frequently criticized. It is said that the general pattern for Costa Rica was established in 1942 and that it needs thorough restudy.[41] One of the effects of the Regional Textbook Center of ODECA and ROCAP and the distribution between 1963 and 1968 of 1,070,400 elementary texts in Costa Rica[42] has been awareness of the need for thorough restudy of the elementary curriculum. In 1966 a special commission was appointed with the goal of achieving a thorough revision of the elementary program by 1969, the centennial year of the act establishing free, obligatory, public primary education.[43] In March 1969 the new curriculum was applied to the first grade; in succeeding years the new program will cover the entire six grades. The design of the first year is modern and exciting. The concepts are relevant to the life of the child and adaptable to differing regions of the country; the approach is an active one on the part of both teacher and pupil. The teacher is given considerable freedom of approach, but the emphasis is clearly upon the development of the child rather than on a rigid intellectual structure.[44]

In general terms the elementary curriculum in 1968 consisted of 360 hours annually of instruction in Spanish, 288 in mathematics, 144 in both social studies and natural sciences, and 72 hours in each of the following: agriculture, art, home economics for girls, music, physical education, religion, and industrial arts for boys.[45]

Overall, it can be said of elementary education in Costa Rica that the long struggle to make primary education available to all has been successful, as statistics on literacy make evident. It is the only Central American country in which the education of teachers is carried on at the level of higher education rather than secondary, and it has a relatively high proportion of teachers qualified at this level. There has been some success in recent years in reducing the student dropout during the school year as well as in improving the academic performance of students. In this last regard, however, much still remains to be done. We believe it can be fairly said of Costa Rican primary education that improvement can no longer be measured in quantitative terms. Henceforth, the evaluation must be made in qualitative terms.

Secondary Education

Until 1887 there were really only two levels of education in Costa

Rica, primary and higher. Graduates of the primary schools entered the University of Santo Tomás and followed a program which did not clearly separate the elements of secondary and higher education. Mauro Fernández, the eminent minister of education, persuaded the Congress in 1886 to pass a new law of public education to distinguish three levels of education. He also dissolved the University of Santo Tomás on the grounds that, until secondary education became strong, it was an unnecesary waste of resources to try to maintain a university. Secondary education really began in 1886 and in 1887 the first modern secondary school opened in San José, the Liceo de Costa Rica.[46]

Secondary education developed slowly until after the Second World War. The Constitution of 1949, as has been noted, emphasized the correlation of the work of the three levels of education. The organic law of the Ministry of Education of 1957 provides for a conventional set of goals for secondary education and for a program in two cycles, one of general culture and one with variable plans.[47] After many years of controversy, a major revision of secondary education was put into effect in 1964.[48] There is now a three-year common program for all students in secondary education. In the academic program of two years a student may choose between an emphasis on science or upon humanities. In the vocational program (industrial, agricultural, or commercial) two or three years are required, but, by contrast to some other countries, graduates from these programs are also eligible to enter the University of Costa Rica.[49]

As shown in Table 28, enrollment has greatly increased in secondary education in recent years.[50] These increases have averaged 9.44 percent

TABLE 28. STUDENT ENROLLMENT IN SECONDARY-EDUCATION PROGRAM

	Enrollment			Percentage of Annual Increase		
Year	Total	Public	Private	Total	Public	Private
1957	19,614	14,265	5,349	17.04	18.19	14.08
1958	23,349	17,588	5,761	19.04	23.29	7.71
1959	26,068	19,664	6,404	11.65	11.80	11.16
1960	28,164	21,660	6,504	8.98	10.15	1.56
1961	30,123	23,268	6,855	6.96	7.42	5.46
1962	32,526	24,807	7,617	7.93	7.05	11.12
1963	35,447	27,220	8,227	9.02	9.28	8.01
1964	38,844	29,986	8,858	9.58	10.16	7.69
1965	44,229	34,290	9,939	13.86	14.35	12.20
1966	51,612	40,976	10,636	16.69	19.50	7.01
1967	57,386	46,506	11,210	11.19	12.69	5.40

per year. Public education in 1967 cared for 80.55 percent of the students, an increase of about 8 percent over 1957. Of the total population between the ages of 13 and 18 in 1967, 24.08 percent were enrolled in the secondary schools. From a U.S. point of view, this is a low percentage; from the point of view of all the other countries in Central America except Panama, this is a very high percentage.[51]

The numbers of schools have increased roughly in proportion to enrollment. In 1957 there were 49 secondary schools in Costa Rica, 26 public schools and 21 private, plus two vocational schools. In 1967 there were 107 schools, 56 public, 43 private, and eight vocational schools.[52] In 1965, 2,301 teachers were employed in secondary education, 1,620 in public and 681 in private schools.[53]

As in the primary schools the dropout rate during the school year is high. In 1967 the initial enrollment in public schools was 42,487; the final enrollment dropped to 36,136 or a loss of 15.18 percent of the students. Unfortunately, too, this percentage was considerably higher than the 10.04 percent of 1957, ten years earlier.[54] The percentage of students passing their year's work in public schools was also very low in 1967— 48.4 percent—and only insignificantly better than ten years before, when the percentage was 47.85.[55]

The retention rate, affected by dropouts and end-of-year failures, was inevitably low. In the public schools, of the 9,479 students who entered the first year in 1963, only 4,166 or 43.95 percent reached the fifth year in 1967. This retention rate, though very low, represented an improvement over the 31.39 percent reaching the fifth year in 1964 in terms of the entering group in 1960.[56]

In the past, teachers for the secondary schools have been prepared in the University of Costa Rica. Beginning in 1968 a higher normal school was opened to share in this function. Study of a sample of Costa Rican teachers in 1966 indicated that 61.5 percent of secondary teachers lacked degrees.[57] The opening of this new school was fought bitterly by the School of Education of the university, but the shortage of qualified secondary teachers offered some justification for the creation of a second source of teachers.

In addition to the problem of a supply of well-prepared teachers, the other major problem of secondary education appears to be the high attrition rate among secondary-school students. The growth of vocational education —from two schools in 1957 to eight in 1967—and the growth of enrollment in the public vocational schools—from 180 in 1957 to 4,019 in 1967—suggests that this important field of secondary education is developing very rapidly.[58]

Higher Education: Nonuniversity

The School of Nursing, three normal schools for the preparation of primary teachers, and the Higher Normal School for Secondary Teachers constitute the nonuniversity level of higher education in Costa Rica.

To this group can be added the prestigious Inter-American Institute of Agricultural Science (IICA), the research and graduate training center of the Organization of American States, located in Turrialba. Between 1946 and 1957 it was the only graduate center for agriculture in Latin America. Between 1960 and 1965 the IICA graduated an average of 21 students per year with the master's degree in agriculture. In 1966 it graduated 42 students. The teaching staff in 1967-1968 totaled 57, all full time in teaching and research. The staff includes 27 with the doctor's degree, 21 with the master's, and five agricultural engineers. There were 91 students enrolled in 1967-1968, representing most of the Latin American countries, only a small percentage being Costa Rican or Central American.[59]

The School of Nursing during recent years has had an average enrollment of something over 100 students in its three-year program. It graduates between 30 and 40 nurses a year. After the opening of the School of Medicine in the University of Costa Rica in 1960, there was discussion of the possibility of incorporating the School of Nursing within the School of Medicine; so far, the relationship is described as an affiliation.[60]

Much of the success of primary education in Costa Rica can be attributed to the three normal schools located in Heredia, San Ramón, and Liberia. Graduation from secondary school is a requisite for admission to the two-year program leading to licensing as a primary teacher. In 1967 the enrollment totaled 1,431 students: Heredia had 961, San Ramón, 274, and Liberia, 196. The teaching staff totaled 64; 36 in Heredia, 13 in San Ramón, and 13 in Liberia. The three schools graduated 471 primary teachers in 1967.[61] Between 1957 and 1967 they graduated a total of 4,084 teachers.[62] The ever-troublesome problem of persuading teachers to leave the metropolitan area and the need to adjust the normal-school program to the needs of both urban and rural teaching are subjects of recent study.[63]

The Higher Normal School created in 1968 was established temporarily as a section of the Normal School in Heredia and first offered courses in the summer vacation of 1968 for experienced secondary-school teachers.[64] The establishment of the school was preceded by prolonged controversy between the minister of education (a university professor and former secretary-general of the university) and the School of Education and the University Council. The minister argued, with some reason, that one of the most critical problems of Costa Rican education was the shortage of qualified secondary teachers. In the previous ten years, he said in 1966, the university had graduated only 362 secondary teachers; the estimated need during the next five years was 2,000 new secondary teachers, and he said no single institution could possibly meet this need.[65] The university argued that it had always been deeply interested in secondary education, that the nation could not financially afford to duplicate facilities by creating a new institution, that the university already possessed the necessary laboratories and library, and that there was the danger that the hasty production of secondary teachers would reduce their quality.[66]

An outside observer might risk some comment on this problem. Clearly the shortage of qualified secondary teachers is a major problem. More people aspire to and expect to study at the secondary level, so the need will grow. Enrollment in the School of Education in the university has not risen in recent years in proportion to total university enrollment increases.[67] Even though there are estimates that the School of Education has facilities for production of 250 secondary teachers per year, clearly there would have to be some violent shifts in student choice of vocation to make this growth possible. The School of Education has had less attrition than most schools in the university, but the attrition rate in the preprofessional program in general studies has been very high.[68] If one believes that a less demanding program in the Higher Normal School will reduce the enrollment in the School of Education, one might oppose the opening of this new school. The higher prestige of the university and more desirable facilities should, under the right circumstances, be attractive to many good students. Thus it is possible to think that Costa Rica may profit also from the existence of two sources for the supply of secondary teachers.

Higher Education: The University of Costa Rica

Despite the existence of the University of Santo Tomás between 1843 and 1888, it is correct to say the University of Costa Rica, founded in 1940, had few, if any, links to its predecessor and hence it is the most recent of the Central American national universities. Created during the presidency of Dr. Calderon Guardia with its rapid social advances and stimulated by the Revolution of 1948 and the concern for social change during the first presidency of José Figueres,[69] it was natural that the university should itself be more open to change and innovation than many older Latin American universities. In 1941 the university consisted of eight schools: Agriculture, Fine Arts, Sciences, Law, Pharmacy, Philosophy and Letters, Engineering, and Education. The School of Dentistry was added in 1942 and the School of Economics in 1943. In 1946 the university began to work toward a variety of profound changes in academic philosophy and structure, in physical facilities, and in its relationship to the government. The First University Congress in 1946 created the necessary atmosphere for five major achievements which took place during the next twenty years:

(1) The economic independence and stability of the university. In 1949 the Constitutional Assembly provided for the autonomy of the uni-

versity and for permanent financial support at an annual level equal to 10 percent of the budget of the Ministry of Public Education.

(2) The construction of a unified university campus. In 1952, under the rectorship of the brilliant Rodrigo Facio Brenes, the university began the planning and construction of a new campus, which by 1970 was almost complete.

(3) The establishment of the common preprofessional program of general studies and the creation in 1957 of a new School of Sciences and Letters.

(4) The departmentalization of the basic academic disciplines.

(5) The use of full-time professors.

Much of this accomplishment took place during the rectorship of the late Dr. Facio between 1952 and 1961. Facio is clearly one of the great forces in the history of education in Costa Rica, and the university campus is appropriately named for him. Since 1961 there has been a multiplication of new academic programs, a rapid increase in the qualifications of staff, and the development of laboratories and a central university library.[70] An early problem of the very high failure rate in general studies has apparently been solved. In 1968 some 85 percent of students passed the first year.[71]

In its academic organization, as a result of the changes just described, the University of Costa Rica differs greatly from the majority of Latin American universities which lack a central school of arts and sciences and departmentalization. This academic organization has been accomplished within the administrative structure common among Latin American public universities. There is the University Assembly composed of the members of the elected University Council, the directors of departments in the School of Sciences and Letters, all professors in active service, delegates from the national professional associations, and students. The principal responsibilities of the assembly are to elect the rector and vice-rector of the university, to approve proposals from the University Council for new schools, and to approve changes in the organic statutes of the university.

The University Council is made up of the rector, the minister of public education, the vice-rector, the deans (including the vice-dean of sciences and letters), and two students. The auditor and administrative director are members with voice but without vote. The functions of the council are to approve major curricular changes and to approve the university budget. In its weekly meetings it creates academic policy and directs academic activities in the university.

The rector presides over both the assembly and the council and has general administrative responsibility for the university. He is elected for a three-year term and may be re-elected.

The various schools elect their deans by votes of professors and representatives of the students. The deans are aided by directive councils made up of professors and student representatives.[72]

In 1968, with the goal of unifying the university, a radical change was proposed in a recommendation that the deans of the schools be ineligible to be members of the powerful University Council and that the members be named by the University Assembly,[73] but as of 1969 the change had not occurred.

The University of Costa Rica is made up of a central School of Sciences and Letters (which offers both the general studies program for all university students as well as specialties in various academic disciplines) and ten professional schools.

The total enrollment of the university in 1968 was 9,333. Table 29 lists the schools and the distribution of enrollments in 1968 in both absolute

TABLE 29. DISTRIBUTION OF ENROLLMENT BY SCHOOLS

School	Students	Percentage
Sciences and Letters	5,402	57.9
Agriculture	231	2.5
Fine Arts	219	2.4
Conservatory of Music (a part of Fine Arts)	236	2.5
Economics	789	8.4
Law	497	5.3
Education	919	9.8
Pharmacy	73	0.8
Engineering	299	3.2
Medicine	215	2.3
Microbiology	105	1.1
Dentistry	52	0.6
Social Service (a part of Economics)	127	1.2
Regional Center of San Ramón	186	2.0

numbers and percentage.[74] The total enrollment increased from 3,801 in 1960 to 9,267 in 1968.[75] The traditional university in Latin America is top-heavy with enrollments in law, medicine, and engineering. The distribution of students in Costa Rica is sharply different, representing the effectiveness of the creation of new careers in recent years, the influences of the general studies program, and the influence of a well-developed program of orientation and vocational counseling.[76]

In 1968 there were 523 faculty members in the University of Costa Rica: 126 full time, 137 half time, 256 part time, and four on short term contract.[77] The rapid changes taking place are illustrated by the fact that of 388 professors in 1963 there were only 59 full time and 76 half time, but 253 on hourly appointment.[78]

In 1967-1968 the budget of the university was 31,544,131 colones ($4,740,000), an increase of almost six million colones from the previous year.[79] The university has received substantial financial aid both from foundations and from international organizations. The average expenditure per student in 1966-1967 was 3,540 colones ($532 U.S.).[80]

In the past few years there have been some major new developments in the university.

(1) A new central library has been recently completed. For some years there was a well-organized central library, working in temporary quarters. The library has grown from 10,000 to more than 100,000 volumes in ten years; it is heavily used, and it is modern in all of its procedures.[81]

(2) Like San Carlos, the university is developing regional centers, first in San Ramón and later in Liberia.[82]

(3) Serious planning for the development of doctoral programs is occurring in several strong fields, such as microbiology, chemistry, and philosophy.

(4) A university television station to complement the traditional cultural and educational activities of the university radio station is planned.

Overall, Costa Rica exhibits an enthusiasm for education and a constant support for it that are extraordinary. The unity of the country and the traditional lack of conflict between the government and the university are unique in Central America. The president of the republic in 1969 was a professor of mathematics and a former dean of both the School of Economic Sciences and the School of Sciences and Letters.[83] There is no absence of disagreement and lively dialogue over educational matters, but there is an innovating spirit. This national unity and the other historical and socioeconomic factors described at the beginning of this chapter explain the high ranking of the Costa Rican educational system in the world of education.

7
EDUCATION
IN
PANAMA

When one asks Panamanian educators and those from the countries to the north whether education in Panama should be treated in a study of education in Central America, the answer is almost always a hesitant "yes and no."

Through the colonial period Panama was a part of the Vice-Royalty of New Granada, the center of which was Bogotá, rather than a part of New Spain centered in Mexico. Thus Panama was not, like the five other Central American countries, under the Captaincy-General of Guatemala. After independence from Spain it was a province of Colombia. Not until 1903 did it become an independent state. Geographically, Panama is a part of the Isthmus and hence of Central America, but, historically, it is not Central American. When the U.S. Agency for International Development created its regional organization to promote the economic and educational development of Central America, it called the organization ROCAP: Regional Organization for Central America and Panama. Panama is a part of the region but different from the other five states. In education, the National University of Panama recently became a full member of CSUCA, the regional organization for public higher education. Panama has also maintained close ties with the cultural and educational activities of ODECA, the Organization of Central American States, and has participated in the largest of ODECA's projects in elementary education, the regional textbook program. Because of these close regional ties the educational system of Panama can be included in a description of education in Central America.

Historical, Geographical, and Economic Background

Hubert Herring describes Panama as "an anomaly among nations. Independent and sovereign, with the full panoply of a free government, Panama is dominated economically and politically by the American-controlled Canal. No matter how sincerely the United States may guarantee the little state its dignities and privileges, the fact remains that Panama exists only because of the Canal. The result is a nondescript state unlike any other in the world."[1] This judgment may be unduly harsh, but there can be no doubt that there has been constant dissatisfaction in Panama over the Canal and constant crisis. The white minority, frequently quarreling within itself, has controlled the politics and economy of the country. In early years the army constantly intervened. At U.S. urging, the army was disbanded and replaced by the National Guard, but the behavior of the National Guard has been no better.[2] The most recent intervention occurred in late 1968 when a junta from the National Guard overthrew the civilian government. Conflict has also been frequent between the National University and both the Panamanian and U.S. governments.

The area of Panama is 29,208 square miles. The estimated population in 1967 was 1,329,000, 53 percent of which was urban. The annual rate of growth between 1960 and 1967 was 3.1 percent, but the urban growth was twice that of the rural. During this period, migration from rural areas led to a 7.9 percent annual growth of Panama City. Like the other Central American countries with high birth rates, the population is heavily youthful; in 1960 55 percent were age 20 or under. The rate of literacy is 76.7 percent; life expectancy at birth is 61 years.[3]

There are two major concentrations of population in Panama: the Canal Zone and nearby Panama City (with a third of the population) and the Pacific lowlands west of the Canal where 75 percent of the rural population lives. Other large areas of Panama are thinly populated. The rural people of the lowlands are mixtures, originating in colonial days, of white, Indian, and Negro. A high percentage of the residents of the Canal Zone are descendants of Jamaican laborers who were brought in for the construction of the Canal. The population of Panama City is very cosmopolitan and reflects the immense service function of this transit center. Perhaps ten percent of the population is white, living chiefly in Panama City and representing upper-class Spanish families going back to the colonial period.[4]

Economically, more than half of Panama's income derives from the commercial and service activities of the transit zone. Agriculture represents only one-fourth of national production and Panamanian agriculture remains the least developed in Central America. Panama is not self-sufficient in food production and imports many commodities from the

United States.[5] Activities relating to the Canal resulted in a per capita gross domestic product of $540 in 1966, the highest in Central America.[6] Since the government of Panama puts a high percentage of its income into education (24.3 percent in 1966), the average level of schooling per capita has reached 4.4 years, a relatively high level for Latin America as a whole.[7]

Legal and Constitutional Bases for Education

The Constitution of 1946 contains 15 articles relating to education. Many of these articles are very similar to those of other Central American countries: the importance of education to the state, the responsibility of the state to organize and supervise it, obligatory attendance in the primary school, academic freedom, the teaching of national history and civics by Panamanian citizens, the requirement that private schools follow the same program as the public schools, the autonomy of the university, the importance of literacy programs, etc. Several provisions differ from those of most of the other countries.

Article 80 states that no school may deny admission to students because of the nature of the union of their parents, or for social, racial or political reasons. The violation of this rule by private schools will result in the loss of public subvention if there is one, the loss of the power to give legal diplomas or certificates, or, if the violation continues, the loss of the right to continue giving instruction. Article 81 provides that private schools may not teach in a foreign language without special permission of the ministry. Article 83 provides that by law incentives will be established to bring about the production of Panamanian textbooks. With reference to the financing of education Article 84 provides that the costs of education will have priority over all other governmental expenditures. Article 89 provides that the state will stimulate the establishment of vocational school and, from the primary level on, the development of vocational counseling. Article 91, the final one, anticlimactically provides for the creation of a department of physical culture.[8]

Organization and Administration of the Educational System in Panama

A report of the ministry in 1967 emphasizes the role of the minister:

The Minister of Education has in his charge everything related to national education and culture, including the direction, organization, and supervision of all public and private educational institutions in the republic, with the exception of those under the responsibility of other ministries, and he has the responsibility for stimulating culture in the entire country in the form most appropriate for the national interest.

The educational system of Panama is centralized.

For the carrying out of its functions, the Ministry has the following organization:

The Minister, the maximum authority in the area, charged with determining the orientation and direction of the educational policy of the state.

The Vice-minister, who collaborates with the Minister in the task of orienting and stimulating national education.

There are, moreover, dependent advisory groups, such as the National Council of Education, the National Planning Council, the National Commission for UNESCO, and the legal office, and a series of offices, departments and sections each headed by an official, all of which collaborate with the Minister and Vice-minister of Education in the orientation, direction, and administration of the system.[9]

The justification for so long a quotation is the emphasis on extreme centralization that it conveys. An organizational chart of the ministry shows that 17 offices report directly to the minister,[10] very much in the spirit of the statement quoted above. There are separate offices, apparently on the same administrative level, for example, for primary education, private schools, adult education and literacy, the national printing office, physical education, secondary education, and cultural affairs.[11]

The general structure of education is like that of other Central American countries: preprimary, primary, secondary, and higher education. The school year of 36 weeks extends from April through December.[12]

Preprimary and Primary Education

The six-year program of primary education has as its official objectives the development in students of the habits, attitudes, and understanding necessary for efficient work and constructive contribution to the economic life of the country, for maintaining health, for enjoying and improving the home, for participation in democratic national life, for using free time wisely, and for acting in a moral and ethical manner.[13]

In general, the plan of study for primary education includes the following subjects and number of hours annually: Spanish, 245; mathematics, 210; social studies and natural sciences, 175 each; agriculture, 105; art, 70; home economics for girls, 105; physical education and religion, 70 each; and industrial arts for boys, 35. Panama is the only Central American country that includes English in the primary schools (70 hours per year in grades five and six).[14]

At the level of preprimary education, the data for some recent years are shown in Table 30.[15] For elementary education the data are shown in Table 31.[16]

TABLE 30. DISTRIBUTION OF STUDENTS AND TEACHERS IN PREPRIMARY SCHOOLS

	1961	1963	1965	1966
Public				
Schools	26	27	28	30
Enrollment	1,777	1,888	1,948	2,095
Teachers	49	49	53	52
Private				
Schools	46	57	71	70
Enrollment	1,756	2,302	2,877	3,078
Teachers	65	82	99	107
Total				
Schools	72	84	99	100
Enrollment	3,533	4,190	4,825	5,173
Teachers	114	131	152	159

TABLE 31. DISTRIBUTION OF STUDENTS AND TEACHERS IN ELEMENTARY SCHOOLS

	1961	1963	1965	1966
Public				
Schools	1,321	1,358	1,520	1,552
Enrollment	161,996	176,512	193,037	199,583
Teachers	5,252	5,563	6,047	6,605
Private				
Schools	51	61	60	68
Enrollment	9,163	10,207	10,392	11,045
Teachers	298	360	344	469
Total				
Schools	1,372	1,419	1,580	1,620
Enrollment	171,159	186,719	203,429	210,628
Teachers	5,550	5,923	6,391	7,044

In 1967 the total of primary and preprimary enrollment in public schools reached 208,801, an increase of 6,700 over 1966.[17] The increases have been substantial in recent years. In Panama, as in Costa Rica, the public system carries the great portion of the burden at the primary level.

Concerning both the successes and the critical problem of primary education in Panama, there is considerable agreement among both planners in the ministry and foreign observers on the following six points:

(1) Although primary enrollment has increased rapidly, in 1967 46,587 children between the ages of 7 and 16 were not in school, 16.7 percent of this age group.[18]

(2) Like all of the other Central American countries except Costa Rica, Panama requires a normal-school diploma at the secondary level for primary teachers. More than 97 percent of primary teachers in the public schools meet this requirement.[19] More than 300 primary teachers (over 5 percent) have university degrees.[20] Some advisers to the ministry are now asking whether it is time to raise the educational requirements for primary teachers.[21]

(3) There is general agreement that the program of ODECA and AID has made substantial contributions to primary education in Panama through the production of textbooks.[22]

(4) The problem of primary schools not offering the full six-year program remains. Of 1,552 public primary schools in 1966, only 865 offered the full primary program. Most of the children (85.9 percent) attended complete schools, however; a great many of the incomplete schools were located in the rural areas where there were 631 one-teacher schools, the majority of which did not offer the full program.[23]

(5) Panama does not experience the same problems of student dropouts during the year and of academic failure that are common in Central America. In Panama in 1966 the dropout during the year was only 2.6 percent. In the same year 80.5 percent of primary students passed their courses. Nevertheless, the overall problem of attrition remains. Of the students who entered the first grade in 1961-1962 in public schools, only 43.6 percent reached the sixth grade.[24] The percentage was even smaller in private schools, and, worse still, there has been little improvement in the past dozen years.

(6) The greatest need of the ministry in 1968 was the completion of a national plan for education, one related to and coordinated with the overall national development plan. Both the Minister of Education and such agencies as AID-Panama are in agreement on this major need.[25]

Secondary Education

The six-year program in secondary education is divided into two three-year cycles. The first cycle consists of general education; the second cycle is diversified: an academic program and professional programs in primary teacher training and in commercial studies, and vocational education in home economics, agriculture, and trades.

Because of the division of responsibility for secondary education in the ministry between an office for public secondary education and an office for all of private education, all Panamanian statistics for this level of education are separate in this manner and not always organized consistently. Apparently for 1966 the data concerning schools and enrollment are as follows: of a total of 180 schools with an enrollment of 50,079 students, 41 public schools had an enrollment of 34,765 students, and 139 private schools had 15,314 students enrolled. The total enrollment in public secondary education rose to 37,443 in 1967.[26]

The data concerning private secondary education are contradictory and confusing. Data attributed to the ministry show 150 private schools and an enrollment of 23,258 for 1965, strikingly different from the 1966 figures given above.[27] By contrast to all other Central American countries, there is also the startling fact that in 1966 the great burden of technical-vocational education was carried by the private sector; only 11.9 percent of the public school students were enrolled in technical-vocational programs in contrast to 64.8 percent of the private school students. The explanation of both the contradictory statistics concerning private-school enrollment and the heavy emphasis on vocational education in the private schools could result from the fact that the Office of Private Schools in the ministry tries to include in its statistics the many private commercial and technical schools run for profit.[28]

The statistics concerning public vocational-technical education, on the other hand, seem consistent and reliable. The distribution of the 4,129 secondary-school students in this field in 1966 was the following: home industries and clothing, 665; commercial education, 1,928; agriculture, 143; industrial education, 1,248; and training of seamen, 145. There is general agreement that vocational education is a high priority of the ministry and that it is developing with some rapidity.[29]

The distribution of students among the various public secondary programs is reflected in the number of graduates in 1965. The total of 2,124 graduates was divided as follows:[30] academic program, 965; primary teachers, 448; commercial studies, 307; home economics, 122; industrial arts, 227; agriculture, 17; and seamanship, 38.

In a country in which half the population is involved in agriculture and in which agriculture is little developed, there is obviously a disproportionately small number of secondary graduates in this field.

The teaching staff for public secondary education numbered 1,804 in 1967. By striking contrast with Costa Rica and other Central American countries, 79.7 percent of those teachers had university degrees, chiefly in secondary education.[31]

In the various recent reports and studies of the ministry concerning secondary education, it is evident that there are more ties between the National University and secondary education than in other Central American countries, natural, perhaps, because of the much higher percentages of university graduates among secondary teachers and administrators than in the other countries. There appears also to be more attention to in-service preparation of teachers in the sciences and languages than elsewhere. The successes of secondary education are obviously represented by the rapid growth of enrollment, the comparatively high qualifications of teachers, and by the percentage of adolescents enrolled in the secondary schools. Only Costa Rica approaches Panama in this last regard.[32]

One can accept, too, a recent diagnosis by the ministry of fundamental problems in secondary education: a lack of articulation between primary and secondary education and between secondary and higher education; deficiencies in academic achievement by the students (particularly in science and mathematics); the high failure rate; an insufficient number of supervisors; scarcity of teachers in such fields as science, mathematics, art, and music education; the deficiencies of preparation of vocational teachers; an inadequate number of classrooms; scarcity of school libraries and laboratories; inadequate student counseling; and insufficient textbooks and teaching materials.[33] Since all of these problems are relative, it is worthwhile making the subjective judgment that the problems are less acute in Panama than in any other Central American country except Costa Rica.

In general, in public elementary and secondary education and in the ministry, it is agreed that a national educational plan is needed to relate to the national development plan. It is also agreed that a more rationally organized and efficient administration is badly needed. Whether in the turbulence of Panamanian national politics these changes can occur is not predictable at this time.

Higher Education

Apart from a small public school of nursing (156 students in 1965, which in its advanced programs is affiliated with the National University),[34] higher education in Panama consists of the National University of Panama, and a small private university, Santa Maria La Antigua.

The history of higher education in Panama has some interesting aspects. During the colonial period King Ferdinand VI of Spain authorized the creation of the Royal and Pontifical University of Saint Xavier in 1749. This university disappeared with the expulsion of the Jesuits in 1767. After independence in the nineteenth century, while

Panama was a part of Colombia, there existed for 25 years the Colegio del Ismo (the School of the Isthmus), which for a time had university status.

Three years after the separation of Panama from Colombia, the National Institute was established in 1907. This secondary school was later to be converted into the National University. During World War I, with the goal of establishing an international institution, the National Congress authorized the president of the republic to negotiate with other governments concerning the establishment of a Pan-American university, but with no result. In 1918 a law school was created and tied to the National Institute, but it disappeared in 1930.

In 1933 a pedagogical institute and a school of pharmacy were established under the Ministry of Education. The National University under the direction of the ministry was created by law in 1935 and opened a year later using the facilities of the National Institute. Panama has often aspired to create higher education of a somewhat supranational character. After a conference of Latin American ministers of education the National Congress in 1943 authorized the change of the name of the National University to the Inter-American University in the expectation that it would become an international institution. Although that move failed, the congress did grant the university a partial autonomy for the first time, giving it the right to choose its own teaching staff. The new National Constitution of 1946 took the further step of giving it legal autonomy and its present name, the University of Panama.[35] One notes the difference between the emphasis in other Central American countries upon the Central American region and in Panama upon a broader Latin American area. In its statement of objectives, for example, the University of Panama speaks of giving the student "an orientation toward social, national and inter-American usefulness."[36]

The government and administration of the University of Panama differ in several ways from those of other universities in the region. The General University Council consists of the permanent professors and of student representation from each school. This council names the rector, the general or principal dean (principal assistant to the rector), and the general secretary of the university, as well as approving modification of university statutes. This council also selects the public members of the *Junta de Síndicos* (the Financial Board).

The *Junta de Síndicos,* made up of the rector, the minister of education, a representative of the alumni association, and four citizens, is responsible for the general financial affairs of the university.

The Administrative Council is made up of the rector, a representative of the minister of education, the general dean, the deans of all the schools, and a student representative from each school. The function of this council is to approve appointments of professors, draw up the general university budget, and to approve academic programs.

The rector is elected for a period of five years and may be reelected.

Academic deans of each school are elected at the beginning of the academic year. They and faculty councils, made up of all of the regular professors and one student for each five faculty members, govern the affairs of the individual schools.[37]

The rector, the general dean, and other officials of the university have commented on the shortage of administrative staff in the university and have explained the absence of a university planning office on this basis. The same reason is given as the explanation for the slow publication of statistical and other data concerning the university. The organizational chart of the university, too, is unnecessarily complex.[38]

By contrast to the other national universities in Central America, Panama has scarcely begun the process of departmentalization. The University is made up of eight *facultades,* each composed of one or more schools with individual curricula: Public Administration and Commerce; Agriculture; Architecture; Natural Sciences and Pharmacy; Law; Philosophy, Letters, and Education; Engineering; and Medicine.

The only evidence of departmentalization in the university (and evidence as well of the complexity of organization) is found in the *facultad* of Natural Sciences and Pharmacy. It is made up of the Schools of Biology (including departments of Zoology, Botany, and Medical Technology), Chemistry, Pharmacy, Nursing, and Mathematics and Physics.[39]

By contrast to the absence of departmental organization, Panama is the only university in CSUCA which uses the U.S. system of letter grades.[40]

Enrollment has risen steadily in recent years, from 5,056 in 1962-1963 to 8,946 in 1967-1968. The number of graduates has risen correspondingly, from 340 in 1962-1963 to 491 in 1967-1968. The distribution of enrollment and graduates in 1967-1968 among the various schools is shown in Table 32.[41]

TABLE 32. DISTRIBUTION OF ENROLLMENT AND GRADUATES AMONG
SCHOOLS, 1967-68

School	Enrollment	Number of Graduates
Law	427	22
Architecture	369	11
Engineering	326	24
Medicine	132	21
Agriculture	125	9
Letters	2,923	226
Public Administration and Commerce	2,672	74
Sciences	1,973	104

In 1966-1967 there were 308 professors, 74 full time and 244 who taught by the hour. Of the 244 professors on hourly appointment, 122 were on the regular staff and 122 were temporary.[42]

In the area of university extension Panama undoubtedly has the most active program among the CSUCA universities. During 1967 it offered extension courses to 2,312 students in various parts of the country.[43]

Despite the fact that the Republic of Panama has the highest per capita income in the region, the university has received the lowest support per student. The data for the total university budget and per capita student expenditures between 1963 and 1967 are shown in Table 33.[44]

TABLE 33. UNIVERSITY BUDGETS AND PER CAPITA STUDENT
EXPENDITURES

Year	Total Budget	Amount per Student
1963	$1,613,660	$315
1964	2,161,906	377
1965	2,700,000	403
1966	3,241,000	412
1967	3,782,484	423

One might readily conclude that the University of Panama needs more support from the national government. As of June 1969, however, the university was closed. In December 1968 military forces of the Panamanian National Guard occupied the university and the autonomy of the university was abolished by a decree of the *Junta Provisional de Gobierno.* Reports from observers in Panama indicated that the university would be closed for at least six months during which time a new board of trustees would select a new rector and carry through a reform of the university. Reports also indicated that the military government had some difficulty finding members willing to serve on the board of trustees.

The decree of December 14, closing the university for six months and announcing the creation of the Board of Trustess *(Junta de Regentes),* also provided a list of 26 points on the basis of which the trustees would create a new set of statutes for the university. One major point was the requirement that the rector be given greater power (deans, for example, will be selected by the schools from a list of three names supplied by the rector); the quotas of admission to the schools will be related to plans for national development; student representatives will be regular students with an academic average of at least B; a program of general studies will be created; and students who fail one or two courses may repeat them only once.[45]

The second university in Panama is the Catholic university, Santa Maria La Antigua. Under a Panamanian law for private universities, passed in 1963, the university was created in 1965 as a dependency of the Conference of Catholic Bishops of Panama and it falls under the authority of the Archbishop of Panama.[46]

The Council of Bishops of Panama elects the members of the Directive Council of the university. The Archbishop of Panama, who has the supreme authority over the university, designates the rector and delegates functions to him. The Supreme Council of the university is composed of all the members of the Directive Council and the Financial Board. It may make changes in the university statutes.

The Directive Council names the vice-rector, general secretary, and other university officials. This council has all of the powers normally possessed by the council of the national university. The council is made up of the grand chancellor, the rector, one dean, and four professors elected by the Council of Bishops.

The Financial Board is made up of the grand chancellor, the rector, and seven private citizens. The private citizens are elected by the Association of Parents of Catholic Secondary Schools and the Committee of Benefactors. The function of the board is to name the treasurer of the university and comment on the budget.

There is also the University Council, made up of the rector, the general secretary, and all of the full professors of the university; the council may include one student from each school in the university. This council is concerned with instructional and disciplinary matters.[47]

The university consists of these schools: the School of Philosophy, Letters, and Education, with departments of philosophy, linguistics, education, and theology; the School of Sciences, with a department of engineering and exact sciences, a department of natural sciences, and a department of psychology; and the School of Law and Administration, with departments of law and of the sciences of administration.[48]

In the first semester of 1968 the total enrollment was 451 students, with the largest numbers in business administration (145), secretarial training (56), and psychology (56). The budget for 1968 totaled $261,000.[49] In 1966 there was a total of 48 professors, 40 half time and 8 full time.[50]

The future of higher education in Panama depends upon some degree of cooperation between the government and the National University. The instability of the government in recent years has hindered all levels of education. Education has progressed in Panama in recent years, but without much planning either in the ministry or in the university. In many respects Panama has an overall educational system better than some others in Central America. With Panama's much greater resources, however, the quality should be higher than it is.

8

EDUCATION
IN
CENTRAL
AMERICA:
Regional Aspects

In the preceding six chapters we have described the educational systems of six countries as if there were no special relationships among them—as if no regional organizations exist. Such organizations do exist, however, parallel with those in the area of economic integration. In the volume of intraregional trade and commerce, it is clear that the organization of the Central American Common Market brought about immense increases in recent years; between 1961 and 1968 the increase was 1,000 percent.[1] It is not so easy to measure the effects of regional cooperation in education. One purpose of this chapter is to describe and evaluate these regional entities as they have confronted regional problems.

The Educational Activities of
The Organization of Central American States

The rapid lifting of the level of life in Central America requires regional integration as one component. Industrial and agricultural development require wider-than-national markets, better prepared and more mobile manpower, and integrated planning and financing. The inability of these small countries to maintain a Central American unity after independence was the result in part of the isolation and the lack of easy communication that followed from the geographical separateness. The development in recent years of effective means of transportation and communication lays the groundwork for all of the types of cooperation not really practical in earlier periods.

The Organization of Central American States (ODECA) was founded in 1951 with a charter that called for political, economic, and social integration. In 1962 a new charter was signed strengthening the administrative structure. One agency of ODECA (which has its headquarters in El Salvador) is the Cultural and Educational Council, made up of the ministers of education of the member countries.

The first meeting of the Cultural and Educational Council took place in El Salvador in December 1956. The most important result of that meeting was the decision to hold a series of seminars relative to the various levels of education with the purpose of comparative analysis and the goal of an agreement concerning common purposes and organizational patterns of education in Central America. With the assistance of experts supplied by UNESCO, the OEA, and International Cooperation Administration of the U.S., five seminars were held during 1957 and 1958 concerning rural and urban primary education, the training of teachers for rural primary schools, vocational and technical education, and academic secondary education.

Something of the spirit of all these meetings can be illustrated by aspects of the seminar on academic secondary education. The seminar produced some 160 recommendations concerning the philosophical bases of secondary education; programs of study; the internal organization of schools; methods of teaching and teaching materials; the preparation and in-service training of teachers; the professional organization of teachers; student counseling, supervision, and evaluation; and the administration of secondary education. In the section concerning programs of study, for example, the seminar recognized the differences in basic organization of secondary education among the countries and declared one of the essential objectives of the seminar to be the search for unified plans and programs in the region "with a view to educational and cultural unity as a basis for future economic and political unity." Thus the seminar specifically recommended to the Cultural and Educational Council of ODECA that secondary education in the Isthmus should have a minimum duration of five years, including a basic cycle of three years and a second academic cycle of at least two years—all with a uniform program of study.[2]

With the stimulus of the Conference concerning Education and Economic and Social Development held in Chile in March 1962, the ministers of education met in El Salvador in June 1962 and ratified an important agreement, the *Convenio Centroamericano sobre Unificación Básica de la Educación,* based on the recommendations of the earlier seminars and incorporating also some of the recommendations adopted in Chile. This agreement was ratified by Costa Rica, Nicaragua, Honduras, El Salvador, and Guatemala and included an article indicating that Panama might join at any time it wished. In February 1968 Panama accepted the agreement and became a part of the Cultural and Educational Council of ODECA.[3]

This agreement for the basic unification of elementary and secondary education in Central America is of fundamental importance, although the fact must be recognized that unification simply means the development of parallel programs, similar structures, and equivalent standards among the six ministries of education, and not in any sense a central control by ODECA or its Cultural and Educational Council. The secretary-general of ODECA, Albino Román y Vega (whose term ended in 1969), wrote in 1968:

> If we confront the problem of education in a joint and integrated fashion, unifying methods, programs and calendars as much as possible, we will solve the problem in less time and with lower costs. If each country, on the contrary, insists on doing things in its own fashion, or ignoring the experiences of the others, certainly it will make larger expenditures, will make frequent useless efforts, and, what is worse, will not benefit its sister countries with its successes.
>
> I think that sometimes, talking about a hoped-for or projected union, we are victims of an error in historical perspective. Perhaps the truth is that Central America is already a fact, a destiny, and a task which weighs upon us, even though sometimes, perhaps, we forget our responsibility.[4]

ODECA has moved slowly in the area of education. In 1969, as ODECA sought a new secretary-general, it was clear that fruitful activity by ODECA depended upon adequate financial support by the member states and upon the willingness of the states to elect a new, prestigious, and imaginative executive officer.

What has ODECA accomplished in the field of education?

(1) The Agreement for the Basic Unification of Education in Central America was a major step taken in 1962. Since the signing of the agreement, there has been a strong tendency on the part of the various ministries, as educational laws and patterns are changed, to bring them into concurrence with the minimum standards of the agreement. The countries, for example, have moved to a three-year basic cycle of general

education which precedes a diversified second cycle.[5] Although the Agreement of 1962 is a good document, the needs of education in Central America, especially with reference to education and national development, go well beyond the recommendations of 1962. Lic. Ovidio Soto Blanco has recently made the following sound comment:

> Even though the Agreement for the Basic Unification of Central American Education was ratified, it has not been a sufficiently flexible document to lead to the coordination that is absolutely necessary for Central American integration. In other words, an integrationist educational policy has been lacking as well as those orientations which permit us to channel our educational efforts towards the success of common aims. Education must constitute a dynamic factor in the economic, social, and cultural development of our countries.[6]

(2) One joint educational effort sponsored by ODECA and supported by ROCAP (the Regional Office for Central America and Panama of USAID) is an excellent illustration of the success that may stem from the kind of regional cooperation that Lic. Soto asks for. On the basis of the 1962 agreement to unify education in the region, the ministers approved an eight-year program aimed at supplying textbooks to all primary-school students in the Isthmus. The Regional Textbook Center was set up under the supervision of ODECA and located in El Salvador. Teams of textbook writers were organized and technical assistance was obtained from other Latin American countries and from the U.S. By the end of 1968, 21 primary-school textbooks were prepared as well as teachers' guides. The various ministries of education select the teachers to participate in the author-teams and approve the books before printing. With support from the local AID Mission each ministry arranges for the printing of the books. Between 1963 and March 1969, 10,134,000 copies were printed and distributed, and a great many orientation programs for school directors, supervisors, and teachers were held to plan for the effective use of the books. An additional 2,500,000 textbooks were scheduled for printing by December 1969.

In the last two years in Nicaragua, for example, according to a February 1969 report, the textbooks were stored in a special warehouse rented by the ministry. Distribution was made by school supervisors using vehicles of the ministry, as well as by private initiative. Between 1964 and 1968, 1,145,726 textbooks, work books, and teachers' guides were distributed. During the previous two years, training in the philosophy and application of new primary programs in relation to the contents of the texts was given to 464 school directors, 92 subdirectors, 83 school inspectors,

22 normal-school professors, 3,092 first-grade teachers, and 2,077 second-grade teachers.[7]

Other countries of the region reported very similar experiences, with perhaps the exception of El Salvador, where distribution and orientation seemed to lag. The overall program obviously is a successful and very important one, not only in the fact that it supplies textbooks to primary-school children, many of whom did not have books earlier, but perhaps more significantly in its effects upon teachers, upon teaching method, and upon curriculum.

The funding of some aspects of the center by ROCAP was due to end in 1970. Very careful plans are being drawn, however, to convert the center into a regional institute. A series of seminars and studies was planned during 1969 to open up new areas of future activity for the institute, such as the provision, for example, of textbooks for the three-year, first general cycle of secondary education.[8]

It is easy to imagine the immense complexity of this textbook project and the difficulties that had to be overcome. Not only were there intricate administrative problems in the organization of the multinational writing teams but equally complex problems in the area of production, distribution, and evaluation of the materials, as well as immense problems in the orientation of teachers and administrators in the six countries. There were nationalistic difficulties, differences in language usage, and cultural sensitivities. The early series of readers oriented primarily toward Guatemala, for example, drew sharp criticisms from Costa Rica and other countries. The success of ODECA and the center in this immense project augurs well for the future.

(3) A most important new activity, the Central American Office for Educational Planning (OCEPLAN), was created by the Cultural and Educational Council in 1967, acting upon the recommendation made by the first meeting of directors of educational planning in Central America. OCEPLAN was restructured in meetings of the council in 1968 and began to function in August 1968.

OCEPLAN has two principal objectives: first, the training and upgrading of its own personnel and that of national offices of educational planning; and, second, to represent the educational sector in the regional effort toward the social and economic progress of Central America, developing regional data and plans and coordinating the work of the national offices of educational planning.

The secretary-general of ODECA is responsible for OCEPLAN; he administers the funds of the office and chooses the personnel, taking into account the need for a multinational base in the organization, the technical competence of candidates, and the advice of the various national offices of educational planning. In 1969 the four competent and experienced planners representing the central staff come from four different countries of the region. In addition there are various experts whose services have been provided by the OEA and UNESCO.

An important group was established by the Cultural and Educational Council of ODECA in August 1968: the Advisory and Coordinating Council of OCEPLAN, a group made up of the directors of educational planning of the Central American countries or delegates of the ministers, representatives of CSUCA (the Higher Council of Central American Universities) and of SIECA (the Permanent Secretariat of the General Treaty of Central American Economic Integration), as well as representatives of other organizations that lend technical assistance to the office.[9]

The budget supplied by the ministries of education is small, $42,000 in 1969. The carrying out of the goals of OCEPLAN requires the help of international agencies. The project submitted to the Inter-American Cultural Council of the Organization of American States was approved. UNESCO and ROCAP continue to support OCEPLAN; in March 1969 in Panama the ministers of education approved a proposal that OCE-PLAN obtain technical aid from a U.S. university.

Apart from intense organizational activities and the preparation of various projects in search of technical aid, OCEPLAN had already undertaken some important substantial tasks by early 1969. At the request of the Cultural and Educational Council of ODECA the staff of OCEPLAN completed an analysis of the second, diversified cycle of secondary education in Central America.[10] The relation between this professional-vocational cycle of secondary education and regional economic development is obvious.

OCEPLAN is also much interested in the problem of the training of technicians. In ODECA there is cooperative planning between the ministers of education and the ministers of labor to provide training for the heavy percentage of school dropouts. The staff of OCEPLAN sees useful models in two Panamanian institutions: INA, *Instituto Nacional de Aprendizaje* (National Institute for Apprenticeship), and IFARHU, *Instituto de Formación Acelerada de Recursos Humanos* (Institute for Accelerated Training of Human Resources).

A second major project, which may set an important precedent, was an analytical study of a proposed reform of secondary education in Honduras. The Consortium of Universities of the State of Florida prepared for the Ministry of Education of Honduras a thoroughgoing revision of secondary education. With the goal of assisting the minister in his decisions and also of evaluating the compatibility of the proposed changes with the principles and structures proclaimed in the Central American Agreement for the Basic Unification of Education, Minister Rafael Bardales requested OCEPLAN to make its analysis and also to convene a seminar for the discussion of the proposals.[11] It is probably fair to say that, as so often occurs in the relationship between U.S. advisors and Latin American educational institutions, the Florida proposal tends to impose a U.S. pattern upon Honduran secondary education. The involvement of a Central American planning office in educational reform in member countries undoubtedly supplies a desirable counterbalance and conduces also toward Central American educational unity.

Finally, the publication in November 1968 by ODECA of Ovidio Soto Blanco's very useful survey of Central American education, which we have so frequently used in this study, provides a good basis for the further collection and analysis of educational data in the region, a goal to which OCEPLAN is committed.[12]

We see a parallel between the development of the educational activities of ODECA and the development of CSUCA, the regional organization of national universities. In its earliest years CSUCA moved slowly as it defined its purposes and procedures. Then, with the establishment in 1959 of a permanent secretariat with a full-time staff, it burst into great activity. The establishment of OCEPLAN may well have the same effect of stimulating fruitful activity in primary and secondary education. In any event, OCEPLAN appears to represent a unique experiment: a regional, international planning office for elementary and secondary education, operating in the context of other vigorous regional activities such as the Central American Common Market and CSUCA.

The Confederation of Central American Universities and the Regional Organization of National Universities

In 1946 Dr. Carlos Martínez Durán, the rector of the University of San Carlos of Guatemala, was concerned about inconsistencies in the recognition of Central American university degrees by the various Central American countries. In most of the countries the national university was responsible for the recognition of professional degrees obtained in foreign countries, this recognition being a requisite for practice of the profession. The lack of uniformity of titles and programs among the Central American universities was the root of the problem. Dr. Martínez suggested to the rector of the University of El Salvador, Dr. Carlos Llerena, that a meeting of Central American national universities be called to discuss the problem of degrees; at that time there were no private universities in the region. The discussions of the two rectors led to a broadening of the purposes of the meeting to a discussion of the possibilities of creating a Central American organization in higher education.

In September 1946 the Higher Council of the University of El Salvador authorized Dr. Llerena to invite the Central American universities to a meeting in El Salvador. Thus in September 1948 the First Central American University Congress was held, attended by delegates from the University of Costa Rica, the University of El Salvador, the University of San Carlos of Guatemala, and the University of Honduras. Students were included in all of the delegations except that of Honduras. The University of Nicaragua did not attend since it still lacked autonomy and the government was not in favor of the meeting. The University of Panama did not participate because, at that time, Panama was not thought of as a part of Central America.

The outcome of the meeting was the creation of the Confederation of Central American Universities with the Higher University Council of Central American Universities (CSUCA) as its highest authority. The same Congress adopted a basic set of unified goals and principles for the Central American universities.[13] The significance of these goals and principles and of the activities of CSUCA during the subsequent ten years is a matter of some controversy. In a recent study of CSUCA, Willard H. Mitchell writes:

> It is not surprising that CSUCA fell into complete inactivity for four years in the middle fifties. There was never more than convention oratory and idealistic pronouncements to bring them together. They had not set up any regionally realizable goals, nor had they created a secretariat with sufficient continuity to promote fruitful cooperation. Indeed, it would appear that the initial motivations for regional meetings never went beyond a desire for exchanges of information and ideas. The notion of regional integration was far from anyone's mind except in the millennial future. The only major accomplishment of these early years was the acceptance of the University of Nicaragua into membership in 1953, following its reorganization.[14]

This comment is not just or accurate except in its reference to lack of continuity of the secretariat. Actually the First Central American University Congress made many concrete proposals for integrated action by the universities, recommendations that were discussed in later meetings of CSUCA. There were serious efforts to unify the plans of study of the universities in law, engineering, economics, accounting, and dentistry; there were proposals for exchange of professors and students and for a Central American summer school; there was recognition of the need for general studies, for departments, and for the stimulus and standardization of the university teaching career.[15] A reason for the lack of real progress during the 1950s was certainly the absence of a permanent secretariat and the dependence upon a rotating secretary and president of CSUCA. Dr. Sergio Ramírez Mercado, now the secretary of CSUCA, made a careful analysis in 1968 of the development of CSUCA during its first twenty years, giving particular attention to the first ten-year period. Dr. Ramírez suggests a more fundamental reason than the absence of a permanent secretariat for the lethargy of CSUCA in the middle fifties. In 1948 only the universities of Costa Rica and Guatemala were autonomous. El Salvador received its autonomy in 1951, Honduras in 1957, and Nicaragua in 1958. The absence of autonomy made free regional cooperation difficult. When, in 1953, the presidency of CSUCA passed to Nicaragua, the newest and one of the least developed of the members of CSUCA, activity came to a stop. In 1958 Lic. Rodrigo Facio of the University of Costa Rica, a university which was undergoing a thorough restructuring, called for an extraordinary meeting of CSUCA and its later vigorous development began.[16]

Dr. Carlos Tünnermann Bernheim, the first full-time secretary-general of CSUCA, summarizes very well the significance of CSUCA by pointing out that the agreements made in 1948 included the basic elements of the university reform movement proclaimed at Córdoba, Argentina, in 1918: university autonomy, university concern for social change, and student participation in university government. The achievement of these goals for all of the Central American universities was a preoccupation of CSUCA in the 1950s, as Dr. Ramírez has noted. But Dr. Tünnermann asserts that the 1948 declaration of principles went far beyond the reforms proposed at Córdoba.

> Anticipating by many years what is today almost the common language of Latin American university circles, CSUCA oriented the university reform movement in a correct sense: toward the reform of the academic structure of the university, which is the essence of the problem. This academic reform promoted by CSUCA is what is transforming our universities today, giving them the look of modern universities, on the basis of general studies, departmentalization, full-time professors, etc. CSUCA has the indisputable merit of having focussed the university reform among us on the central point: structural reform and the overcoming or transcending of the professional or Napoleonic pattern. The recovery of the concept of university unity and the search for a balance between humanities and science in the education of the student are very dear principles for CSUCA.[17]

Regional integration of higher education involves planning and coordination. CSUCA went through three stages in its first twenty years. The first stage extended from the First Central American University

Congress in 1948 until the creation of the permanent secretariat of CSUCA in 1959 with its location in Costa Rica. During this first period, without a full-time general secretary, CSUCA attempted to establish minimum programs of study for various professional fields, discussed projects for regional schools of economics and public administration, discussed regional institutes for research (in industrial technology, for example), and talked also about unifying university statutes. Little concrete result came from these efforts except the strengthening of these ideas.[18]

The second stage began in 1959 with the creation of the permanent secretariat, with the agreement in 1960 to set up a technical commission for the regional integration of higher education in Central America, and with the approval in June 1961 of the plan. The principal aspects of the plan included the establishment of preprofessional programs in the basic disciplines in all of the member universities; the creation of regional postgraduate programs in the various existing professional fields; the creation of regional programs in undergraduate professional fields where programs did not already exist in the member universities; the creation of regional research institutes; the search for outside sources of funds; interchange of students and professors; the promotion of regional seminars and round tables in the various fields; and a study of the possibility of creating a Central American university press.[19]

A third stage began in December 1965 with the decisions of CSUCA to meet more frequently, to make an evaluation of the regional programs, to convert the Coordinating Commission for the Plan for Regional Integration into the Central American Commission for University Planning, and to create a planning office within CSUCA. The principal members of the new commission were to be the directors of planning offices in the member universities or those who were performing a similar role.[20]

The evaluation of regional programs was made in 1966, an evaluation which is, on the whole, still valid. The list of regional activities in 1966 was the following:

(1) Regional research institutes
   a. Central American Institute for Social and Economic Research—University of Costa Rica.
   b. Central American Institute for Statistics—University of Costa Rica.
   c. Central American Institute for Comparative Law—University of Honduras.
   d. Central American Institute of Penal Law—University of El Salvador.
   e. Institute for Research and Educational Improvement (IIME)—University of San Carlos of Guatemala.
(2) Schools and departments which offer regional courses

a. Undergraduate level
School of Veterinary Medicine—University of San Carlos of Guatemala.
School of Microbiology—University of Costa Rica.
b. Graduate level
School of Microbiology—University of Costa Rica.
Department of Chemistry—University of Costa Rica.
Regional School for Sanitary Engineering—University of San Carlos of Guatemala.
School of Medicine (Anatomy, Physiology, Pharmacology, and Cardiology)—University of El Salvador.
School of Medicine of El Salvador and San Carlos (Clinical Medicine).[21]

The evaluation also included a check as to whether the various professional schools were meeting the minimum curricular standards set by CSUCA. The conclusions and recommendations drawn by the evaluating committee were approved by CSUCA.

Where fellowships were available, as for the graduate program in sanitary engineering, there was a regional student body. Where reasonable amounts of funds were available, as for a period with IIME in its program with Michigan State, there was much research activity. Where strong leadership was available, even with limited funds, there was important activity, as in the Institute for Comparative Law in Honduras. On the whole, in 1966 these regional activities left much to be desired although there was still a general belief in their importance and in CSUCA in all of the universities.[22]

The Planning Office of CSUCA and the Central American Commission for University Planning have worked hard since 1966 on basic data on every aspect of university education in Central America; much of this data was used in the earlier chapters of this study.

A major landmark in CSUCA's history was the Second Central American University Congress held in El Salvador in September 1968 on the twentieth anniversary of the founding of the Federation of Central American Universities and of CSUCA in 1948. The Congress approved a revision of the principles and goals adopted in 1948. The new statement still stresses the importance of university autonomy, university unity, and the balance between science and the humanities; but it puts more stress than the earlier document upon the universities' role in the economic and social needs of the region, the importance of university teaching as a permanent career, and upon planning.[23]

The programs within the new regional development plan were approved, but the proposal to restructure CSUCA in order to give it more control over regional activities was given to a new commission for a deeper analysis and an early report to CSUCA. This proposal involved a change in the present organization in which the rectors represent the universities but must take back to their own university councils for approval most important matters. It is agreed that a CSUCA group which included representatives of professors and students in the manner of the university councils could take more decisive action than the present council.

CSUCA has maintained certain basic principles, such as insistence upon university autonomy, since its beginning. The University of Panama became the sixth member of CSUCA in 1965. When the new military government of Panama closed the University in 1968, CSUCA protested the violation of university autonomy. In February 1969 CSUCA voted to suspend relations with the University of Panama, declaring that the new university authorities were illegally imposed. In the same meeting it approved and funded the long-desired Central American University Press. The program for activities for 1969 included the strengthening of regional programs in academic and professional studies, an evaluation of the general studies programs in academic and professional studies, an evaluation of the general studies programs in the member universities, and the promotion of socioeconomic and educational research.[24]

Our contact with CSUCA and the Central American universities since 1959 perhaps justifies attempting some personal observations here.

(1) All CSUCA universities have advanced tremendously during the last ten years. Important and basic structural changes referred to above by Dr. Tünnermann have occurred in all the member universities.

(2) Most university leaders in the region have participated through the years in the development of CSUCA and believe in CSUCA and its importance. In 1959 the establishment of the permanent secretariat was made possible by a contribution of $2,000 by each of the five member universities. Outside funds were helpful during succeeding years. In 1969 the annual contribution of $13,000 by each of the member universities made possible a nucleus of staff in CSUCA sufficient to guarantee at least a minimum level of operation, regardless of outside funds.

(3) It is sometimes said that CSUCA has been better known outside the region than inside. In the past, communication was poor even inside the national universities and much worse among them. University reorganization and the development of CSUCA have resulted in greatly improved communication.

(4) The general studies program of CSUCA has been a success not merely in terms of its direct goals of the better preparation of university students, but also in its long-run indirect consequences. From the first, university leadership saw general studies as a means of unifying the universities. These preprofessional programs in the basic disciplines led to departmentalization in the basic academic disciplines, and departmentaliza-

tion led to the preparation of a new type of university professor. This new professional university teacher (rather than the professional man teaching part time in the university) resulted not only in better teaching but also in some interest in serious research. In the University of Costa Rica—which has the oldest general studies program—this progress is the most evident. Even the abolition of the general studies organization in San Carlos in 1969 does not mean a totally backward step.

(5) The regional research institutes and the regional graduate programs—in the minds of university leaders for many years—were probably created too rapidly and most are not yet really successful. The years since the adoption of the basic plan for regional integration in 1961 have represented too brief a period for the full modernizing of the individual universities and too brief a period for the development of the stable, well-prepared nuclei of university professors necessary for the effective carrying out of these regional research and teaching programs. In 1969 various of these regional programs had the basis for rapid development. The opportunities for outside funds and the encouragement of outside advisors probably stimulated the creation of some institutes and regional educational programs much earlier than even the Central Americans thought wise. The situation in 1969 was very different from that of 1959 in terms of the talent and resources for the growth of these regional centers. The next decade is the period in which many of these programs will flourish.

(6) The wide recognition of CSUCA as a pioneer in regional university planning is well deserved.

Private Universities in Central America

Until 1961 the only universities in Central America were public, the five members of CSUCA. By contrast, at both the primary and secondary levels, there was a long tradition of private schools, the great majority under auspices of the church. Particularly at the secondary level, the participation of the private schools was very heavy. In Nicaragua in 1961 when the first private university was established, there were 7,600 students in public and 4,700 in private secondary schools. In Costa Rica the proportion was smaller, but in Honduras, El Salvador, and Guatemala it was higher.[25]

We have seen in earlier chapters that the relationship between the national governments and the national universities was often difficult, especially the authoritarian governments of Nicaragua and El Salvador. Conservative elements of society, too, often distrusted the national university, especially its apparent politicization, its student participation in the management of the university, and its demands for social and economic change.

When, for political reasons, the government of Nicaragua closed the university center in the capital in 1945 and the university center in Granada in 1951, there remained in the country only the National University in León with its student body of about 1,200 and its tiny budget. When the Jesuit order sought to found a new university, the legislature in 1961 authorized the Catholic Central American University in a five-line legislative decree and without consultation with the National University. The National University opposed the creation of the new university on three principal grounds: that the country could hardly afford a second university when the needs of the National University were so great; that duplication of efforts should be avoided since there was a great need to develop new programs; and that the private university should conform to standards set by the National University and be subject to technical supervision by it. The Central American University argued that it had just as much right to autonomy as the National University and asserted that competition would be good for both.[26]

When the *Ministerio de Gobernación* approved the statutes of the new university under its power to approve charters of various types of civic associations, the university argued that what was needed was a national law setting the standards for private universities. In April 1961 as the Technical Commission of CSUCA was drawing up the Plan for Regional Integration, it included a statement of criteria for national laws regulating private universities and defining their relationships with the national universities, a statement later formally approved by CSUCA and still today accepted as basic principle by CSUCA. This statement, in its main points, asserts that a national university should have the exclusive right to determine nomenclature of degree, minimum curricular requirements, and minimum standards for courses. It should also be the national agency to evaluate proposals for new universities, to set standards for professors, to inspect the private universities, to approve examinations, and to determine the validity of all foreign degrees and professional titles. The Central American University turned to the minister of education of Nicaragua and received approval of its right to set its own standards and approve its own degrees.[27]

In 1964 in El Salvador the Association of Catholic Parents proposed to the Legislative Assembly a law for private universities. The University of El Salvador opposed it vigorously and defended the necessity of including the CSUCA criteria. The law was passed, including some CSUCA criteria, such as a requirement that curricula be equal to those of the National University. The law also created a three-member board, made up of a representative from the private university, one from the Ministry of Education, and one from the National University, with the purpose of supervising curricula; but the University of El Salvador refused to participate. The Jesuit University José Simeón Cañas was then set up in September 1965.[28]

In Guatemala the situation developed differently. The Guatemalan Constitution already included the provisions upon which the CSUCA criteria had been modeled. The three private universities in Guatemala were thus authorized under the supervision of the University of San Carlos. Subsequently, the 1965 Constitution of Guatemala modified the powers given to San Carlos, creating a commission for the supervision of private universities and transferring to it the powers earlier held exclusively by San Carlos.

In Panama a law regulating private universities was created before the University of Panama joined CSUCA, and the private University Santa Maria La Antigua was authorized in 1965.[29]

In 1968, there appeared to be cooperative relationships between the private and the national universities in Nicaragua and Guatemala, including discussions of the possibility of creating national associations of universities. In El Salvador the National University did not recognize the private university; in Panama the National University was closed by the military government.

Regionally, the six private universities in the CSUCA area, as well as the private university in British Honduras, have organized an association of private universities, FUPAC, the Federation of Private Universities of Central America. The association meets regularly but does not have a central staff. Some rectors speak of the possibility of joining CSUCA but there is little or no willingness to enter on the basis presently provided by the CSUCA statutes: a provision that private universities which meet the minimum criteria may be members with voice but without vote.

Overall, it would appear that the private universities meet a need, as is evidenced by their growing enrollments. Although the private universities have offered a few new programs, their necessity to support themselves by student tuition fees and their severe financial problems force them to concentrate their programs in traditionally popular fields, law, economics and business administration, engineering, and education, very frequently duplicating long existing programs of the national universities. There is thus a problem of both national and regional duplication and a consequent problem of national and regional planning. In some respects, too, their programs are more traditional in the fact that students enter the professional program directly from secondary school. In the long run we believe there will be some useful aspects in the existence of more than one university in each country and there are clearly some moves toward cooperation. In 1967 there were only 3,782 students enrolled in the private universities by contrast to 36,382 in the public universities. This proportion may not change very rapidly unless there is an unexpectedly rapid growth in family incomes or in philanthropy in Central America.

Outside Aid to Regional Development in Education

Outside assistance to Central American education has taken two principal forms: the setting up of new institutions and aid to existing ones. Some of the new institutions have been described earlier, such as IICA, the Inter-American Institute of Agricultural Sciences in Turrialba, Costa Rica, sponsored by the Organization of American States, and the Pan American School of Agriculture in Zamorano, Honduras, supported initially by the United Fruit Company and later by AID. The education program of INCAP (the Institute of Nutrition of Central America and Panama) in cooperation with the University of San Carlos of Guatemala has also been mentioned earlier. ICAITI (the Central American Institute for Research in Industrial Technology), located in Guatemala, has a tiny educational program.

Two important regional educational institutions have not been mentioned earlier. The Central American Institute of Public Administration (INCAP, earlier known as ESAPAC) is located in San José, Costa Rica, and was founded in 1954 by the six Central American countries with the help of the United Nations. Recently it has emphasized the offering of seminars and short courses for civil servants, particularly in relation to activities involved in regional integration.

INCAE (the Central American Institute for Business Administration), located in Managua, was established in 1963 by Central American businessmen, aided by Harvard University and the AID. Its purpose is to offer courses in advanced business management and executive development.

Most of these independent schools and institutes operate in more or less formal isolation from the universities of the region. This independence is a reflection of the lack of national unity of most of the Central American countries and of the lack of trust and of communication that frequently exists among government, the private sector, and the national university. It is also a reflection of the weakness and disunity of the traditional university, one which since 1961 is being overcome. Closer ties are developing as the universities become more unified and as professional university teachers and researchers grow in numbers. The shortage of highly qualified people in Central America makes the independence of these various institutes, competing with the universities for staff, especially unfortunate.

In terms of aid on a regional basis to existing institutions, the four most prominent outside organizations have been UNESCO, ROCAP, the Bank for Inter-American Development, and the Ford Foundation. After the creation of the Alliance for Progress and recognizing the importance of the Central American movement toward integration, the U.S. Agency for International Development set up in 1962 its Regional Office for Central America and Panama (ROCAP) with headquarters in Guatemala. Its assistance to education, although only a small part of its support for regional development, has been important. On the other hand, ROCAP's aid to education has been only a small part of the support of the Agency for International Development to education in Central America, for there are AID missions in each of the countries which have also made important contributions. ROCAP's principal activities in education have been the regional program for the development of textbooks for the primary schools and its contributions, through CSUCA, to the development of general studies in the national universities. Both of these major programs have been successful.

UNESCO has been active in Central American education for ten years or more, placing its early emphasis on elementary education, but more recently it has also contributed technical aid to educational planning in the ministries in various levels of education. It has cooperated in joint programs with the World Bank, in its educational loans. In 1967 UNESCO set up a regional office for Central America, locating it in El Salvador.

The Ford Foundation has been active in Central America since 1962, principally at the level of higher education. From time to time it has had a representative in Central America, but since 1967 its activities have been under the charge of the Ford representative in Mexico. Between 1962 and 1967 Ford granted about $2,500,000 to CSUCA and to its member universities in support of the administrative activities of CSUCA and of the general studies programs of the universities.[30] These Ford funds, matched in various degrees by CSUCA and university funds, accelerated the development of CSUCA and the universities in a significant way.

The BID has made many development loans in Central America. In the field of education its loans of almost $3,000,000 to the national universities in 1963 and 1964 in support of basic education in science did much to assist in the building of new campuses and in the providing of scientific equipment.[31] These loans came from the Social Progress Trust Fund (representing only U.S. funds). Other loans in aid of education for science, technology, and agriculture have also been made to Central American universities.

Anticipating a conclusion that might perhaps better be placed in the last section of this chapter, we assert that these external funds have been absolutely essential to the development of education at all levels in Central America. On the whole, it is completely clear that the dimensions of need in elementary, secondary, and higher education in Central America cannot be met from the funds of the region, now or in the immediate future.

Some Final Comments

It has been the purpose of this study to describe the organization, the recent developments, and the current situation of education in Central America. The diagnosis of problems has largely been, we hope, that made by Central Americans. The presentation in this relatively brief study of the significant data on six national systems of education, as well as their attempts at regional cooperation, has demanded some choice and some value judgments, since the quantity of information, often conflicting, is immense. We do not intend to offer formulas for faster progress or to make dogmatic judgments in these final pages; but we would like to essay some brief generalizations and evaluations. The systematic study of all levels of education in these six countries, at the same time very similar and so very different from each other, does provoke us to measure against these descriptions some of the general problems of education and educational development that are currently being discussed.

(1) Can education as a whole or institutions within it advance more rapidly than the society of which they are a part?

(2) What is the degree of importance of educational planning?

(3) What is the effect of university autonomy and of a democratic university government upon the possibilities of innovation and progress in higher education, or the effect of centralization of power in ministries of education in the same areas?

(4) Where do the ideas for change come from in a developing country —directly from developed countries or from other sources?

(5) Among all of the possibilities, what are the criteria of evaluation that should be applied to education in developing countries? Where does Central America stand now?

Turning to the question of the rate of change of educational institutions with reference to change in the society of which they are a part, the point of view of the anthropologist Richard Adams is explicit. In a 1967 study of Latin American development, he comments that changes in the universities occur ". . . no faster than . . . changes in other sectors of the culture."[32] In a more recent paper, he is more pessimistic (from the university point of view):

In discussing education in the present context it should first be made clear where education stands in the general society. A popular myth, now considerably shaken, is that education stands at the forefront of development, and that through it a nation may expect rapid progress. The contrary is closer to the truth. An educational system can be no further developed than is the society as a whole. And developments in educational systems inevitably appear to lag noticeably behind other phases of social evolution. The first point of importance is, then, that the educational system develops as general development occurs, and that changes in it follow, not precede, changes in the larger society.[33]

If one looks at the six countries of Central America in terms of general level of development, it is clear that there are wide differences. Table 34 includes data on literacy, gross domestic product per capita, and life expectancy for the six Central American countries and for two South

TABLE 34. COMPARATIVE LEVELS OF DEVELOPMENT IN CENTRAL AMERICA, CHILE, AND BOLIVIA

	Percentage of Literacy	Gross Domestic Product per Capita (1966)	Life Expectancy at Birth
Guatemala	37.9 (1964)	$290	47
El Salvador	49.0 (1961)	270	52
Honduras	45.0 (1961)	220	49
Nicaragua	49.8 (1963)	330	69
Costa Rica	84.4 (1963)	415	66
Panama	76.7 (1960)	540	61
Chile	83.6 (1960)	385	59
Bolivia	32.1 (1950)	150	50

American countries, Chile and Bolivia.[34] Obviously there are general similarities between the data on Bolivia and those for Guatemala, El Salvador, and Honduras, and similarities in the data for Chile and those for Costa Rica and Panama. We are clearly dealing with Central American countries at different levels of general development. Despite these differences we believe that the descriptions in earlier chapters indicate that all of the national universities of Central America except Panama have undergone profound modernizing changes in their academic structures during the past decade, and in 1969 in Panama the military government was attempting to impose similar structural changes upon the University of Panama. This modernization has moved in a parallel manner with efforts at regional economic integration but has in no sense followed it or the economic development of individual countries.

In the area of primary and secondary education in the Central American countries, on the other hand, there has been innovation and progress, not in a degree comparable to that of higher education, but in a manner that perhaps illustrates Professor Adams' thesis.

If one turns to the second question—the effects in Central America of university autonomy and democratic university government upon the possibilities of innovation in higher education, or the effects of centralization of power in ministries of education in the same areas—we believe one finds some explanation for the educational changes in Central America. The autonomous universities, working together through CSUCA, have stimulated each other to modernization. Innovations, especially in the University of Costa Rica, the University of El Salvador, and the University of San Carlos of Guatemala, have been carried to all of the universities. National associations of universities, for example in Colombia, have sponsored useful changes, but we have the impression that the inevitable competition for funds, professors, students, and prestige among universities of the same country makes cooperation less easy than in a regional but international association. The opportunities for CSUCA to obtain funds from international agencies interested in supporting Central American integration have made cooperation among the member universities not only theoretically but practically profitable.

On the other hand, the centralization of elementary and secondary education in the ministries of education and the complete identification of the minister with his national government has probably, we think, reduced the possibilities of innovation both nationally and regionally. None of the individual ministries of education has made changes comparable in degree to the changes in the corresponding national university, and ODECA has been slower to develop in the area of education than CSUCA.

In the area of university autonomy and university government in Central America, there is something to be learned about these complex problems. The head of the planning office of CSUCA describes the system of government of the member universities as similar in structure to the republican form of government of the Central American countries. The university community is made up of all of the professors, students, and graduates; and all power in the university resides in this community. The university assembly or general council is made up of delegates from these three sectors and has primarily the function of electing administrators. A second body, variously called the higher university council, the university council, the *junta universitaria,* or the *junta administrativa,* has the legislative power. This body is made up of the rector, perhaps other administrators from the rectory, the deans of schools, and various proportions of professors and students. The executive function is carried by the rector and his assistants.[35]

The proportion of student participation varies between 50 percent in Honduras and less than 10 percent in Nicaragua. On the one hand, it is not possible to establish any correlation between the proportion of student participation and the degree of politicization of the student body or the number of student strikes; on the other, it is clear that with (or in spite of) a system of autonomy and co-government in each of the universities there has been remarkable modernization of the universities in recent years. In 1964 Dr. Kalman Silvert made an interesting analysis of the influence of university students in terms of the level of the society and its universities. He has four categories, in three of which he places various Central American countries.

(1) Situations of Stable Societies. "In very rudimentary, almost bi-class social structures, necessarily governed under crude dictatorial forms, students normally play a very limited role in innovation and political activity." Dr. Silvert places Nicaragua in this category.

(2) Situations of Beginning Modernization and Disarray. "Students assume a most important role in the importation and adaptation of ideology, in the organization of power as well as ideas, and in government itself. Factionalism is one of the earliest signs of modern pluralism." Here Dr. Silvert places El Salvador, Guatemala, and Panama.

(3) More Mature Situations of Temporary Resolution. Student groups are active here but limited by other established sectors. No Central American country falls into this category.

(4) Situations of Institutional Complexity and Relative Strength. Students exert little power here. Costa Rica falls into this group.[36]

We think that this classification may fit the Central American data of the 1950s more accurately than it does that of the late 1960s. One effect of university academic reform, especially the development of groups of full-time professors, the new emphasis on science and technology, and the development of many new programs, is probably, for the moment at least, to reduce student activism in all of the universities of the Isthmus, or to separate it at least from on-going university academic functions. The development of the private universities, too, tends to siphon off from the national universities the more conservative professors and students and to leave the universities more unified. In 1969, in terms of Dr. Silvert's categories, we were inclined toward leaving Panama, Guatemala, and Costa Rica where he placed them, to move El Salvador up one step, and to be quite uncertain as to where Nicaragua fits, perhaps placing it with Panama and Guatemala.

How do innovations come about in Central American education? Where do the ideas originate and how are they adapted? There are

Education in Central America: Regional Aspects

projects like the new *plan básico* television effort in El Salvador that can be installed where a minister of education, backed by a strong president in agreement with a U.S. president, decides to act. On the other hand, the files of every university and ministry are full of studies done by outside advisory teams that apparently came to nothing. By contrast, the concept of general studies, first talked about in Costa Rica immediately after World War II, or the concept of departments advocated by the First University Congress of Central American Universities at El Salvador in 1948 slowly matured, were discussed by regional commissions, were supported by a variety of outside technical advisers, and finally materialized. Although outside advisers often imagine that their assistance and the proposal for outside funding represent the origin of the change, this is rarely true. The regional meetings of administrators and disciplinary groups in Central America are sometimes criticized as costly and unproductive. They actually represent, however, a most essential step in the communication process, one that both disseminates the innovative notion and adapts it to the regional or national situation into which it must fit if it is to thrive. No revolution is likely to occur in Central American education. Over a decade or more, however, there has been an evolution and a modernization.

The development of both ODECA and CSUCA over twenty years from a stage of meetings and exchange of ideas, to a stage of working commissions, to a final stage of educational research and formal planning is the measure both of the maturing of these organizations and also of the basic mechanism by which ideas occur and develop in Central America.

Where does Central American education stand today? We can remember a welcoming reception held in the Club Unión in San José in 1959 in honor of the creation of the permanent secretariat of CSUCA. Many of the Costa Ricans present told us that nothing much was likely to result from this step; there was not really much in common among the countries of the Isthmus. Much has occurred, however, a great deal in the regionalization of higher education and less but a substantial amount in elementary and secondary education. An evaluation of the current situation might be made with a variety of criteria. It is not useful or appropriate to use the standards of the developed countries. We remember a Caribbean rector's comment after a visit to U.S. universities that if his university had half the money it could do twice as much. One does not expect a 1,000,000 volume university library, however, in the Central American university. In 1968 a group of Latin American university administrators made the following comment concerning the 100,000 volume library of the University of Costa Rica: "We recommend that there be a study not only of the very important technical processes it uses, but also of the exact mechanisms of its high productivity and effectiveness. In spite of its small personnel and budget, we recommend it as a model for Latin American universities."[37]

Using the criteria of degree of modernization (of academic reform of the traditional Latin university) in terms of relative financial resources, we think all of higher education in Central America, both public and private, deserves high marks. In trying to understand this quality, we think one has to recognize the strong effects of regional cooperation. It is this regional cooperation, too, which we believe makes it possible to expect steady continuing change in a positive direction during the next decade.

In the area of primary and secondary education the progress is slower, the problems are greater, the effort is more completely on a national basis. The differences in achievement toward the goal of universal primary education are sharp; the same is true in secondary education, especially in the adaptation of the second cycle to the development needs of the region. The educational leadership of ODECA and of the new planning commission OCEPLAN is still more hope than reality.

In all levels of education in Central America the task is immensely larger than present regional financial resources can provide for. Progress in the short run depends on continued and increased international aid. Both ODECA and CSUCA are excellent channels of evaluation and communication and both merit support, not only in terms of Central American needs but also as useful models for other regional cooperative ventures in education.

In the long run, Central America has opportunities to muster the resources to do what the Central Americans want to do. In the past, which endures in the present, these resources of land and people have been, at the least, underdeveloped, with choices as to the use of these resources in the hands of a privileged few. The will to change will have to come either from them, or from some essentially now-powerless majority.

Obviously, a regional entity is potentially more than simply the sum of its six parts because of the multiplicity of interactions it makes possible. The question will be resolved only when more powers of local or national character are ceded to larger regional enterprises and common organizations. Loyalties to or interests fostered by existing national governments may always be an obstacle to a political federation, which may indeed be an unrealistic goal. Cooperation and common action, however, need not be impeded.

Central America's burden is its high population of people born to live and die without access to political or economic voice in their own destinies, people legally free but with neither the means nor the education to make choices. Regional markets must be further developed and the means to supply them. Above all, what wealth the region can produce must cease being siphoned off. Massive investment must be made by the private and public sectors in Central America for the development of its human resources. Contemporary educational institutions, already greatly enhanced by cooperation, have their nuclei of competent and gifted men and women capable of creating appropriate systems of education.

NOTES

CHAPTER 1

1. Alberto Herrarte, *La unión de Centro-américa (tragedia y esperanza)*, 2nd ed. (Guatemala: Centro Editorial del Ministerio de Educación Pública, 1964), p. 29.

2. *Ibid.*

3. Lewis Hanke, *Mexico and the Caribbean*, 2nd ed. (Princeton, N.J.: D. Van Nostrand Co., 1967), I: 14.

4. *Socio-Economic Progress in Latin America, 1967* (Washington, D.C.: Inter-American Development Bank, 1968). Total of country-by-country estimates for mid-1967.

5. Robert C. West and John P. Augelli, *Middle America: Its Lands and Peoples* (Englewood Cliffs, N.J.: Prentice-Hall, Inc., 1966), p. 35.

6. Franklin D. Parker, *The Central American Republics* (London and New York: Oxford University Press for the Royal Institute of International Affairs, 1964), p. 14.

7. Hubert Herring, *A History of Latin America* (N.Y.: Alfred A. Knopf, 1967), pp. 31-32.

8. *Ibid.*, p. 33.

9. See Parker, *op. cit.*, pp. 33-36, for a summary of linguistic patterns to realize the complexities of the relationships.

10. See Herring, *op. cit.* Chapter three has a well-written background on Iberian history, from which part of this section is all too greatly condensed.

11. *Ibid.*, p. 77.

12. Américo Castro, *The Structure of Spanish History*, trans. Edmund L. King (Princeton, N.J.: Princeton University Press, 1954), p. 29.

13. *Ibid.*, footnote, pp. 182-183.

14. *Ibid.*, p. 630. The early seventeenth-century Spanish critic who complained of the quantity of lackeys also described the Spaniard's propensity to resist governments and laws as a matter of personal honor, an act of nobility.

15. *Ibid.*, pp. 631, 632.

16. *Ibid.*, p. 609.

17. To account for contemporary social structure on purely cultural or philosophical grounds is, of course, a distortion. The French and English, for example, left the remnants of their own class-divided societies in the Americas, Africa, and the Orient—wherever the colonial pattern of economy prevailed. To that same exploitive economic pattern, whether dominated by foreign or local interests, must be attributed much of the backwardness and inequity which characterize the societies of which we write.

18. West and Augelli, *op. cit.*, p. 256.

19. *Ibid.*, p. 257.

20. See West and Augelli, *op. cit.*, chapter 9, for an account of the period of conquest and settlement which emphasizes the multiple interactions of the Spaniards, the lands, and the indigenous peoples.

21. Herring, *op. cit.*, p. 157.

22. Mario Rodríguez, *Central America* (Englewood Cliffs, N.J.: Prentice-Hall, Inc., 1965), p. 51.

23. Rodrigo Facio Brenes, *La federación de Centroamérica, sus antecedentes, su vida, y su disolución* (San José: Escuela Superior de Administración Pública América Central, 1965), p. 5.

24. *Ibid.*, pp. 11-12.

25. West and Augelli, *op. cit.*, pp. 268, 269.

26. *Ibid.*, pp. 383, 465.

27. James Petras and Maurice Zeitlin, eds., *Latin America: Reform or Revolution* (N.Y.: Fawcett World Library, 1968), p. 37.
28. *Ibid.*, p. 39.
29. John Tate Lanning, *The University in the Kingdom of Guatemala* (Ithaca, N.Y.: Cornell University Press, 1955), p. 101. For a detailed account of the founding, see José Mata Gavidia, *Fundación de la Universidad de Guatemala, 1548-1688* (Guatemala: Editorial Universitaria, 1954).
30. Lanning, *op. cit.*, p. 109.
31. *Ibid.*, p. 111.
32. *Ibid*, p. 114.
33. *Ibid*.
34. *Ibid.*, p. 120.
35. *Ibid.*, p. 204.
36. *Ibid.*, pp. 221-256.
37. *Ibid.*, pp. 262-263. Italics added.
38. Claudio Velez, ed., *Latin America and the Caribbean: A Handbook* (London: Anthony Blond, 1968), p. 196.
39. *Ibid.*, p. 197.
40. Parker, *op. cit.*, p. 80.
41. Hubert Herring, *A History of Latin America*, 2nd ed. rev. (N.Y.: Alfred A. Knopf, 1968), pp. 296, 451. See also Rodríguez, *op. cit.*, pp. 93-98, for examples of the confused relationships of "liberals" and "conservatives" in the area.
42. Carlos M. Castillo, *Growth and Integration in Central America* (N.Y.: Frederick A. Praeger, Inc., 1966), p. 6.
43. *Ibid.*, pp. 31, 32.
44. Rodríguez, *op. cit.*, p. 92.
45. Parker, *op. cit.*, p. 82.
46. Petras and Zeitlin, *op. cit.*, p. 16.
47. *Ibid.*, p. 25.
48. Herring, *op. cit.*, p. 158. See also Luis Ratinoff's chapter "The New Urban Groups: the Middle Class" in *Elites in Latin America*, ed. Seymour Martin Lipset and Aldo Solari (N.Y.: Oxford University Press, 1967). He points out that the middle class in its emerging stages identified with democratic goals, but characteristically identifies in time with the traditional elites.
49. Frank Bowles, *Access to Higher Education* (Paris: UNESCO and the International Association of Universities, 1963), I: 46.
50. See Barbara Ashton Waggoner, "The Latin American University in Transition," *Viewpoints on Education and Social Changes in Latin America* (Lawrence, Kan.: Center of Latin American Studies, Occasional Publications No. Five, Dec. 1965), pp. 5-17.
51. Facio, *op. cit.*, pp. 66-69.
52. *Ibid.*, p. 84.
53. See Parker, *op. cit.*, pp. 84-89, for more details of activities in ODECA's early years.
54. *El Imparcial*, Feb. 21, 1969. It should not be overlooked that in the same issue of *El Imparcial* and on the same day in Guatemala's *Diario El Gráfico* there were editorials and stories on the acute, even desperate conditions, among the indigenous population. Moreover, internal political tensions and random violence were at the same time manifested in the presence of armed soldiers at many street corners in the capital.
55. *Ibid.*
56. Comments of Costa Rican economists Claudio González and Eduardo Lizano Faith. Interviews, April 1969.
57. Data from the Central American Bank, furnished by González and Lizano.
58. Velez, *op. cit.*, p. 552. In the same vein Carlos Castillo says ". . . the integration program was launched by means of a simple resolution, without fanfare and without the signature of any formal treaty. Yet it was to be the most successful joint effort in the region since independence." *Op. cit.*, p. 78.
59. *Ibid.*, p. 553.
60. *Ibid.*
61. The "football war" which burst into armed conflict between El Salvador and Honduras in mid-1969 seriously interrupted land travel in the isthmus, and, in typical fashion, impeded certain regional cooperative ventures. How long lasting the consequences will be no one can say. It is only another of the examples of misfortune derived from intense nationalisms and the dysfunction of political boundaries. Football was only a spark to set off the ready fuse.
62. *Miami Herald*, July 13, 1968. "The regional balance of payments deficit has ballooned from $157 million in 1965 to $242 million in 1967. . . ."
63. For example, Costa Rica in 1966 spent $21,415,000 for new electrical construction materials, only $71,000 of which was purchased in Central America. *La*

Prensa Gráfica, San Salvador, July 13, 1968.
64. Castillo, *op. cit.,* p. 171.
65. *La Prensa Libre,* San José, July 25, 1968.
66. Associated Press story in *San Antonio Express,* July 2, 1968.
67. *Síntesis del mercado común Centroamericano,* transcrito del Boletín de la Integración No. 35 de octubre de 1968,

editado por el Instituto para la Integración de América Latina (INTAL). Mimeog. report of Banco Central de Costa Rica, departamento de Estudios Económicos, San José, 21 Feb. 1969, pp. 5-9.
68. *Ibid.,* p. 10.
69. *Ibid.,* pp. 11-13.
70. Castillo, *op. cit.,* p. 169.

CHAPTER 2

1. J. Mata Gavidia, *Fundación de la Universidad en Guatemala, 1548-1688* (Guatemala: Editorial Universitaria, 1954), pp. 10, 14, 36-37, 43.
2. *Ibid.,* p. 42.
3. *Ibid.,* pp. 176-179. John Tate Lanning, *The University in the Kingdom of Guatemala* (Ithaca, N.Y.: Cornell University Press, 1955), p. 61.
4. *Socio-Economic Progress in Latin America, 1967* (Washington, D.C.: Inter-American Development Bank, 1968), p. 177.
5. *Ibid.,* p. 177.
6. *Ibid.,* pp. 168, 176. La Oficina de Planeamiento Integral de la Educación reports that, according to the 1964 census, life expectancy was 49.09 years. Using 1968 statistics, *Socio-Economic Progress in Latin America, 1968* (Washington: BID 1969), p. 178, gives an estimate of 49 years, equal to the figure for Honduras.
7. Comisión de Planeamiento, Universidad de San Carlos de Guatemala, *La realidad nacional y la Universidad de San Carlos de Guatemala,* Plan de Desarrollo de la Universidad, 1967-1973, mimeog., n.d., p. 86.
8. *Socio-Economic Progress in Latin America, 1967,* p. 176.
9. *La realidad nacional . . . San Carlos,* p. 75.
10. *Ibid.,* pp. 40-41. An analysis of the decline in the position of the indigenous farmers after 1954 is given in Richard Adams, *El sector agrario inferior de Guatemala, 1944-1965,* Institute of Latin American Studies, Reprint Series, No. 64 (Austin, Texas: The University of Texas, 1967).
11. Adams, *op. cit.,* p. 20. *Socio-Economic Progress in Latin America, 1968,* pp. 168-169. The planning office of the

Ministry of Education estimates the population in 1967 as 4,664,331. Oficina de Planeamiento Internal de la Educación, Ministerio de Educación, *Boletín estadístico de la educación,* III (Sept. 1968), p. 19.
12. *La realidad nacional . . . San Carlos,* pp. 21-22.
13. *Socio-Economic Progress in Latin America, 1967,* p. 168.
14. *La realidad nacional . . . San Carlos,* p. 23.
15. *Ibid.,* p. 30.
16. Robert C. West and John P. Augelli, *Middle America: Its Lands and Peoples* (Englewood Cliffs, N.J.: Prentice-Hall, 1966), p. 6.
17. *La realidad nacional . . . San Carlos,* pp. 24-25; Franklin D. Parker, *The Central American Republics* (London: Oxford University Press, 1964), p. 50.
18. *La realidad nacional . . . San Carlos,* pp. 24-25.
19. *Ibid,* p. 26.
20. West and Augelli, *op. cit.,* p. 393.
21. *La realidad nacional . . . San Carlos,* p. 29.
22. *Ibid.,* pp. 25-26.
23. Dr. Robert Hinshaw, an anthropologist of the University of Kansas and a visiting professor in the University of San Carlos in 1968-1969, makes the following comments on the statements in this paragraph:
"After posing the alternative approaches to the challenge of assimilation (i.e., reducing cultural isolation and distinctiveness vs. reducing economic inequities), you suggest that education will be the primary key to assimilation. But to which of these kinds of assimilation principally, or to both equally? Possibly a clearer distinction should be made between greater access to and

involvement of Indians in Ladino economic life and the narrowing of cultural distinctiveness and isolation to the point where a shift in identity occurs. I strongly suspect education has had and will continue to have in the foreseeable future much, much more impact upon economic assimilation than upon cultural assimilation.

"Let me pursue further the importance of clarifying these differing implications of assimilation. Your assumption is rather explicit that Indian life is miserable and that therefore education must supplement increased economic opportunity to achieve not only economic power but also a Ladino status. Many operate with this assumption both within Ladino circles and within North American circles, and this leads naturally enough to posing Indian Guatemala as a national 'burden.' Of course, from half the country's point of view, Ladinos are the burden, if not a national one, and while Indians want to be able to compete more successfully with Ladinos economically, they would not remain Indians if they did not prefer their more local identity and life style to the more national orientation of Ladinos. The importance of at least recognizing these alternative assumptions concerning what is in the Indians' best interests is that the assumption Indian life is something they want or should want to move away from leads to possible misunderstanding of Indian attitudes toward education.

"For example, you give two reasons for the high rate of attrition in rural schools (i.e., economic pressure and lack of facilities through sixth grade); both reasons seem to imply that Indians are rather generally frustrated in realizing as much education as they want. I think this is not the case, and in pursuing this it is worth asking what Indians want from formal schooling. True, it is an obvious means to becoming non-Indian, and a few exploit available schooling as fully as possible in climbing the ladder of social mobility. I suspect very few value education for this, however, and in fact many more object to more education than is 'needed' simply because appreciation of Ladino life style is implied. Indians' definition of what is 'needed' usually boils down to functional

literacy, to be able to read and write letters, legal documents and petitions, and to handle basic arithmetic. This usually is achieved by third and at the most by fourth grade, so more grades than these are seldom deemed necessary within the Indian community. Where Ladinos constitute a significant minority, more grades are introduced, but even where this happens, Indian utilization of the increased facilities is surprisingly low."

24. Ovidio Soto Blanco, *La educación en Centroamérica* (San Salvador: Publicaciones de la Secretaría General de la Organización de Estados Centroamericanos (ODECA), 1968), p. 23.

25. *Ibid.,* pp. 23-26.

26. Ministerio de Educación, *Ley orgánica de educación nacional, decreto-ley número 317* (Guatemala: Centro Editorial José Pardo de Pineda Ibarra, 1965).

27. *Leyes, estatutos y reglamentos generales de la Universidad de San Carlos de Guatemala* (Guatemala: Imprenta Universitaria, 1961), pp. 5-18. Edmundo Vásquez Martínez, *La universidad y la constitución* (Guatemala: Editorial Universitaria, 1966), p. 17.

28. Vásquez Martínez, *op. cit.,* p. 25.

29. Ministerio de Educación, *Ley orgánica de educación nacional* (Guatemala: Centro Editorial José Pardo de Pineda Ibarra, 1965), Título II, Art. 5.

30. See, for example, such valuable publications as: *Diagnóstico de la educación de Guatemala* (Guatemala: OPIE, 1965), and *Anuario estadístico de la educación, 1965* (Guatemala: OPIE, 1966).

31. *Ley orgánica de educación nacional,* Título II, Arts. 13-29.

32. *Ibid.,* Arts. 31-40.

33. *Ibid.,* Arts. 41-44.

34. *Ibid.,* Art. 60.

35. *Socio-Economic Progress in Latin America, 1967* (Washington: Inter-American Development Bank, 1968), p. 177.

Statistics in Central America are often somewhat in conflict. A recent report of the Office for Integral Planning of Education of the Ministry of Education shows 45.8 percent of the children between ages 7 and 14 enrolled in primary school in Jan. 1966, although my recalculations of the percentage from the data given shows 48.4. Calculation of

the percentage for 1967 gives 47.5. In any event there has been progress since 1960 when the percentage was only 36. OPIE, *Boletín estadístico de la educación,* III (Sept. 1968), p. 19.

36. Oficina de Planeamiento Integral de la Educación, *Diagnóstico de la educación en Guatemala* (Guatemala: Ministerio de Educación, 1965), p. 8. This table does not include evening programs or literacy programs, according to Lic. Tomás Barrientos of OCEPLAN (Feb. 18, 1969).

37. *Ibid.,* p. 9.

38. OPIE, *Boletín estadístico de la educación* (Guatemala: Ministerio de Educación, II, June 1967, pp. 10-12.

39. *Diagnóstico de la educación en Guatemala,* p. 13.

40. Oficina de Planeamiento Integral de la Educación, *Anuario estadístico de la educación, 1965* (Guatemala: Ministerio de Educación, 1966), p. 135; and OPIE, *Anuario estadístico de la educación, 1967* (Guatemala: Ministerio de Educación, 1968), p. 14.

41. Unpublished report on rural primary education made by the U.S. AID Mission in Guatemala, June 28, 1968, p. 3. *Diagnóstico de la educación en Guatemala,* p. 10.

42. *Anuario estadístico de la educación, 1967,* p. 398.

43. *Ibid.,* pp. 215-216. The information regarding the number of rural normal schools was given us in Feb. 1969 by Sra. Gloria de Romero of OPIE. In 1967 the private normal school in Huehuetenango had only five students and all of the rural normal schools had a total enrollment of only 239. *Anuario, 1967,* pp. 59-60.

44. Javier Ruíz Paniagua, *La educación normal en Guatemala* (Estudios de la educación media en Centro América) (Guatemala: Instituto de Investigaciones y Mejoramiento Educativo, 1964), p. 8. Corrections in the program were supplied by Lic. Tomás Barrientos of OCEPLAN, Feb. 1969.

45. *Ibid.,* pp. 15-16.

46. *Diagnóstico de la educación en Guatemala,* p. 11; unpublished report on rural primary education, USAID, Guatemala, June 28, 1968, p. 3.

47. Soto, *op. cit.,* p. 54.

48. Unpublished report on textbook develop-

ment, ROCAP, Jan. 1-Mar. 31, 1968, Table 15.

49. Unpublished report on rural primary education, USAID, Guatemala, June 28, 1968.

50. OPIE, *Proyecto para la extensión y el mejoramiento del nivel de educación primaria en la república de Guatemala: resumen* (Guatemala: Ministerio de Educación, 1968), pp. 1-3.

51. *Diagnóstico de la educación en Guatemala,* p. 14.

52. *Ley orgánica de educación nacional,* pp. 32-33.

53. *Boletín estadístico de la educación,* III (Sept. 1968), p. 19.

54. OPIE, *Proyecto para la extensión . . . de educación media* (Guatemala: Ministerio de Educación, 1968), p. 4.

55. *Boletín estadístico de la educación,* III (Sept. 1968), pp. 5-7.

56. *Diagnóstico de la educación en Guatemala,* p. 16. A later report for the 1965 school year shows no significant improvement. Of all of the teachers in both public and private schools in the basic cycle, for example, 0.8 percent had obtained a university degree in secondary education in any subject matter or any other degree related to pedagogy. *Boletín estadístico de la educación,* II (June 1967), p. 8. In the academic program leading to the university, both in public and private schools, only 12 teachers among 776 had degrees in secondary education. *Anuario estadístico de la educación, 1965,* p. 144. In 1968 OPIE still estimated that only 1 percent of secondary teachers are qualified. OPIE, *Proyecto para la extensión . . . de educación media* (Guatemala: Ministerio de Educación, 1968), p. 5.

57. Universidad de San Carlos de Guatemala, *Catálogo de estudios 1967-1968* (Guatemala: Imprenta Universitaria, 1967), p. 103.

58. *El sistema educativo en Guatemala* (Estudio de Recursos Humanos en Centroamérica No. 2) (San José: CSUCA, 1964), p. 75 and footnote.

59. Article 146 of the *Ley orgánica de educación nacional, 1965,* is as follows: "It is an indispensable requisite for teaching in the schools, public or private, that a person possesses the professional degree (or title) legally authorized. Nevertheless, while the state cannot

count on the necessary number of teachers qualified at the secondary level, persons who do not possess the appropriate educational qualification may teach in a provisional category, always providing that they have the necessary aptitude and preparation, and that they fill the other conditions which the regulations establish."

60. Oficina de Planificación, *Boletín informativo,* No. 1 (Guatemala: Universidad Rafael Landívar, May 1968), n.p.

61. *Ibid.*

62. *Catálogo de estudios, 1967-1968,* pp. 16-17, 103-124.

63. Universidad de San Carlos de Guatemala, Oficina de Registro, *Boletín estadístico universitario, 1967* (Guatemala: n.d.), pp. 18, 37, 38.

64. *Proyecto para la extensión . . . de educación media,* pp. 5-7.

65. *La realidad nacional . . . San Carlos,* pp. 27-28.

66. *Ibid.,* pp. 60-63; p. 90.

67. *La realidad nacional . . . San Carlos,* p. 62; OPIE, *Fundamentos para una política educativa en el desarrollo* (Guatemala: Ministerio de Educación, June 1966), Chart No. 26-9.

68. *Anuario estadístico de la educación, 1965,* p. 149.

69. *La realidad nacional . . . San Carlos,* p. 63.

70. *Ibid.,* pp. 64-65; *Socio-Economic Progress in Latin America, 1967,* pp. 383, 403; mimeog. memo, Office of the Registrar, University of San Carlos, enrollments up to Mar. 19, 1968.

71. Comisión de Estudio, *Informe sobre universidades privadas* (San José: CSUCA, July, 1968), pp. 15, 32-35.

72. *Estatutos de la Universidad Rafael Landívar* (Guatemala: Universidad Rafael Landívar, 1966), pp. 4-8. Information concerning recent modifications supplied by Jorge Toruño, S.J., in Feb. 1969.

73. *Informe sobre universidades privadas* (San José: CSUCA, 1968), pp. 32-34. Information concerning the new 1969 programs was supplied by Father Toruño in Feb. 1969.

74. *Ibid.,* pp. 34-35.

75. *Ibid.,* pp. 35-38; information concerning recent changes was obtained from Lic. Adalberto Santizo Román, the Rector, in Feb. 1969.

76. *Ibid.,* pp. 39-42.

77. OPIE, *Diagnóstico preliminar de la educación en Guatemala* (Guatemala: Ministerio de Educación, 1964), p. 13.

78. OPIE, *Fundamentos para una política educativa en el desarrollo* (Guatemala: Ministerio de Educación, 1966), p. 27 and Cuadro 24-29.

79. *Ibid.,* p. 27.

80. *Ibid.,* p. 15.

81. Universidad de San Carlos de Guatemala, Oficina de Registro, *Boletín estadístico universitario 1968* (Guatemala: 1968), p. 44.

82. Carlos González Orellana, *Historia de la educación en Guatemala* (México: Colección Científica Pedagógica, 1960), pp. 390-392.

83. Guillermo Lara López, *Análisis de la educación universitaria Centroamericana* (Ciudad Universitaria Rodrigo Facio, Costa Rica: CSUCA, 1968), mimeog., pp. 3, 5; CSUCA, *Catálogo de estudios de las universidades nacionales de Centroamérica, 1967-1968* (San José: Secretaría Permanente, n.d.), pp. 31-32.

84. *Resumen del informe de la Comisión de Educación de la Facultad de Ciencias Médicas* (Guatemala: Universidad de San Carlos de Guatemala, Jan. 1968), p. 25.

85. The most recent data concerning types of professors is less favorable than indicated here. In 1967 there were 1,008 teachers, 74 full-time, 216 half-time, 527 hourly, and 179 teaching assistants. Comisión de Planeamiento, Universidad de San Carlos de Guatemala, *Plan de desarrollo de la universidad, 1967-1974,* Capítulo IV, "La organización y el personal de la Universidad de San Carlos de Guatemala," p. 20.

86. Comisión de Planeamiento, Capítulo II, "Los objetivos de la Universidad de San Carlos de Guatemala," *Plan de desarrollo de la universidad, 1967-1973,* Edición Preliminar, Documento de Trabajo, mimeog., n.d., pp. 92-96.

87. Universidad de San Carlos de Guatemala, *Proyecto de la escuela de estudios generales* (Guatemala: Facultad de Humanidades, June, 1962); *El Imparcial,* Aug. 10, 1968, p. 1.

88. *Plan de desarrollo de la universidad, 1967-1973,* pp. 14, 16, 17, 21, 136-142.

89. G. Lara López, *Análisis,* pp. 51-52. The scattered activity in social science will

be reinforced if a current plan is carried out to create a new research institute for the economic and social development of Guatemala, an institute depending directly on the office of the Rector. See Calvin P. Blair, *Social Science Research in Guatemala and the Role of U.S.*

Personnel, 1950-1967, mimeog., LASA and EWA, 1969, p. 19.

90. Universidad de San Carlos, *Boletín estadístico universitario*, 1967, pp. 68-69.
91. G. Lara López, *Análisis*, p. 79.
92. *Boletín estadístico universitario 1968*, p. 57.

CHAPTER 3

1. Franklin D. Parker, *The Central American Republics* (London: Oxford University Press, 1964), pp. 148-149.
2. *Ibid.*, p. 174.
3. *Ibid.*, p. 145; Robert C. West and John P. Augelli, *Middle America: Its Lands and Peoples* (Englewood Cliffs, N.J.: Prentice-Hall, 1966), p. 407; *Socio-Economic Progress in Latin America, 1967* (Washington: Inter-American Development Bank, 1968), p. 157.
4. West and Augelli, *op. cit.*, pp. 408, 409-410; *Socio-Economic Progress in Latin America, 1967*, pp. 159-160, 166.
5. West and Augelli, *op. cit.*, p. 407.
6. *Ibid.*, pp. 409-412; *Socio-Economic Progress in Latin America, 1967*, pp. 157-158; observations made by Mr. Theodore Foley, an economist with USAID, El Salvador.
7. West and Augelli, *op. cit.*, p. 410.
8. *Ibid.*, p. 409.
9. *Socio-Economic Progress in Latin America, 1967*, p. 157.
10. Guillermo Lara López, *Descripción general de la región* (San José: CSUCA, 1968), mimeog. draft, pp. 9-12.
11. *Socio-Economic Progress in Latin America, 1967*, p. 157.
12. Parker, *op. cit.*, p. 165.
13. *Ibid.*, pp. 152-153. Professor Lieuwen, a well-known student of the Latin American military, comes to similar conclusions: "The colonels introduced modest welfare measures, but faced by firm resistance from the planters, they no longer even mentioned agrarian reform or sweeping social changes. The net results of the 1948 revolution were the substitution of colonels for generals...." Edwin Lieuwen, *Arms and Politics in Latin America* (N.Y.: Frederick A. Praeger, 1963), p. 96.
14. Parker, *op. cit.*, p. 155.
15. *Ibid.*, pp. 156-159.
16. *Socio-Economic Progress in Latin America, 1967*, pp. 117, 157, 168, 192, 218, 230.
17. Parker, *op. cit.*, pp. 161-162.
18. Legitimacy was in colonial days a criterion for access to education as well as other privileges. In a society where, for a variety of reasons, parental union is not always legally blessed, the protection of children from the stigma of illegitimacy is meaningful.
19. Ovidio Soto Blanco, *La educación en Centroamérica* (San Salvador: Publicaciones de la Secretaría General de la Organización de Estados Centroamericanos (ODECA), 1968), pp. 26-27.
20. Departamento de Planificación, *Diagnóstico de la educación, Septiembre de 1964* (San Salvador: Ministerio de Educación, 1967), pp. 1-45.
21. *Ibid.*, pp. 46-56; Soto, *op. cit.*, p. 46.
22. Unpublished memorandum of USAID, El Salvador, May 17, 1968; conversations with ministry officials and those of UNESCO mission to the ministry, July 1968.
23. Sección de Estadística del Departamento de Planificación, Ministerio de Educación, San Salvador, *Cifras suministradas para el anuario estadístico de 1966*, mimeog., n.d.
24. *Diagnóstico de la educación*, p. 101.
25. *Memoria de las labores del Ministerio de Educación, 1966-1967* (San Salvador: Ministerio de Educación, Aug. 1967), pp. 7-9.
26. *Socio-Economic Progress in Latin America, 1967*, p. 165; *Cifras Suministradas para el Anuario Estadístico de 1966:* this report shows 2944 schools in 1964.
27. *Memoria . . . del Ministerio, 1966-1967*, Anexos, Cuadros Nos. 01-0100 and 0102.
28. *Diagnóstico de la educación*, p. 130.
29. *Memoria . . . del Ministerio, 1966-1967*, p. 32: USAID El Salvador, unpub. memo, May 17, 1968, pp. 15-16. Looked at in another way there is, of course, no

excess of teachers; there is simply a shortage of funds to create the schools and teaching posts to care for the more than 30 percent of primary-age children not in school.

30. USAID, El Salvador, unpub. memo, May 17, 1968, p. 7; *Memoria . . . del Ministerio, 1966-1967*, p. 9.
31. *Diagnóstico de la educación*, p. 126.
32. USAID, El Salvador, unpub. memo, May 17, 1968, p. 1.
33. Soto, *op. cit.*, p. 54.
34. *Memoria . . . del Ministerio, 1966-1967*, pp. 12-22.
35. Manuel Luis Escamilla, "La educación media como problema nacional," *Educación*, II (July-Dec. 1965), 8-9; UNESCO, *World Survey of Education*, III, 443.
36. Félix Hernández Andrino, *La educación media en Centro América* (Guatemala: IIME, Universidad de San Carlos, 1965), p. 51.
37. Hernández, *op. cit.*, p. 16.
38. *Cifras suministradas para el anuario estadístico de 1966.*
39. *Memoria . . . del Ministerio, 1966-1967*, Cuadros 02-0100 ff.
40. *Diagnóstico de la educación*, pp. 161-162.
41. USAID, El Salvador, unpub. memo, May 27, 1968.
42. Escamilla, "La Educación Media," pp. 10-16.
43. USAID, El Salvador, unpub. memo, May 27, 1968.
44. *Diagnóstico de la educación*, p. 41.
45. USAID, San Salvador, unpub. memo, May 27, 1968, p. 16.
46. *Diagnóstico de la educación*, pp. 82 ff.
47. *Ibid.*, p. 91.
48. *Memoria . . . del Ministerio, 1966-1967*, p. 42.
49. The law permitting the establishment of private universities was passed despite strong objection by the national university. The relationship between the national universities of Central America and the new private universities is discussed in chapter eight.
50. *Prospecto general de la Universidad José Simeón Cañas, 1968*, San Salvador; Universidad Centroamericana José Simeón Cañas, *Datos estadísticos curso 1968*, mimeog., p. 2.
51. *Informe sobre universidades privadas* (San José: CSUCA, 1968), pp. 28-29.

52. Antonio Pérez, S. J., dean of the new school, Feb. 18, 1969.
53. *Datos estadísticos curso 1968*, pp. 4-5, 31.
54. *Catálogo de estudios de las Universidades Nacionales de Centroamérica, 1967-1968* (San José: CSUCA, n.d.), pp. 15-16; *Guía, Universidad de El Salvador, 1962* (San Salvador: Editorial Universitaria, 1962), pp. 13-19.
55. *Guía, Universidad de El Salvador, 1962*, pp. 20-21, 29.
56. Parker, *op. cit.*, pp. 152-157; *Guía, Universidad de El Salvador, 1962*, pp. 25-30.
57. *Memoria de las actividades desarrolladas por las autoridades universitarias en el período, 1967-1968* (San Salvador: Universidad de El Salvador, 1968), pp. 1-2 to 1-10.
58. *Catálogo universidades Centro Americanas, 1967-1968*, pp. 25, 32-33.
59. Manuel Luis Escamilla, "La reforma Universitaria de El Salvador," *Educación*, III (April-Sept., 1966), 19.
60. *Ibid.*, p. 20.
61. G. R. Waggoner, *Problemas en la profesionalización de la carrera docente universitaria en Centroamérica* (San José: CSUCA, 1964), p. 11.
62. *Cuarto censo de población Universitaria Centroamericana, 1966* (San José: CSUCA, 1966), p. 40. These statistics do not include 24 professors of agronomy.
63. Escamilla, "La reforma Universitaria de El Salvador," pp. 20-36.
64. *Ibid.*, p. 21.
65. *Memoria . . . 1967-1968*, pp. 1-48.
66. *Catálogo universidades Centro Americanas, 1967-1968*, pp. 54-55. The School of Law was departmentalized in 1968: see *Informe de la Facultad de Jurisprudencia y Ciencias Sociales de la Universidad de El Salvador a tercera mesa redonda de facultades de derecho, reunida en San José, Costa Rica*, mimeog., n.d., p. 13.
67. *Informe de la Facultad de Jurisprudencia*, p. 55; Escamilla, "La reforma Universitaria de El Salvador," pp. 47-51.
68. Angel Gochez Marín, *Facultad de Ciencias y Humanidades, proposición del rector a la comunidad universitaria* (San Salvador: Universidad de El Salvador, 1968), p. 3; *El Universitaria*, May 22, 1968; June 14, 1968.

69. *Acuerdo de creación de la Facultad de Ciencias y Humanidades* (San Salvador: Universidad de El Salvador, n.d.).
70. Letter from Dr. Gustavo Adolfo Noyola, Secretary General of the University, July 11, 1968.
71. *Ibid.*
72. Guillermo Lara López, *Análisis de la educación universitaria Centroamericana* (San José: CSUCA, 1968).
73. *Memoria . . . 1967-1968,* pp. 1-52.

CHAPTER 4

1. Guillermo Lara López, *Descripción general de la región* (San José: CSUCA, 1968), pp. 5, 9.
2. Franklin D. Parker, *The Central American Republics* (London: Oxford University Press, 1964), p. 181.
3. *Descripción general de la región,* p. 13; Hubert Herring, *A History of Latin America* (N.Y.: Alfred A. Knopf, 1967), p. 460.
4. R. C. West and J. P. Augelli, *Middle America: Its Lands and Peoples* (Englewood Cliffs, N.J.: Prentice-Hall, Inc., 1966), p. 417.
5. *Ibid.,* pp. 424-425.
6. *Ibid.,* p. 427.
7. Parker, *op. cit.,* p. 207.
8. *Education in Honduras,* unpub. USAID report, Tegucigalpa, Honduras, Feb. 20, 1967, pp. 22. The BID report (*Socio-Economic Progress in Latin America, 1967,* Washington, 1968, p. 194) indicates that in 1965 Honduras had 2,200 miles of roads of which only 240 miles were paved—the smallest road system in Central America, both in absolute figures and with relation to area.
9. *Socio-Economic Progress in Latin America, 1967,* p. 192.
10. *Ibid.,* pp. 157, 192.
11. *Ibid.,* p. 192.
12. West and Augelli, *op. cit.,* p. 419.
13. *Socio-Economic Progress in Latin America, 1967,* pp. 157.
14. Parker, *op. cit.,* p. 185.
15. W. S. Stokes, *Honduras, An Area Study in Government* (Madison: University of Wisconsin Press, 1950); reprinted in part in Lewis Hanke, *Mexico and the Caribbean* (Princeton: D. Van Nostrand, 1967), pp. 184-185.
16. *Ibid.,* p. 185; Herring, *op. cit.,* p. 459; Parker, *op. cit.,* p. 218.
17. Victor F. Ardón, *Datos para la historia de la educación en Honduras* (Tegucigalpa: Imp. la República, 1957), pp. 5-6.
18. *Ibid.,* pp. 7-8.

19. *Ibid.,* pp. 9-14.
20. *Ibid.,* pp. 18-19.
21. *Ibid.,* pp. 20-23.
22. *Ibid.,* p. 35.
23. *Ibid.,* pp. 56, 60-61.
24. *Ibid.,* pp. 84-85.
25. *Ibid.,* p. 119.
26. *Ibid.,* p. 120.
27. Unpub. memo, USAID, Honduras, Feb. 20, 1967, pp. 4-5.
28. Ovidio Soto Blanco, *La educación en Centroamérica* (San Salvador: Publicaciones de la Secretaría General de la Organización de Estados Centroamericanos (ODECA), 1968), pp. 27-29.
29. *Ibid.,* p. 27.
30. Unpub. memo, USAID, Honduras, Feb. 20, 1967, pp. 11-13.
31. *Informe que el Ministro de Educación Pública presenta al Congreso Nacional de la República de Honduras en sus sesiones ordinarias de 1967* (Comayagüela: Ministerio de Educación Pública, 1967), p. 6.
32. OPIE, *Primer boletín de estadísticas educativas* (Tegucigalpa: Ministerio de Educación, 1968), p. 1.
33. *El sistema educativo en Honduras* (San José: CSUCA, 1965), pp. 16-17.
34. *Ibid.,* p. 16.
35. Unpub. memo, USAID, Honduras, Feb. 20, 1967, p. 2.
36. *Informe . . . Ministro de Educación Pública, 1967,* p. 8.
37. *Socio-Economic Progress in Latin America, 1967.*
38. *Informe . . . Ministro de Educación Pública, 1967,* p. 8.
39. *Ibid.,* p. 7.
40. *Ibid.,* pp. 6-7.
41. *Ibid.,* p. 7.
42. Oficina de Planeamiento Integral de la Educación, *Los costos de la educación, 1959-1965* (Tegucigalpa: Ministerio de Educación Pública, 1967), p. 43.
43. *Informe . . . Ministro de Educación*

Pública, 1967, p. 9; *El sistema educativo en Honduras,* pp. 22-24.

44. *Informe . . . Ministro de Educación Pública, 1967,* pp. 11-12.
45. Soto, *op. cit.,* p. 54.
46. Unpub. memo, USAID, Honduras, Feb. 20, 1967, pp. 4-6.
47. *Ibid.,* p. 4.
48. *Los costos de la educación, 1959-1965,* p. 4.
49. Soto, *op. cit.,* p. 11.
50. Unpub. memo, USAID, Honduras, Feb. 20, 1967, p. 2.
51. *El sistema educativo en Honduras,* p. 33; *Informe . . . Ministro de Educación Pública, 1967,* pp. 18-19. A very complete statistical study of the academic, normal, and commercial secondary programs was made in 1966; OPIE, *Encuesta nacional del nivel de educación media* (Tegucigalpa: Ministerio de Educación Pública, 1966), 217 pp.
52. *Informe . . . Ministro de Educación Pública, 1967,* p. 19.
53. Unpub. memo, USAID, Honduras, Feb. 20, 1967, p. 5.
54. *Informe . . . Ministro de Educación Pública, 1967,* p. 20.
55. *El sistema educativo en Honduras, 1965,* p. 33.
56. USAID, Honduras, reports that in 1966 there were 1,572 secondary teachers; the Ministry of Education reports that in 1967 there were 2,275 teachers; CSUCA states that in 1962 there were 1,404 teachers. Unpub. memo, USAID, Honduras, Feb. 20, 1967, p. 3; *Informe . . . Ministro de Educación Pública, 1967,* p. 20; *El sistema educativo en Honduras,* p. 39; *Prospecto* (Tegucigalpa: Escuela Superior del Profesorado Francisco Morazán, 1968), pp. 4-5.
57. Soto, *op. cit.,* p. 55.
58. OPIE, *Plan de acción educativa nacional: educación vocacional* (Tegucigalpa: Secretaría de Educación Pública, 1967), Cuadro 2.
59. Unclassified Capital Assistance Paper, Agency for International Development, *Honduras: Secondary Education,* Washington, June 20, 1967, p. i. In 1967 a loan of $7,000,000 was granted for development of secondary education.
60. *El sistema educativo en Honduras,* pp. 44-48.

61. *Ibid.,* pp. 46-48.
62. *Ibid.,* pp. 45-46.
63. *Prospecto* (Tegucigalpa: Escuela Superior del Profesorado Francisco Morazán, August 1967), p. 5; *Catálogo de estudios* (Tegucigalpa: Universidad Nacional Autónoma de Honduras, 1967), pp. 150-153; information from Professor John P. Wolf, Apr. 15, 1969.
64. *Prospecto* (1967), p. 5; *Informe . . . Ministro de Educación Pública, 1967,* pp. 3, 106-107.
65. *Honduras: Secondary Education,* p. 25.
66. *Catálogo universidades Centroamericanas* (San José: CSUCA, 1968), pp. 16-17; *Catálogo de estudios* (1967), pp. 12-13; Parker, *op. cit.,* p. 212; *World Survey of Education* (Paris: UNESCO), IV, p. 573.
67. *Catálogo universidades Centroamericanas* (1968), pp. 31-34; *Ley orgánica de la Universidad, Decreto No. 170* (Tegucigalpa: Universidad Nacional Autónoma de Honduras, n.d.), 22 pp.
68. *Catálogo universidades Centroamericanas* (1968), p. 68.
69. *Catálogo de estudios* (1967), p. 33.
70. Guillermo Lara López, *Análisis de la educación universitaria Centroamericana* (San José: CSUCA, 1968), p. 41.
71. *Memoria de la Universidad Nacional Autónoma de Honduras, 1966-1967* (Tegucigalpa: Univ. Nacional Autónoma de Honduras, 1967), p. 182. For 1968 the source is the Oficina de Planeamiento Universitario.
72. *Informe . . . Ministro de Educación Pública, 1967,* p. 19; *Catálogo de estudios* (1967), p. 33; *Memoria . . . Honduras, 1966-1967,* p. 205.
73. G. R. Waggoner, *Problemas en la profesionalización de la carrera docente universitaria de Centroamérica* (San José: CSUCA, 1964), pp. 13-14; *Cuarto censo de población universitaria Centroamericana* (San José: CSUCA, 1966), p. 40.
74. Guillermo Lara López, *Análisis de la educación universitaria Centroamericana* (San José: CSUCA, 1968), p. 79.
75. News release, Inter-American Development Bank, Washington, D.C., July 11, 1968.

CHAPTER 5

1. Mario Rodríguez, *Central America* (Englewood Cliffs, N.J.: Prentice-Hall, Inc., 1965), p. 41.
2. *Socio-Economic Progress in Latin America, 1967* (Washington: BID, 1968), pp. 177, 225.
3. Franklin D. Parker, *The Central American Republics* (London: Oxford University Press, 1964), pp. 222-223; *Nicaraguan Election Factbook, 1967* (Washington: Institute for the Comparative Study of Political Systems, 1967), pp. 8-9.
4. Parker, *op. cit.*, pp. 224-234.
5. Robert C. West and John P. Augelli, *Middle America: Its Lands and Peoples* (Englewood Cliffs, N.J.: Prentice-Hall, Inc., 1966), p. 427.
6. *Socio-Economic Progress in Latin America, 1967*, p. 218.
7. West and Augelli, *op. cit.*, pp. 428-429; *Socio-Economic Progress in Latin America, 1967*, p. 218.
8. *Socio-Economic Progress in Latin America, 1967*, p. 218.
9. West and Augelli, *op. cit.*, p. 431.
10. *Socio-Economic Progress in Latin America, 1967*, pp. 218-219.
11. Ovidio Soto Blanco, *La educación en Centroamérica* (San Salvador: Publicaciones de la Secretaría General de la Organización de Estados Centroamericanos (ODECA), 1968), pp. 29-31.
12. *Ibid.*, p. 48.
13. *Proyectos prioritarios de educación para el desarrollo: Nicaragua* (Paris: UNESCO, 1965), pp. 31-32.
14. Soto, *op. cit.*, p. 108.
15. *Proyectos prioritarios . . . Nicaragua*, p. 35.
16. Soto, *op. cit.*, p. 40; *Socio-Economic Progress in Latin America, 1967*, p. 227.
17. *Socio-Economic Progress in Latin America, 1967*, p. 226.
18. *Oficina de Planeamiento, Informe No. 7: año escolar, 1964-1965* (Managua: Oficina de Planificación, Consejo Nacional de Economía, 1966), p. 7.
19. *Estudio de la educación en Nicaragua, 1964-1965* (Managua: Oficina de Planificación, Consejo Nacional de Economía, 1966), p. 7.
20. *Proyectos prioritarios . . . Nicaragua*, p. 5.
21. *Ibid.*, p. 5.
22. Soto, *op. cit.*, p. 54.
23. *Ibid.*, p. 72.
24. *Ibid.*, p. 74.
25. *Estudio de la educación en Nicaragua, 1950-1964*, pp. 26, 30-31.
26. *Socio-Economic Progress in Latin America, 1967*, p. 226.
27. Soto, *op. cit.*, pp. 11-12.
28. *Ibid.*, p. 86; *Informe No. 7: año escolar, 1964-1965*, p. 23.
29. Soto, *op. cit.*, p. 100.
30. *Ibid.*, p. 100.
31. *Ibid.*, p. 99.
32. Félix Hernández Andrino, *La educación media en Centro América* (Guatemala: IIME, 1965), p. 55.
33. *Estudio de la educación en Nicaragua, 1950-1964*, p. 45.
34. Soto, *op. cit.*, p. 78.
35. Unpub. statistics concerning graduates of the National University between 1960 and 1967 obtained from the office of the rector.
36. Hernández, *op. cit.*, p. 32.
37. *Estudio de la educación en Nicaragua, 1950-1964*, p. 178.
38. These comments are based on personal observations on various visits beginning in 1962.
39. *Estudio de la educación en Nicaragua, 1950-1964*, p. 44.
40. *Ibid.*, p. 45.
41. Comments of Dr. Norman Ziff, Cultural Affairs Officer, U.S. Embassy, Managua; UNESCO report, p. 22; *Estudio de la educación en Nicaragua, 1950-1964*, p. 63.
42. *Socio-Economic Progress in Latin America, 1967*, p. 226.
43. *Estudio de la educación en Nicaragua, 1950-1964*, pp. 65-66.
44. *Ibid.*, p. 75.
45. Javier Ruiz Paniagua, *La educación normal en Nicaragua* (Guatemala: IIME, 1966), p. 8.
46. *Estudio de la educación en Nicaragua, 1950-1964*, pp. 81-89.
47. *Ibid.*, pp. 89-97; the data concerning the budget is taken from Dirección General del Presupuesto, *Presupuesto general de ingresos y egresos de la República* (Managua: Ministerio de Hacienda y Crédito Público, 1967). The average expenditure per student in the National University in 1967-1968 was $638.

48. *Estudio de la educación en Nicaragua, 1950-1964,* pp. 97-107.
49. *Ibid.,* pp. 107-111.
50. *Ibid.,* pp. 188-193.
51. UNESCO, 1965, p. 30.
52. *Estudio de la educación en Nicaragua, 1950-1964,* pp. 204-206.
53. *Ibid.,* pp. 203, 208.
54. These historical data are drawn from the following sources: "Cronología universitaria," *Revista conservadora del pensamiento Centroamericano,* XIII (Oct. 1965), 13-15; *Estudio de la educación en Nicaragua, 1950-1964,* p. 124; Mariano Fiallos Gil, "Los primeros pasos de la reforma Universitaria en Nicaragua," *Ventana,* I (July 1965), 59-68; C. Tünnermann Bernheim, *El CSUCA y la integración de la educación superior Centroamericana,* unpub. MS, n.d., pp. 11-13.
55. *Memoria, 1959-1962* (León: Universidad Nacional de Nicaragua, n.d.), pp. 9, 20, 116-125, 159, 176-185.
56. *Catálogo universidades Centro Americanas, 1967-1968* (San José: CSUCA, 1968), pp. 26-27.
57. For the grading system, see Guillermo Lara López, *Análisis de la educación universitaria Centroamericana* (San José: CSUCA, 1968), p. 40. For university government, see *Ley orgánica estatutos reglamentos* (León: Universidad Nacional Autónoma de Nicaragua, 1965), pp. 8-14.
58. K. H. Silvert, "The University Student," in *Continuity and Change in Latin America,* ed. J. J. Johnson (Stanford: Stanford University Press, 1964), p. 222.
59. René Dávila Boza, "Ciencia y técnica al servicio de Nicaragua," *Revista conservadora del pensamiento Centroamericano,* VIII (Oct. 1965), 30.

60. Ronald J. Fundis, *Población estudiantil, 1960-1967* (Managua: UNAN, 1967), p. 36.
61. *Catálogo universidades Centroamericanas, 1967-1968,* pp. 59-60.
62. Fundis, *op. cit., passim:* mimeog. report of enrollment for the academic year 1968-1969 made by the Office of Registration and Statistics, UNAN; *Estudio de la educación en Nicaragua, 1950-1964,* p. 145.
63. See, for example, Carlos Tünnermann B., *Lección inaugural para los cursos, 1968-1969* (León: UNAN, 1968), pp. 25-26; Comisión de Planeamiento Universitario, Recinto Universitario Rubén Darío, *Plan general* (Managua: UNAN, 1968).
64. R. J. Fundis and L. Chavez, *Resumen de la información presentada en el documento preliminar de estudio del manual de informaciones y principios* (Managua: Recinto Universitario Rubén Darío, 1968), p. 23.
65. Fundis, *Población estudiantil, 1960-1967,* p. 33.
66. *Plan general,* pp. 30-31.
67. G. R. Waggoner, *Problemas en la profesionalización de la carrera docente universitaria en Centroamérica* (San José: CSUCA, 1964), p. 15.
68. *Estudio de la educación en Nicaragua, 1950-1964,* p. 173.
69. C. Tünnermann B., *Informe del Rector* (León: UNAN, 1968), p. 7.
70. *Informe sobre universidades privadas* (San José: CSUCA, 1968), pp. 3-5.
71. *Folleto informativo, facultad de ciencias económicas y administrativas* (Managua: Universidad Centroamericana), 1967, pp. 6-7.
72. *Universidad Centroamericana, datos estadísticos, cursos 1967-1968* (Managua: UCA, 1967), *passim.*

CHAPTER 6

1. K. H. Silvert, "The University Student," in *Continuity and Change in Latin America,* ed. J. J. Johnson (Stanford: Stanford University Press, 1964), pp. 219, 224.
2. Aldo Solari, "Secondary Education and the Development of Elites," in *Elites in Latin America,* ed. S. M. Lipset and A. Solari (N.Y.: Oxford Univ. Press, 1967), p. 458.

3. Quoted by Hubert Herring, *A History of Latin America* (N.Y.: Alfred A. Knopf, 1967), p. 469.
4. Carlos Monge Alfaro, *Historia de Costa Rica* (San José: Imprenta Trejos Hnos., 1963), p. 5.
5. *Ibid.,* pp. 93-138; Carlos Meléndez Ch., *La ciudad del lodo (1564-1572)* (San José: Universidad de Costa Rica, 1962), p. 24. The site of Cartago was selected

in 1563; the city was founded in 1564.

6. *Ibid.*, pp. 150-155.
7. Franklin D. Parker, *The Central American Republics* (London: Oxford Univ. Press, 1964), pp. 259-260.
8. *Ibid.*, pp. 261-262.
9. *Ibid.*, pp. 265-277.
10. *Socio-Economic Progress in Latin America, 1967* (Washington: BID, 1968), pp. 117-118.
11. *Ibid.*, pp. 123-125.
12. R. C. West and J. P. Augelli, *Middle America: Its Lands and Peoples* (Englewood Cliffs, N.J.: Prentice-Hall, Inc., 1966), pp. 436, 440.
13. *Ibid.*, p. 440. Eighty-five percent of Costa Rica is suitable for agriculture or forestry; only 40 percent is now used.
14. *Socio-Economic Progress in Latin America, 1967* p. 127.
15. Ovidio Soto Blanco, *La educación en Centroamérica* (San Salvador: Publicaciones de la Secretaría General de la Organización de Estados Centroamericanos (ODECA), 1968), pp. 31-32.
16. *Ibid.*, p. 50; John F. Helwig, *A Definitive Study of the Status of Costa Rican Public School Teachers*, unpub. master's thesis, University of Kansas, 1968, p. 1.
17. *Organización del sistema educativo de Costa Rica* (San José: Ministerio de Educación, 1968), p. 1.
18. *Memoria del Ministerio de Educación, 1966* (San José: Imprenta Nacional, 1967), pp. 14-15.
19. Helwig, *op. cit.*, p. 1.
20. Soto, *op. cit.*, pp. 43-44, 49.
21. *Ibid.*, p. 12.
22. *Socio-Economic Progress in Latin America, 1967*, pp. 117, 126.
23. *Memoria anual, 1966* (San José: Ministerio de Educación Pública, 1967), p. 21.
24. Soto, *op. cit.*, p. 105.
25. UNESCO, *World Survey of Education*, II, 269.
26. *Organización del sistema educativo de Costa Rica*, p. 3.
27. *Informe sobre el estado de la educación Costarricense, 1957-1967* (San José: Ministerio de Educación Pública, 1968), pp. 9, 38.
28. *Ibid.*, pp. 16, 43. Educational statistics for Costa Rica are often contradictory and confusing. In the publication *Organización del sistema educativo de Costa Rica* (by the Statistics Section of the Department of Research and Statistics of the Ministry), July 1968, p. 3, we find the statement that in 1967 total primary enrollment was 315,256 (public, 305,481; private, 9,775). On the same page, it is stated that in 1967 there were 316,751 children between 6 and 12 of which only 277,756 were enrolled. Perhaps the discrepancy is due to the fact that 37,500 enrolled primary students were above the age of 12, but this seems a high figure.

The ten-year study of education published by the same department in June 1968, p. 15, gives a total matriculation of 351,481 (close to the earlier figure but not identical); 305,277 in public schools and 9,775 in private schools. On page 17 there is a total for public primary enrollment in 1967 identical with that in *Organización del sistema educativo*, but different from the figure on p. 15 of the same volume.

The BID figure for primary enrollment in 1967 is 312,857, different from all of the figures just given above (*Socio-Economic Progress in Latin America, 1967*, p. 125).

The data regarding teachers in private primary school included in the ten-year study are as follows:

Year	From Page 38	From Page 43
1967	399	399
1966	412	366
1965	297	312
1964	204	258
1963	341	300
1962	349	349
1961	134	341
1960	258	204
1959	178	297
1958	366	412
1957	300	399

For some reason, the figures agree only for the years 1962 and 1967.
29. *Memoria anual, 1966*, p. 15. Data from the Department of Statistics of the Ministry indicate that 87.69 percent of the 6 to 12 age group were enrolled in primary school in 1967 (*Organización del sistema educativo de Costa Rica*, p. 3). The 1968 BID report (*Socio-Economic Progress in Latin America, 1968*, p. 125) gives different data: "In 1965, 93.5 percent of all primary school age children six to thirteen years old were enrolled in school." As a possible

explanation of some of the differences, it should be noted that the minister's figures for 1966 are based on ages 7 to 14 (the compulsory period), while the other two figures are based on 6 to 12 and 6 to 13; it does not seem reasonable, however, that there could be a sharp decline in the percentage between 1965 and 1967, and no source indicates that there was a decline.

30. *Informe sobre el estado de la educación,* p. 22.
31. *Ibid.,* p. 35.
32. *Ibid.,* p. 26.
33. Soto, *op. cit.,* pp. 68-69. The total numbers of schools given here differs somewhat from those on p. 8.
34. *Informe sobre el estado de la educación,* p. 18.
35. *Algunas consideraciones en relación con la reforma a la enseñanza primaria* (San José: Consejo Superior de Educación, 1965), p. 4.
36. Soto, *op. cit.,* p. 68. D. A. Lemke, *Las escuelas normales—una evaluación e interpretación* (San José: Consejo Superior de Educación, 1966), pp. 18-19, takes the position that school consolidation is the first great step toward quality in the rural schools.
37. *Memoria anual, 1966,* p. 15.
38. Helwig, *op. cit.,* pp. 12, 17-18.
39. *Ibid.,* p. 61.
40. *Ibid.,* pp. 21-23.
41. *Algunas consideraciones en relación con la reforma a la enseñanza primaria* (San José: Consejo Superior de Educación, 1965), p. 6.
42. Report from C. C. Boyd, educational adviser for the RTC (Regional Textbook Center), to ROCAP, March 1968, Table 15-A.
43. Helwig, *op. cit.,* p. 5.
44. *Nuevos programas de educación primaria* (San José: Ministerio de Educación Pública, 1969), 40 pp.
45. Soto, *op. cit.,* p. 54. Much greater detail is available in *Fines, planes y contenidos para programas de educación primaria* (San José: Ministerio de Educación Pública, 1964).
46. Monge, *op. cit.,* pp. 216-227; Parker, *op. cit.,* p. 292; UNESCO, *World Survey of Education,* III, 385.
47. UNESCO, *World Survey of Education,* III, 386.
48. *Memoria anual, 1966,* pp. 5-13.

49. *Concepto de estructura educativa y planes de estudio de la enseñanza media en Costa Rica* (San José: Universidad de Costa Rica, Facultad de Educación, 1968), pp. 5-6.
50. *Informe sobre el estado de la educación,* p. 56.
51. *Ibid.,* p. 55.
52. *Ibid.,* p. 54.
53. *Anuario estadístico, 1965* (San José: Ministerio de Educación Pública, 1967), p. 197.
54. *Informe sobre el estado de la educación,* p. 61.
55. *Ibid.,* pp. 64-65.
56. *Ibid.,* p. 69.
57. Helwig, *op. cit.,* p. 44.
58. *Informe sobre el estado de la educación,* p. 78.
59. *Centro de enseñanza e investigación del IICA* (Turrialba, Costa Rica: Instituto de Ciencias Agrícolas de la OEA, n.d.), pp. 1-19.
60. *El sistema educativo en Costa Rica* (San José: CSUCA, 1964), p. 64; *Informe del Rector, 1967-1968* (Ciudad Universitaria Rodrigo Facio: Universidad de Costa Rica, 1968), pp. 198-199.
61. *Organización del sistema educativo de Costa Rica,* p. 7.
62. *Informe sobre el estado de la educación,* p. 94.
63. Donald A. Lemke, *op. cit.,* pp. 59-60.
64. *Organización del sistema educativo de Costa Rica,* p. 7.
65. *Memoria anual, 1966,* p. 14. It is said that most of the 362 university graduates were in-service teachers who took part-time university work. Few were new to teaching.
66. *Informe del Rector, 1967-1968.* In the lengthy discussions of this problem, pp. 253-325, see, for example, pp. 290-291, 316-317.
67. In 1963, 742; 1964, 677; 1965, 662; 1966, 672. Secondary teaching does not have the same prestige in most universities as either the traditional careers of law, medicine, and engineering or as some of the newer careers, such as those in the natural sciences. As entrance into the University of Costa Rica becomes increasingly more difficult each year (in Oct. 1968, 5,578 students took the admission examination, competing for only 2,700 places—*La Nación,* Jan. 19, 1969, p. 36), apparently those who succeed in

winning admission are not seeking preparation for secondary teaching in the increasing numbers necessary to staff the secondary schools. It may well be that unsuccessful applicants for the university will turn to the Higher Normal School.

68. Milo Stucky, *A Report on the Teacher Preparation Program of the School of Education of the University of Costa Rica, with Emphasis on the Secondary and Administration Areas* (San José: 1967), pp. 13, 19.

69. Parker, *op. cit.,* pp. 264, 271.

70. Jorge Emilio Padilla, "Breve historia de la Universidad de Costa Rica," in *Noveno seminario de educación superior en las Américas,* ed. by G. R. Waggoner and Anita Herzfeld (Lawrence, Kan.: Univ. of Kansas, 1968), pp. 18-22.

71. Information from Lic. Chester Zelaya, Director of General Studies, Feb. 1969.

72. *Catálogo universidades Centroamericanas, 1967-1968* (San José: CSUCA, 1968), p. 30.

73. *Informe del Rector, 1967-1968,* pp. 232-233.

74. Report of the Registrar, University of Costa Rica, Feb. 1969.

75. Guillermo Lara López, *Análisis de la educación Universitaria Centroamericana* (San José: CSUCA, 1968), p. 47.

76. The University of Costa Rica offers a great variety of programs, as follows:

A program in primary education and in secondary education with specialties in Spanish language and literature, French, English, philosophy, biology, physics and mathematics, chemistry, geography and history, fine arts, industrial arts, general science, classical studies, and psychology.

Bachelor's degrees in biology, the sciences of man (psychology, anthropology, and sociology), physics, mathematics, history and geography, chemistry, philosophy, sciences of education (primary and kindergarten), classical studies, and English, French, and Spanish philology.

Licenciaturas in biology, economic and social sciences (business administration, public administration, economics, statistics, and insurance), sciences of education (counseling and administration), pharmacy (community pharmacy, hospital pharmacy, industrial pharmacy, and medical visiting), engineering (agricultural, civil, electrical, mechanical, and chemical), philosophy, physics, French, history and geography, English, chemistry, mathematics, medicine and surgery, microbiology, law, political science, journalism, dentistry, and social service.

Catálogo universidades Centroamericanas, 1967-1968, pp. 46-47, and information concerning recent programs from the Office of the Registrar. The total of enrollments in the school is 9,333. Because some students are enrolled in two programs the total enrollment of persons is lower.

77. Information supplied by Lic. Luis Torres, Registrar, Feb. 1969.

78. G. R. Waggoner, *Problemas en la profesionalización de la carrera docente universitaria en Centroamérica* (San José: CSUCA, 1964), p. 17.

79. *Informe del Rector, 1967-1968,* p. 411.

80. Carlos A. Caamaño Reyes, report to the 9th Seminar on Higher Education in the Americas, San José, April 1968.

81. *Noveno seminario de educación superior en las Américas* (Lawrence, Kan.: University of Kansas, 1968), pp. 30-31.

82. *Consideraciones preliminares sobre la erección de los centros universitarios regionales* (San José: Universidad de Costa Rica, 1967), 32 pp.; *Informe del Rector, 1967-1968,* pp. 30-43.

83. See, for example, José Joaquín Trejos F., *Reflexiones sobre la educación* (San José: Editorial Costa Rica, 1963), 168 pp.

CHAPTER 7

1. Hubert Herring, *A History of Latin America* (N.Y.: Alfred A. Knopf, 1961), p. 473.

2. *Ibid.,* pp. 474-478; Mario Rodríguez, *Central America* (Englewood Cliffs, N.J.: Prentice-Hall, Inc., 1965), pp. 42-47.

3. *Socio-Economic Progress in Latin America, 1967* (Washington: BID, 1968), pp. 230-231.

4. R. C. West and J. P. Augelli, *Middle America: Its Lands and Peoples* (Englewood Cliffs, N.J.: Prentice-Hall, 1966), pp. 452-453.

5. *Ibid.*, p. 453.
6. *Socio-Economic Progress in Latin America, 1967,* p. 230.
7. *Ibid.*, pp. 230, 239.
8. Ovidio Soto Blanco, *La educación en Centroamérica* (San Salvador: Publicaciones de la Secretaría General de la Organización de Estados Centroamericanos (ODECA), 1968), pp. 32-34.
9. *Síntesis sobre el sistema educativo Panameño* (Panamá: National Office of Planning and Evaluation of the Ministry of Education, 1967), pp. 1-2.
10. Soto, *op. cit.*, p. 50.
11. *Ibid.*, p. 58.
12. *Síntesis sobre el sistema educativo Panameño,* p. 5.
13. *Informe previo para un planteamiento integral de educación Panameño* (Panamá: Ministerio de Educación, 1966), pp. 11-12.
14. Soto, *op. cit.*, p. 54.
15. For 1961, 1963, and 1965: *Panamá en cifras* (Panamá: Dirección de Estadística y Censo, 1966), p. 60. For 1966: *Memoria que el Ministro de Educación presenta a la Honorable Asamblea Nacional . . . 1967* (Panamá: República de Panamá, 1967), Parte Narrativa, p. 39.
16. See note 15.
17. *Memoria . . . Ministro de Educación, 1967,* Parte Expositiva, p. 11.
18. *Ibid.*, p. 12.
19. *Síntesis sobre el sistema educativo Panameño,* p. 5.
20. *Memoria . . . Ministro de Educación, 1967,* Parte Expositiva, p. 12.
21. *Profile of Education in Panamá,* USAID, Panamá, unpub. memo, Mar. 8, 1967, p. 25.
22. *Memoria . . . Ministro de Educación, 1967,* Parte Expositiva, p. 14.
23. *Ibid.*, Parte Narrativa, p. 42.
24. *Ibid.*, Parte Narrativa, p. 48.
25. USAID, Panamá, unpub. memo, Mar. 8, 1967, p. 4.
26. *Memoria . . . Ministro de Educación, 1967,* Parte Expositiva, pp. 15, 20.
27. *Panamá en Cifras,* p. 61.
28. *Memoria . . . Ministro de Educación, 1967,* Parte Expositiva, p. 20.
29. *Ibid.*, Parte Expositiva, p. 17.
30. *Informe previo para un planteamiento integral de educación Panameña,* Cuadro XII.
31. *Memoria . . . Ministro de Educación, 1967,* Parte Expositiva, p. 15.
32. Aldo Solari, "Secondary Education and the Development of Elites," in *Elites in Latin America,* ed. S. M. Lipset and A. Solari (N.Y.: Oxford Univ. Press, 1967), p. 459. In 1960 Costa Rica enrolled 28 percent; Panamá, 30 percent.
33. *Síntesis sobre el sistema educativo Panameño,* p. 12.
34. *Panamá en cifras,* p. 61.
35. *Catálogo universidades Centroamericanas, 1967-1968* (San José: CSUCA, 1968), pp. 20-21; *La autonomía universitaria* (Panamá: Universidad de Panamá, 1966), pp. 2-4.
36. *Catálogo universidades Centroamericanas,* p. 27.
37. *Ibid.*, pp. 36-38; Guillermo Lara López, *Análisis de la educación universitaria Centroamericana* (San José: CSUCA, pp. 4-5; UNESCO, *World Survey of Education,* IV, p. 894.
38. The organizational chart published in the rough draft of CSUCA's analysis of higher education in Central America carries the note that it was taken from a loan proposal made by the university in 1966. G. Lara López, *Análisis,* p. 21.
39. *Catálogo universidades Centroamericanas, 1967-1968,* p. 62.
40. *Ibid.*, p. 63.
41. G. Lara Lopéz, *Análisis,* p. 47.
42. *Ibid.*, p. 53.
43. *Ibid.*, p. 59; publications of the University of Panamá show higher totals in earlier years: 1964, 2,952; 1965, 5,281. *Informe escuela de temporada, 1966* (Panamá: Universidad de Panamá, 1966), p. 6. See also *La universidad llega a todo el país* (Panamá: Universidad de Panamá, n.d.).
44. G. Lara López, *Análisis,* p. 79.
45. Presidencia, República de Panamá, *Fundamentos para la restructuración de la Universidad Nacional de Panamá,* Panamá, Dec. 14, 1968.
46. There exists an extremely detailed description of the process of founding Santa María, from the original conception of the need for the University, the process of enacting the law for private universities, the consultation over plans, etc. This description is useful as an illustration of the process of founding a new private university in any of the Central American countries. See *La*

Antigua, No. 1, Extraordinario (Panamá: Universidad Santa María Antigua, 1968), 287 pp.

47. *Informe sobre las universidades privadas* (San José: CSUCA, 1968), pp. 44-45.

48. Universidad Santa María la Antigua, *Boletín informativo, año lectivo,* 1968, p. 21.

49. Information received from the General Secretary, Gaspar Estribe, in Aug. 1968.

50. *Informe sobre universidades privadas,* p. 45.

CHAPTER 8

1. "5-Nation Trade Unit Chalks up Strongest Gains," *Miami Herald,* Feb. 25, 1969.

2. *Hacia la integración educacional de Centro América* (Guatemala: ODECA, 1959), pp. 322-323.

3. Secretaría General de la Organización de Estados Centroamericanos, *Convenio Centroamericano sobre unificación básica de la educación* (San Salvador: ODECA, n.d.), mimeog., pp. 26-27.

4. Ovidio Soto Blanco, *La educación en Centroamérica* (San Salvador: Publicaciones de la Secretaría General de la Organización de Estados Centroamericanos, 1968), p. ii.

5. *Estudio sobre la diversificación de las modalidades de la enseñanza media en Centroamérica* (San Salvador: Secretaría General de la Organización de Estados Centroamericanos (ODECA), Feb. 1969), mimeog., pp. 5-7.

6. Soto, *op. cit.,* p. 2.

7. *II reunión de la Comisión Asesora del Centro Regional de Libros de Texto de la ODECA, 10-12 Febrero de 1969. Informe de la reunión* (San Salvador: Secretaría General de la Organización de Estados Centroamericanos (ODECA), n.d.), mimeog., p. 10. Statistics concerning textbook production were supplied in April 1969 by Dr. Donald Lemke of the Textbook Center.

8. *Plan de operaciones del proyecto de conversión del Centro de Libros de Texto de la ODECA en un Instituto Regional período Marzo-Junio 1969* (San Salvador: Secretaría General de la Organización de Estados Centroamericanos (ODECA), Feb. 1969), mimeog., 15 pp.

9. *Informe de labores de la Oficina Centroamericana de Planeamiento de la Educación* (OCEPLAN) (San Salvador: Secretaría General de la Organización de Estados Centroamericanos (ODECA), Mar. 1969), mimeog., 13 pp.

10. *Estudio sobre la diversificación de las modalidades de la enseñanza media en Centroamérica,* 73 pp.

11. *Informe final de la reunión de trabajo sobre el proyecto de reforma al plan de estudio de la enseñanza media de Honduras* (San Salvador: ODECA, Dec. 1968), mimeog., 14 pp. and appendices.

12. Soto, *op. cit.*

13. The preceding material concerning CSUCA is drawn from *Memoria de las reuniones del Consejo Superior Universitario Centroamericano, 1949-1959* (León, Nicaragua: Publicaciones de la Secretaría Permanente del Consejo Superior Universitario Centroamericano, 1969), pp. 5-84, and from comments by Dr. Carlos Tünnermann Bernheim of the National University of Nicaragua in Jan. 1968.

14. Willard H. Mitchell, *CSUCA: A Regional Strategy for Higher Education in Central America* (Lawrence, Kan.: Center of Latin American Studies, University of Kansas, 1967), p. 19.

15. *Memoria de las reuniones . . . 1949-1959.*

16. Sergio Ramírez Mercado, *Veinte años de integración regional* (San José: CSUCA, 1968), mimeog., p. 6.

17. Carlos Tünnermann Bernheim, *Lección inaugural para los cursos 1968-1969* (León, Nicaragua: Universidad Nacional Autónoma de Nicaragua, 1968), pp. 21-22.

18. Ramírez Mercado, *op. cit.,* pp. 5-6.

19. Secretaría Permanente del Consejo Superior Universitario Centroamericano, *Plan para la integración de la educación superior Centroamericano* (San José: CSUCA, 1961), mimeog., 45 pp.

20. CSUCA, *Resoluciones de la X reunión ordinaria del CSUCA* (San José: Secretaría Permanente, 1965), mimeog., pp. 1-67.

21. CSUCA, *Informe del comité de evaluación preliminar* (San José: Secretaría Permanente, 1966), mimeog., pp. 3-4.

22. *Ibid.,* pp. 14-16.

23. *Noticias del CSUCA,* Ciudad Universitaria, Costa Rica, V (Oct. 1968), 6-7.

24. "CSUCA declaró ilegal a Universidad de Panamá," *La Nación,* San José, Costa Rica, Feb. 1, 1969. See also Carlos Monge Alfaro, *La universidad frente al poder castrense* (San José: Publicaciones de la Universidad de Costa Rica, Jan. 1969).

25. *Informe sobre universidades privadas* (San José: CSUCA, 1968), mimeog., p. 2.

26. *Ibid.,* pp. 81-94.

27. *Ibid.,* pp. 6-7, 95.

28. *Ibid.,* pp. 11-14.

29. *Ibid.,* pp. 14-17.

30. Data from the Ford representative in Mexico, July 1968.

31. *Socio-Economic Progress in Latin America, 1967* (Washington: BID, 1968), p. 441.

32. Richard N. Adams, *The Second Sowing: Power and Secondary Development in Latin America* (San Francisco: Chandler Publishing Co., 1967), pp. 139-140.

33. Richard N. Adams, *Some Developmental Consequences of the Technological Gap in Latin America, with Special Reference to Higher Education,* mimeog., paper presented to AAAS meeting, Dec. 31, 1968, pp. 13-14.

34. All of these statistics are taken from the basic data reports for each country in *Socio-Economic Progress in Latin America.*

35. G. Lara López, *Análisis de la educación universitaria Centroamericana* (San José: CSUCA, 1968), mimeog., pp. 1-2.

36. K. H. Silvert, "The University Student," in *Continuity and Change in Latin America,* ed. J. J. Johnson (Stanford: Stanford University Press, 1964), pp. 222-224.

37. *Noveno seminario de educación superior en las Américas,* Apr. 3-May 15, 1968 (Lawrence, Kan.: University of Kansas, 1968), p. 31.